LINKS

UNIVERSITY PRESS OF FLORIDA
Florida A&M University, Tallahassee
Florida Atlantic University, Boca Raton
Florida Gulf Coast University, Ft. Myers
Florida International University, Miami
Florida State University, Tallahassee
New College of Florida, Sarasota
University of Central Florida, Orlando
University of Florida, Gainesville
University of North Florida, Jacksonville
University of South Florida, Tampa
University of West Florida, Pensacola

Gainesville

Tallahassee

Tampa

Boca Raton

Pensacola

Orlando

Miami

Jacksonville

Ft. Myers

Sarasota

University Press of Florida

LINKS

My Family in American History

William A. Link

17   16   15   14   13   12   6   5   4   3   2   1

Library of Congress Cataloging-in-Publication Data

Link, William A.

Links : my family in American history / William A. Link.

p. cm.

Includes bibliographical references.

ISBN 978-0-8130-3794-3 (alk. paper)

1. Link, Arthur S. (Arthur Stanley), 1920–1998. 2. Link, Margaret
Douglas, 1918–1996. 3. Link family. 4. Historians—United
States—Biography. 5. College teachers—New Jersey—Princeton—
Biography. 6. Princeton University—Faculty—Biography. 7. United
States—Social conditions—20th century. I. Title.

E175.5.L56L56 2012

378.1'2092—dc23

[B]   2011037517

The University Press of Florida is the scholarly publishing agency
for the State University System of Florida, comprising Florida
A&M University, Florida Atlantic University, Florida Gulf Coast
University, Florida International University, Florida State University,
New College of Florida, University of Central Florida, University of
Florida, University of North Florida, University of South Florida, and
University of West Florida.

University Press of Florida

15 Northwest 15th Street

Gainesville, FL 32611-2079

http://www.upf.com

For John, Jim, and Dave

CONTENTS

PREFACE

After retirement in 1992, my parents, Arthur and Margaret Douglas Link, came home, after almost a half century, to North Carolina. My father liquidated his large collection of books, giving them to me and various libraries. Arthur and Margaret both loved books. They left a house full of them when they died, my mother in 1996 and my father two years later. During most of the summer after my father's death, my siblings and I sifted through their possessions, spending many hours thinking about them. They led fortunate lives. Participants in a world that changed wholly, they abandoned parochial, small-town life, found each other, and spent their lives living fully in and inquiring about the world around them. Both from the South, Margaret and Arthur left their homes, took up a different existence, questioned bedrock values of their upbringing, but also expressed a persistently strong identity as southerners.

Arthur's home office was packed with books and artifacts relating to Woodrow Wilson. As a Wilson biographer and editor, he wrote numerous books, including a five-volume biography. He also edited a sixty-nine-volume collection of Wilson's papers. My father's books were translated into Japanese, Chinese, Portuguese, German, and Polish; over the years, he received honorary degrees from colleges and universities around the country. When he retired after four decades as a faculty member at Princeton University, he donated his office correspondence to the university's Seeley G. Mudd Manuscript Library. Arthur maintained his papers meticulously, and from his early adulthood carefully preserved his correspondence.

My mother, in contrast, liked nothing better than to dispose of clutter, though this was an impulse Arthur kept in check. For in the attic of my parents' retirement home in North Carolina, four boxes of personal correspondence remained wrapped in their original envelopes. Beginning during the summer after my father's death, I read through their letters, arranged them into file folders, and then decided to write someday an account of two southerners' growth and displacement from their homes. Their letters form an amazing collection. Included are letters from my mother to her parents, from her parents to her, and from my father's mother and siblings to him during World War II. The correspondence also includes all the letters that my brothers, sister, and I wrote to my parents during our years in college, and after—this in the 1960s, 1970s, and 1980s, when people still wrote letters as a primary means of communication.

Most fascinating of all was the correspondence between my parents during the 1940s and 1950s. For long stretches during these years, they were separated. Friends at graduate school at the University of North Carolina beginning in 1941, they went their separate ways in the spring of 1943. Thereafter, their relationship developed through an intensifying correspondence that continued over the next two years and culminated in their engagement in late 1944. After their marriage in 1945, Arthur and Margaret were frequently separated while he traveled on long research trips and she returned to summer with her parents in North Carolina. Theirs was an emotionally deep relationship and a partnership framed on the basis of ideas and belief. Their separations were consequently painful, but their time apart offered the chance for both to express their inner thoughts and ideas about their social and political surroundings.

This book looks at the roots and development of my parents' partnership, and, as such, it is most concerned with them as individuals and their social context. Both of them came from the South, though from far different backgrounds. Both experienced the changes that came to the region during the Depression; both were living examples of how World War II changed the lives of southerners, dispersing them to new places, undermining their traditional faith, and introducing them to new ways of viewing the world. During much of their courtship, Arthur and Margaret remained separated. Accordingly, they courted by correspondence. They came to know each other through their words, and through their words they discovered a mutual dependence and satisfaction that was at the center of what became their marriage.

The rich lode of correspondence between my parents provided a tempting opportunity to explore their inner worlds, thoughts, and actions, and this process helps to bring them both back to life. The documentary record is especially rich because both were observant letter writers, in different ways. Arthur was funny and quirky, but also methodical, analytical, and richly descriptive. Margaret understood human beings in the rarest sort of way. Her letters expressed her personality—mainly, her interest in people and her basic compassion.

The death of my father in May 1998, the passing of my last parent, was a major event: like other children who lose their parents, I lost a protective and emotional umbrella. My father died after a long struggle with lung cancer; my mother had died two years earlier, from complications resulting from gastric thrombosis. Her death hastened his decline. Arthur could not function without Margaret, his partner and best friend. My siblings and I worried about Arthur's ability to cope, his loneliness, his depression. My mother was not only his best friend; she was also the emotional center of our family. She was the one we turned to for advice and emotional support. Margaret loved to listen to people's problems, and her best friends were always needy people, sometimes a little obsessive and neurotic; she liked to analyze them and problem-solve. When I was a teenager, she typically invited my friends into the kitchen, sat them down and fed them, and then gently subjected them to her probing questions, interview-style. Very often she seemed to extract information about whatever was on their minds, and in a number of instances she became a kind of counselor.

I profoundly mourned my mother's departure. She was an unusual woman who knew instinctively how to reach out to people, and I spoke to her on the telephone daily, relying on her intelligence and inquisitiveness. When we visited, my mother liked nothing better than to talk late into the night and find out everything happening with me and my wife, Susannah, and our three daughters. I also mourned the reality that Margaret would miss my daughters' childhood and young adulthood; I felt that her presence, her ability to watch them and affect their lives, had been prematurely taken. My feelings about my father's death were entirely different. I missed the departure of a close friend, missed the interesting conversations, his good humor, his sense of irony about human beings, and his enthusiasm for the world around him. But I lacked an emotional connection. Against his positive qualities, he was profoundly flawed, intensely selfish, often too concerned about recognition, and jealous of attention. Arthur's death was somehow liberating. As the youngest of four children, I came to understand my father's temperament, and he was frankly easy to manipulate. He was a loving parent, outwardly strict but inwardly flexible. He liked ideas and enjoyed conversations in which he was the center of attention, and he had a sense of humor that often emerged, in a wry way, in his observations about people. He loved to read, and consumed books at such a rate that it was difficult to keep his bedside table fully supplied.

My parents' rich correspondence has made them, to me, much more complicated, much more the product of their time and circumstances. In this book, I have tried to mix these qualities in the course of storytelling. In an attempt to understand the role of my parents in their environment, this is also a memoir of my own experiences with my parents, my own impressions of how they became who they were.

In one of his expansive moments, Arthur once told me that he was a "citizen of the world." It was a typical example of his hyperbole, his tendency to exaggerate, and his willingness to put himself in the spotlight. I remember my mother exclaiming, "Oh, Arthur!"—which she often did. But, in retrospect, his proclamation rings true, of him and of Margaret. Both of them were two white southerners who tried to come to terms with who they were and how the world around them was changing. Born into a generation of depression and world war—and a new Cold War world that followed it—they witnessed a wholesale transformation of their native region. Both of them grew up in North Carolina small towns, about twenty-five miles apart from each other. In their childhoods, they learned a strict moral code in a world that possessed a limited social vision. As they grew up, that way of life was challenged—by the Depression and war, by the New Deal and the expansion of federal interference in state and local affairs, and by the rebellion of African Americans. The traditional, small-town South was also undermined by its integration into a national mainstream that came sharply into focus around the middle of the twentieth century. In their life experiences, Margaret and Arthur became exiles from this small-town world, as did many southerners of their generation. This book charts their alienation from their upbringing.

Like so many people of their generation, the Great Depression defined my parents' lives. The Depression experience made them very cautious about money, something they never took for granted. As children growing up with these parents, my siblings and I never went without. But my father especially had experienced privation, and he always let us know that money meant something. As children we were served orange juice in little glasses; enjoying a large tumbler of juice became a secret pleasure. My father kept the thermostat at a low temperature; he expected his family to wear long johns to keep warm. If we left lights on, we were scolded. Some of my father's thriftiness was like a nervous tic: he insisted, for example, that two slices of bread should be toasted at the same time so as not to waste electricity. In a sense, at least in terms of energy conservation, Arthur was way ahead of his time.

In writing this book, I have incurred many obligations. Because this book is a very personal project, I found it difficult to achieve the sort of psychic distance that usually comes in producing, revising, and reconsidering a more scholarly work. Writing this book required me, even more than usual, to impose on a number of friends, relatives, and colleagues to read various drafts and to provide advice. Amanda Avery, James Axtell, Vernon Burton, Beth Carmichael, Pete Carmichael, Davison M. Douglas, John M. Douglas, Michele Gillespie, Glenda Gilmore, Nancy Hewitt, Chuck Holden, Cheryl F. Junk, D. G. Martin, Steven Lawson, Susannah Link, Peggy Link-Weil, Nancy Weiss Malkiel, Charles Neu, and Louise Newman all read part or all of the manuscript and offered very useful suggestions. I interviewed many people who knew Arthur and Margaret, and I thank all of them for their assistance. In the end, I'm still not sure that I got it quite right, but I am certain that this is a much better book as a result of their help and support. I also appreciate the help and housing provided by my oldest Princeton friend, Martin D. Kahn. I first met Martin when we were both third-graders at the Nassau Street School. We have been fast friends ever since. The same thing goes for my dear friend Steven Lawson, a person I met many years later. Nancy Hewitt listened with her usual patience and good sense, and thankfully kept Steven on a short leash. Steven and Nancy put me up in locales as diverse as England and New Jersey, listened to endless babble about this project, always provided the best advice, and even, at the last minute, helped with archival research. In the end, they both came to know my parents much better. Meredith Babb of the University Press of Florida has been an unflagging supporter, and I benefited from her suggestion about how to streamline things. The book would not have been possible without her enthusiastic involvement. I also very much appreciate the careful editing of Susan A. Murray.

At the University of Florida, I was assisted by my graduate students working in what is known as the "Milbauer Office": Jim Broomall, Heather Bryson, Angela Diaz, Allison Fredette, Matt Hall, Chris Ruehlen, and Angie Zombek. They assiduously checked documents, transcribed interviews, hunted down references, and in many other ways provided invaluable assistance. My daughter Maggie assembled research materials at different stages of the project, and didn't mind offering reality checks at frequent intervals. Josie and Percy were equally enthusiastic about a book about their grandparents.

I am also appreciative of the help of archivists and librarians: Jan Blodgett at the Davidson College Archives; Hansford Eppes, Davidson College; Susan Boone, Smith College Library; Marianne Bradley, Agnes Scott College Library; Laura Clark Brown at the Southern Historical Collection; Janice Holder, University Archives at the University of North Carolina; Winnie Bryce, Queens University Library; Elizabeth B. Dunn at the Manuscripts Department, Duke University Library; Janet Olson at Northwestern University Archives; and Dan Linke at Mudd Library, Princeton University. Joe Steelman pointed me in the direction of his very rich correspondence with Arthur dating to the 1940s, when they were students together at UNC. Dan Carter shared his observations about *The Papers of Woodrow Wilson* with me—the best such assessment in existence, in my opinion. George H. Nash very generously provided me with his recollections of the February 1983 dinner with Ronald Reagan.

In this instance, as in all instances, my family has been a source of support and enthusiasm. My Douglas cousins Dave, Jim, and John Douglas eagerly supported this book from start to finish. Dave generously shared memories and documents, and he gave the manuscript several thorough, thoughtful, and exceptionally acute readings. The dedication is to all three of them, who themselves value family and exemplify characteristics of intelligence, social justice, and caring.

My daughters, Percy, Maggie, and Josie, put up with this book in various forms over the past decade. During that time, having grown up all their lives in the South, they grew into young women with a sensitive understanding of their surroundings. I am eager for them to read this book, perhaps as a way to comprehend their own past more fully, and certainly to learn more about their grandparents. It's not easy to write a book about one's parents, but my siblings have been unusually supportive. I must thank my sister, Peggy, especially, who provided her usual upbeat energy, and pretty much insisted that the book be written. She also frequently shared her thoughts about our parents, but, above all, wanted me to tell this story faithfully and truthfully—even when she disagreed with me. My brother Stan was generous in sharing recollections. My brother James checked my impulses occasionally, but remained interested and supportive. Susannah put up with me about this project, and, as always, I benefited from her intelligent skepticism. As always I depend on her, my best friend, for the wisest counsel and soundest advice.

LINKS

PROLOGUE

MARGARET AND ARTHUR

As the youngest of four, I was born when my parents were older: my mother was thirty-six, my father, thirty-four. Early on, I became an observer of family interactions, even while I often felt overshadowed by my more outgoing, self-confident older siblings. Like most families, in ours my older siblings bore the brunt of parental scrutiny; they felt that I had things easy. My eldest brother, Stan, left the household when I was ten; my second brother, Jimmy, when I was fourteen; and my sister, Peggy, when I was fifteen. It's probably true that by the time I arrived, my parents were ready to move on, ready for an easy relationship with a child.

My father and I shared many qualities, but we had fundamentally different personalities. Arthur loved the spotlight; indeed, he demanded it, and insisted on remaining the center of attention. He was legendary for his prodigious work habits and productivity. A close friend once observed, "Arthur Link with a high fever writes more coherently than most scholars do with a normal temperature."[1] I share the same drive and ambition and similar work habits, but, unlike him, I don't seek the limelight. I like to listen to people and learn from them; Arthur liked to talk to them and hold forth. Arthur was a loving father, but also detached and remote; a raconteur of great charm and charisma, he had a great deal of difficulty dealing with conflict and emotional crisis. He depended on my mother so much that sometimes his children competed with him for her attention.

Perhaps one of the best ways to understand Arthur is to realize his fascination with the game of bridge, something he learned from his family at an early age. Bridge served as a metaphor for his life. His playing reflected his larger-than-life personality. Often bidding outlandishly, he played aggressively and cleverly, always exaggerating his strengths and minimizing his weaknesses. If his opponents misplayed, he liked to remind them of their mistakes in the bridge equivalent of trash-talking. Arthur often told me that the measure of a great player was the ability to exceed the capacity of the cards you were dealt. And if you misused the "tickets"—the cards—they would eventually turn against you by punishing your ability to make your contract.

His favorite bridge partners in middle age were his best male friends, Blan Aldridge and Dick Gilbert; both offered foils to his persona. Arthur insisted that the husbands play the wives, and, according to Dick, he would often have to "pull his chestnuts out of the fire" after an exaggerated bid. Dick saw Arthur's bridge behavior as an example of his propensity for what he called "Arthurian superlatives." Arthur loved hyperbole, especially in dealing with family and the people he loved.

As children, we often annoyed my father. After my sister, at about the age of fourteen, knocked over a glass of milk, Arthur called her a "wild, free creature." Another time, when she tried to go out the door wearing a skimpy pair of shorts, he said that she looked like a "fallen woman." Arthur used to clean house obsessively, especially our mountain house in western North Carolina, in Montreat. Sometimes he would start cleaning at eleven at night, and he always insisted that the best method to clean the hardwood floors was to use a broom and then a dust mop. My sister once returned to the Montreat house late at night and found him washing the car. At my sister's wedding reception in 1994, Arthur sat down at a table and held court. But the dance band that Peggy had hired was noisy. Sitting with Arthur was Dick Gilbert. Arthur grabbed Dick by the arm, and said, "Dick, you must go down and tell that band to stop playing." When Dick demurred, Arthur insisted: "Here's what you tell them: I'm paying for this, and I want them to cut it out." Dick got no further than Peggy, who vetoed the idea.[2]

Arthur had many eccentricities. He wore clothes that were sometimes beyond their time; he didn't wear deodorant; he kept his hair short even after this went out of fashion in the late 1960s and early 1970s. Arthur smoked in a curious way, holding his cigarette out differently, inhaling and exhaling in exaggerated fashion. He even walked eccentrically, usually charging ahead of his wife and children. These were all qualities that embarrassed his children when we were teenagers, though these personality quirks seemed more endearing later on. He often greeted graduate students and academic visitors in his bathrobe and slippers, which he loved to wear. His slippers were elaborate: in the summer of 1976, while visiting England, he noticed that his friend, Wilson scholar and law judge Lord Patrick Devlin, was wearing velvet slippers with an emblem of a bird embroidered on the toe. My mother and sister found the pair at Fortnum & Mason's in London for his birthday, and the "bird slippers" became one of his trademarks for years.[3]

Sometimes Arthur even forgot that he had the slippers on. Once, while we were vacationing at the beach in Ocean Drive, South Carolina, my brother Jimmy, then an underaged teenager, snuck off and made a secret trip to the town's bars. One of the better-known of these bars in the 1960s and 1970s was an establishment known as the Pad. Somehow, Arthur learned that Jimmy was at the Pad, and he rushed out—in his bedroom slippers—to bring him home. Amazingly, he ran into one of his Princeton undergraduates during the search, which proved fruitless.

Margaret was kind and gentle, a natural but nonjudgmental listener. My sister, Peggy, believes that there was a "duality" to our mother in her curiosity and openness, but her intense sense of tradition. Peggy remembered that one evening while she lived in Washington she took Margaret out to a singles' bar, and Margaret was fascinated with observing the scene in a sort of "anthropological outing"—but also open to what was an alien form of interaction. At the same time, Margaret possessed a refined discrimination about people. She believed in what she called "good breeding," that is, less in class or wealth than in a family background that included strong ethical values. She measured people by this standard. With a highly developed sense of right and wrong, Margaret was both a traditional but also a highly modern person who could adapt to the cultural changes of her era.

For both of my parents, religion existed at the center of their lives. When my father revised his statement to the *Who's Who in America* in the late 1990s, he provided a long listing of various accomplishments. But, revealingly, he added these words, which spoke to his approach to life: "I have no thoughts on life," he wrote, "that do not stem from my Christian faith. I believe that God created me to be a loving, caring person to do His work in the world. I also believe that He called me to my vocation as a teacher and scholar."

Arthur's work on Woodrow Wilson was wrapped up in his view of God, whom he saw as personal, intelligent, all-powerful. He subscribed to a belief "in the sovereignty and inscrutable purposes of the Almighty," Arthur wrote late in life, and "his salvation-work in history."[4] He once described Wilson as the "prime embodiment, the apogee, of the Calvinistic tradition among all the statesmen of the modern epoch." The Calvinistic tradition—the belief in the power of history, justification by faith, and God's sovereignty and divine providence—were all part of how Wilson was wired, how he shaped his worldview. These were also fundamental parts of what wired Arthur Link, what motivated him and drove him on a day-to-day basis. Although he was not raised a Calvinist, he became one, and Calvinism—at least the twentieth-century Reformed faith—informed his life. Wilson's comment that his life "would not be worth living if it were not for the driving power of religion, for *faith*, pure and simple" would also apply to Arthur. He would also agree with Wilson's conclusion that those people who "believe only so far as they *understand*" were "presumptuous and set their understanding as the stand of the universe."[5]

My mother's religious views were more worldly, less intellectual, but nonetheless powerful. Hers was a more social Christianity: she saw the power of God in human interactions. She grew up in a Presbyterian environment that oozed Calvinism at every turn. But it was also a Reformed ethos that stressed probity and biblical purity, action rather than inactivity, spiritualism over materialism. Margaret saw human imperfection in a very Presbyterian way, inevitable, ever-present, but nonetheless intriguing. The duty of a good Christian, she believed, was to improve the world. Margaret in the 1970s helped to sponsor a crisis ministry in alliance with other Princeton churches that reached out to the poor with counseling, clothing, and food. The crisis ministry also incorporated the poor, homeless, and mentally ill into church services—sometimes over the objections of church members. With her children grown and gone, Margaret became an activist through the church in work for human rights, the poor, and the mentally ill. On the latter issue, Margaret became particularly interested after my brother, Jimmy, became afflicted with mental illness in 1968 and suffered recurring bouts over the next decades. In the 1980s,

Margaret served as president of the Association for Advancement of Mental Health (AAMH), which she helped to found in Princeton in 1974. The AAMH's purposes were to sponsor, as the organization website puts it today, "social care and rehabilitative services" for the mentally ill that would "allow them to live in the community with dignity and respect."[6]

Margaret was a more assertive advocate of these causes than was Arthur; she was always ahead of him on civil and human rights issues and more of a doctrinaire liberal. By the 1970s and 1980s, she became more willing to test boundaries. When Arthur and Margaret moved into a retirement community near Winston-Salem, North Carolina, in 1992, Margaret often took delight in announcing to friends and neighbors, nearly all of whom were Republicans, that she was a liberal Democrat. The explosive civil rights issue facing Presbyterians in the 1980s and 1990s was homosexuality; it remains the denomination's most divisive subject. When the issue of ordaining gay ministers exploded in the Presbyterian church nationally—with a conservative, antigay backlash erupting—both my parents were steadfast in their support of civil rights, and they endorsed ordination for a gay seminary student.

Arthur abhorred narrow-mindedness. He was especially outspoken about the equality of women in public affairs. He always said, long before it became fashionable, that he would never join any club or organization that excluded women—and he abided by that principle. After the pastor of the Montreat Presbyterian Church led an effort to prevent the installation and ordination of women as ruling elders—which was happening in Presbyterian churches around the country in the early 1970s—Arthur objected strenuously.[7]

I never detected much doubt in Margaret's faith, though I'm sure she must have had it. But, like Arthur, she had little tolerance for smug certainty or for bigotry of any kind. Arthur's Christianity was theological, academic, and scholarly—but more intellectual than worldly. Arthur was Calvinist, "but a more modern John Calvin," said Blan. "In many ways, Arthur was a traditional Christian, somewhere in between liberal and conservative" theologically. Though he was committed to causes, social action was "not his main thrust," Blan Aldridge said. He was "not as oriented in that respect" as was Margaret.

My parents took their children to church every Sunday. We attended Presbyterian churches in Evanston, Illinois, and Princeton, New Jersey. There was never much question that we would go to church. Like most children, many times we didn't want to; many times we sat through interminable sermons that had no appeal to children of the 1950s and 1960s. But we were encouraged to question and think, and during adolescence when we challenged our elders' assumptions, my parents responded with dialogue and discussion. My cousin Dave remembered talking to Margaret on the phone in 1986, before she had surgery for breast cancer. He would be thinking of her the next day during her operation, Dave assured her. "Dave," she gently chided, "I want you to do more than to think of me; I want you to be praying for me."

Arthur insisted on listening to good sermons on Sunday, and he was easily bored by pedestrian theology. When he heard a sermon in July 1964 by a Princeton pastor, he deemed it as not one of his "better efforts." And since "his best" was "not very good, his performance this morning was pretty bad."[8] Despite his intensely intellectual approach to Christianity, Arthur was committed to social justice, especially in civil rights. When the northern Presbyterian church issued a new statement of principles about social justice—the Confession of 1967—Arthur helped to draft the document.[9] Several other experiences are revealing. During the presidential contest of 1960 between John F. Kennedy and Richard Nixon, Arthur and Dick Gilbert visited L. Nelson Bell, Billy Graham's father-in-law, in Montreat. Bell, formerly a Christian missionary who was expelled from China after the 1949 revolution, was strongly anticommunist and politically conservative. Bell's house lay down the hill from our cottage, and Arthur went with Dick to meet with Billy Graham and his family. In the presidential election of 1960, Bell favored Nixon. In front of Arthur, he announced that he believed that JFK's wife, Jacqueline Kennedy, was deliberately posing as being pregnant in order to get a sympathy vote in the election. Arthur was "furious," according to Dick. "I will not listen to this," he announced. "This is the kind of silly rumors and hypocrisy that does no one any good. Come, Dick!" Although Dick wanted to spend more time with Billy Graham, he left with Arthur. Bell was conservative on race: Dick described him as "bigoted." Montreat considered permitting black teenagers to attend summer conferences; Bell opposed the measure. Arthur turned to Bell and said ironically: "Nelson, I thought you were born-again."[10]

In 1963, my older brother Stan was interested in joining Young Life, an interdenominational youth group with conservative evangelical leanings. Ordinarily, my father rarely interfered in the organizations we joined. In this case, however, he put his foot down and refused to permit Stan to join this group. Like many adolescents today, Stan was attracted to Young Life because of its social activities and because many of his friends belonged. Young Life, said Arthur, was like Pinocchio's "Donkey Island"—it sucked in young people and then converted them into unthinking puppets. Later, when I was in my teens, I questioned the existence of God. How could anyone with an intelligent view of the universe believe in a medieval view of divinity? I asked. My father's response was automatic: How could any thinking person *not* believe in God? How could a loving God condemn humans to hell? I asked. There was no hell, my father responded; everyone went to heaven. Hell, he said, was here on earth, in the grinding consequences of human sin.

One final example is illustrative of Arthur's religious beliefs, which were orthodox in many respects but unorthodox in others. In 1984, Arthur attended a family wedding and was seated at the rehearsal dinner next to the mother-in-law of a soon-to-wed relative. Arthur, as usual, was provocative. The wedding took place just a few weeks before the presidential election that pitted incumbent President Ronald Reagan, a darling of the Religious Right, against liberal Democrat Walter Mondale. Whom did she support for the presidency, Arthur asked his dinner companion? "As a Christian, I am, of course, voting for Reagan," she replied. Arthur's response reflected his reflexive bristling against a brand of Christianity that he grew up with and ultimately rejected. For many years, Arthur and the bridegroom had had many discussions about religion. Arthur's young relative had veered toward conservative evangelicalism, and Arthur enjoyed tweaking him about his beliefs and challenging him on a number of theological and biblical points. Arthur knew theology and he knew the Bible, which he read regularly, and his authority was difficult to question. He didn't refrain from taking on the new mother-in-law. "How do you know," he asked her, "that God is not a Communist?"

Margaret and Arthur were not heroes: they possessed mainstream views, and as southern whites they did not lead the charge and engage in social protest. In many ways, they were very conventional and old-fashioned, and while my siblings and I were growing up, it seemed to us that our parents really did not understand the generation of their children, the generation of the 1950s and 1960s. Although opposed to white supremacy, Arthur was dismayed when the civil rights movement seemed to implode in the late 1960s. When protesters disrupted Princeton University after Richard Nixon ordered the invasion of Cambodia in April 1970, my father had little sympathy with campus radicals—though he was also opposed to the American war in Indochina, the protests closed the university and denied him access to his office in Firestone Library.

Neither Margaret nor Arthur "would have been happy with anyone else," observed a friend, who thought Margaret needed a person "so dedicated to a mission in life." She accepted his character defects, his intense self-centeredness, because she bought into his "credo" of a mission in life. Living with him was an interesting ride: Margaret enjoyed the conversations and the intellectual stimulation that came with Arthur. She thoroughly enjoyed his power, status, and prestige; in another day and time, she would have wanted these through her own work, not through his. But at the same time, she tempered and civilized Arthur, mediating things when there were conflicts or when his "declamations" became annoying. She was a "great foil" to his rough edges.[11]

One of Margaret's closest friends in Princeton in later years was Margaret "Mag" Wardlaw Gilbert, whom she knew from childhood days in Montreat. Mag's father was a Presbyterian minister; she was part of the nexus existing between the highly Presbyterian Davidson College and the church community at Montreat. Mag's husband, Dick, was a Presbyterian minister who had started out in advertising, earned a seminary degree, and then worked as the head of the northern Presbyterian church's media operation in New York City. Mag and Dick were unconventional, iconoclastic, and always attracted interesting friends and acquaintances. Mag Gilbert often spoke her mind to Margaret: she thought Arthur's behavior was "outrageous." He was "just plain selfish and a bully," but she realized that he was "Margaret's bully, and she knows how to spoil him, and then she knows how to guide him, and she also knows how to manipulate him." Margaret, Mag would often say, "raised four children and Arthur." But the truth was that Arthur was utterly dependent on Margaret. This meant that she possessed "all the power in that relationship," according to Peggy, because she understood the marriage's emotional dynamics.[12]

Although we spent many years in New Jersey, both my parents considered the culture of that state to be far beneath North Carolina values of gentility and civility. If New Jerseyisms crept into their children's speech, we were corrected. If we used phrases such as "youse" instead of "you all," if we pronounced "blouse" as "blous" rather than "blouz," if we used the word "already" too much ("I took the trash out already"), if we put the preposition "at" at the end of a sentence, or if we did not properly acknowledge kindnesses and presents, we were scolded. Arthur believed deeply in southern civility: as one former student correctly put it, "he didn't privilege family, but he did privilege manners."[13] As children, we were expected to be polite and respectful in dealings with our fellow human beings—something that was antithetical to what my mother especially thought was true of New Jersey. My parents always made sure that we realized where our roots lay—in the South, especially in North Carolina. I always thought that my mother was far too hard on New Jersey, and I grew up loving the state and its people. In retrospect, it's clear to me that she projected a feeling of foreignness, of otherness, about New Jersey. But I always knew that I would live in North Carolina, and attending college and moving there with my own family seemed my natural fate.

But there were also significant differences between my parents. Arthur grew up poorer, Margaret more solidly middle class. Arthur's family can be characterized as a middling sort, respectable but not affluent. Though his parents were the first in their families to attend college, both were highly intelligent and enterprising. The Links were, however, eccentric, quirky, and iconoclastic, sometimes biting in their dealings with each other—possessing what Arthur once called the "proverbial Link contrariness."[14] In the case of Arthur, his parents' bad marriage and his father's demons haunted his family. The Links did not enjoy interpersonal communication and the discussion of emotional problems, and like many families, they evaded problems rather than confronting them. With a good deal of emotional and psychological bruising, Arthur sought to escape from family relations, rather than to embrace them.

In contrast, Margaret's family was emotionally rich and connective. She was outgoing and empathetic, eager to deal with problems and offer counsel. An astute judge of people, Margaret took the full measure of people, though she was always willing to tolerate their weaknesses. She had a habit of sheltering people under her wing and mentoring them, and she sympathized with the weak. Arthur was self-absorbed, perhaps instinctively defensive, but also intensely gregarious and interested in those around him. He loved celebrity, loved associations with famous people.

My parents' lives as southerners also informed my own fascination with the South, and the process of change and dislocation that affected southerners in the twentieth century. The story of my parents' lives offers a unique perspective on how the South changed: as they grew up, and especially once they came to the University of North Carolina, they came to question basic precepts of their home, even while they maintained a strong regional identity. This book explores the moments at which they left home, how they came to understand themselves as a result, and how they found, in the end, that the South was always their home.

CHAPEL HILL

1

During the fall of 1941, while hard times lingered and world war loomed, Arthur Link and Margaret Douglas had both enrolled as new graduate students at the University of North Carolina. They were drawn to Carolina because it was a dynamic intellectual and cultural center of the South in the 1930s and 1940s. Under the leadership of a series of visionary presidents—Edward Kidder Graham in the 1910s, Harry Woodburn Chase in the 1920s, and Frank Porter Graham in the 1930s and 1940s—UNC attracted unmatched brainpower to its campus. The university became known as an island of freethinking and experimentation, a reputation that sometimes cast it at odds with the state's conservative population and political leadership. UNC was especially strong in the humanities and social sciences, and in those disciplines faculty pushed the politically acceptable boundaries of knowledge in a reexamination of the South's race, labor, and agricultural problems.[1]

Margaret and Arthur were swept up in this ethos. Seeking an advanced degree in sociology, Margaret was also interested in history; seeking an advanced degree in history, Arthur was also interested in sociology. Although their family backgrounds were very different, in 1941 they were already experiencing the upheaval that would come to the South during World War II. More than any other force, the war undermined the social foundations and traditional structure of the American South. Like many of their contemporaries, Arthur and Margaret were thrown into strange new situations, forced to confront the world at large in a way that white southerners had never done. The idyllic world of UNC, at once both removed from and a part of the new social forces coming to mid-twentieth-century North Carolina, served as a center of changes coming to the South.

Arthur and Margaret first met at UNC's Institute for Research in Social Sciences (IRSS), where both worked as research assistants. The institute was created in 1924 under UNC sociologist Howard W. Odum. Born in rural Georgia, Odum studied sociology at Columbia and then joined Carolina's faculty in 1920. He was recruited to expand UNC's School of Public Welfare and the Department of Sociology; both were viewed as critical to the university's attempt to involve itself in the public affairs of North Carolina. In 1922, Odum started *Social Forces*, a journal dedicated to analyzing southern social problems. Two years later, he won a major grant from the Laura Spelman Rockefeller Memorial, part of the Rockefeller philanthropic empire. Founder of the famous Southern Regionalist school of sociology, Odum became a leading interpreter of the American South. During and after the New Deal, he was widely consulted for his views on race, farm tenancy, and the cotton textile industry. The IRSS sponsored UNC scholars and affiliated researchers, while it also funded graduate students.

Family lore has it that Arthur and Margaret met each other on the steps of Carolina's Alumni Hall on October 12, 1941, University Day at UNC. As institute research assistants, they shared an office on the fourth floor of that building. A few years later, Margaret recalled the institute's "rattletrap" typewriter and how she used it one morning and disturbed Arthur's margins. My father was always fussy about things like that, and he found Margaret's use of the typewriter annoying. On the other hand, she found him brash and self-absorbed.[2] But during the 1941–42 year they became friends, though at some point during that year Margaret became seriously involved with Clifton H. Kreps, a graduate student in economics at UNC who received a master's degree in the spring of 1942. After working for the National War Labor Board and the Office of Price Administration during the war, Kreps moved to Duke to complete his dissertation in 1948. Sometime during her first year at Carolina, Margaret fell head over heels in love with Kreps. "I'm more sure every day that Clif is the only one for me," she wrote her parents in August 1942. Margaret was certain that she had found true love, and there was "just no doubt in my mind now." She planned to marry Kreps, though she admitted that he didn't "know this yet." All she had to do was to "wait around a couple of years till he's ready & able to marry me."[3]

During the first several years that they knew each other, Margaret did not take Arthur very seriously on a romantic level. In private correspondence, she made it clear that she considered him boorish. Arthur commented later, in March 1943, about "our little discussions up in 408 Alumni" where he "let slip some statements which appeared dogmatic and intolerant."[4] Margaret was not alone in her initial assessment of Arthur, which was shared by many of his UNC peers. Ben Wall, a contemporary in graduate school, described Arthur as "very, very pompous" and "very self-centered." Arthur especially loved to correct his peers on points of fact. He was known to irritate fellow students with his precise memory, his encyclopedic knowledge, and his wide reading.[5]

Arthur was also awkward socially. On occasion, he joined his classmates to watch basketball or baseball games. One of them complained: "He talks so goddamn much, don't let him come."[6] His arrogance set him off from other students. Jane Zimmerman, another UNC graduate student, complained that she was "terrifically disappointed" in Arthur. Although she acknowledged his brilliance and his ability to do great things, she said that he was "in so many ways . . . unattractive." Arthur's fellow grad students were sometimes "jealous of brilliant students like Link," but their annoyance at him wasn't all jealousy. Perhaps, Zimmerman observed, he was still immature. But a conversation that she had with him in early 1945—in which he told her that he considered himself, at the age of twenty-four, the world's leading authority on Woodrow Wilson—was, for her, the last straw. She was "very mad" at him, "with all of his 'airs.'"[7]

Starting UNC in the fall of 1937, Arthur gravitated toward historians Fletcher Green and Howard K. Beale. These two mentors were quite different, each possessing complementary strengths. A historian of the South, Green was recognized widely by his peers as a leader of southern historians who trained a generation of graduate students. Over the course of his long career at UNC, Green directed more than 100 doctoral students and 150 master's students. Arthur worked with Green on a senior honors thesis on the history of the buildings at UNC—a project for which he was paid out of funds from the New Deal's National Youth Administration. The thesis, which earned Arthur highest honors, was a 292-page tome that is the definitive work on the subject—and today remains one of the most frequently used items in the North Carolina Collection at the UNC–Chapel Hill library.

Set against Green was Beale, a scholar of the Reconstruction era and subsequently a biographer of Theodore Roosevelt. Arriving on the UNC campus in 1935 after receiving a Harvard Ph.D., teaching stints at Grinnell and Bowdoin, and work at the National Archives, Beale was an intellectual dynamo—his best-known student at UNC was C. Vann Woodward—and he drew Arthur into his circle. Beale also stirred things up at Carolina, and his commitment to pacifism and racial justice ran contrary to the History Department's conservative tendencies. Isaac Copeland, a grad student in the 1940s, later observed that Beale "never understood the southern mind, or the small-town or rural South."[8] Historian George Tindall described him as "a curious bundle of contradictions, lavish prodigality and narrow scrimping, liberal impulses and ingrained snobbery, a man with a gift for putting noses out of joint, a running adventure in culture shock for countless Southerners and not a few fellow Yankees."[9] Beale was arrogant and dispensed with the niceties of southern gentility. "Howard is all right, but he can be a bit of a shit at times," one of Beale's very close friends once told Arthur.[10] Beale was an insistent complainer. He objected to southern food, which he described as "horrible" despite its reputation "for being so good." He missed the urban environment of New York, Chicago, and Washington. The students at Carolina, he wrote one friend in 1936, exhibited good manners, but they also exhibited "complacency" and "indifference" about the world around them.[11] Beale, a northerner and an activist, suffered from a "frightful loneliness" at Carolina.[12]

Beale recognized an extraordinary talent in Arthur, though perhaps he also saw similar qualities of arrogance. Arthur, for his part, recognized Beale's penchant for contention and controversy, later describing him as the "queerest combination of contradictions I've ever seen in one man." Beale heavily recruited Arthur during his senior year, inviting him to dinner and transporting him to Raleigh for classical music concerts. When Arthur considered applying to doctoral programs, Beale encouraged him to apply to Harvard and Chicago. In his letter of recommendation, Beale described Arthur as "the best undergraduate who has majored in history" in his six years at UNC, and as "superior to most graduate students I have taught." In the fall of 1940, Beale encouraged Arthur to attend his first Southern Historical Association meeting in Charleston, South Carolina, and even provided a ride there and subsidized the trip.

Arthur faced a choice during his senior year in 1940–41, as relations between his two advisers soured over Beale's personal and professional style. Despite his flirtation with Beale, Arthur decided to remain at UNC to work under Green's direction because he was known as a master teacher who took special care overseeing his graduate students. Their styles meshed: both Green and Arthur were empiricists who believed in documentary sources. Both were workaholics who were always in the library. Green's high standards made an impression. Arthur would never conduct scholarship "without thinking of Fletcher looking over my shoulder and thinking: This was right; this was wrong. I never had that feeling about my other teachers."[13] Arthur admired Green as a mentor, he wrote in July 1944, because there was "absolutely no guile or deception about him; you always know how he will act—always straight and above-board." Arthur thought that he was "frank, sometimes brutally frank," but that he possessed a genuine affection for his graduate students.[14]

But there was a price to be paid in Arthur's choice of Green: the end of his relationship with Beale, at least for the time being. Beale had promised to employ Arthur as a research assistant during the summer of 1941, between graduation and the beginning of graduate school, but once Arthur chose Green as a mentor, Beale dropped him "like a hot potato," canceling the summer offer.[15] Arthur was frozen out. Beale, who had invited Arthur to visit at his summer house in Thetford, Vermont, abruptly canceled the invitation.[16]

In 1942, Beale left UNC in the heat of controversy, with what he called "wild and loose talk about me emanating from my own department." He had opposed American entry into World War II, even after the Japanese attack on Pearl Harbor, and he protested Franklin D. Roosevelt's decision to intern Japanese Americans in concentration camps. Ben Wall recalled that the department had "split wide open" on the question of the war, though it was difficult to determine whether the real issue was the war or Beale. During the war, Beale took an extended leave and worked in San Francisco as the West Coast director of the National Japanese American Student Relocation Council, which was organized by the American Friends Service Committee to coordinate efforts to place 2,500 Japanese

American students in American colleges and universities. Beale also visited the internment camps, where he found conditions "pretty bad," and he described the "pathetically loyal" Japanese Americans who were "baffled" by how their government had treated them.[17]

During the war, Beale had only intermittent contact with Arthur. In the spring of 1944, they ran into each other when Beale breezed in and out of the Manuscripts Division of the Library of Congress while Arthur was working there. "You know Beale," Arthur wrote a friend. "He had already seen everyone of importance in Washington except the President."[18] Throughout his life, Arthur always remained susceptible to the seduction of associating with prominent people. Beale definitely exuded prominence.[19] Arthur was persistent, and in the spring of 1945 they renewed contact. Beale, for his part, became interested in Arthur once again only after he had become an established scholar. He was "so glad at all the good things I have heard," Beale wrote to Arthur in June 1945.[20] After Arthur had been appointed to his first permanent job at Princeton in August, Arthur praised Beale for his "splendid and fine and truly Christian" work with interned Japanese American students during the war.[21]

In contrast to Beale, Fletcher Green maintained an ever-patient relationship with Arthur. Perhaps, as Wall speculated, Green believed that "time would erode some of Arthur's barnacles." Ray Newsome observed that Arthur's brilliance and achievements did not "make for popularity with his fellow graduate students," but he believed that he possessed no "serious personality defect or social ineptitude which more experience will not take care of." Arthur was not unaware of fellow grad students' hostility. Later in life, he admitted to me that his years in graduate school involved constant sniping from his peers—or so he perceived things. In 1947, two years after receiving his degree, he admitted to a friend that he never took his peers seriously, and "they hated me most cordially." "Especially if you try to do as much and as well as you can," he wrote, "you are sure to incur their displeasure."[22]

Under Green's direction, Arthur mapped out an ambitious research agenda. The summer before he began graduate school, in June 1941, he took a course on twentieth-century American history taught by visiting scholar Chester M. Destler. He urged Arthur to exploit the Woodrow Wilson Papers, which had just opened up to researchers at the Library of Congress in Washington. Arthur was interested in Wilson, but only

Links: My Family in American History

in the context of another topic: he wanted to rewrite the history of the South's liberal tradition. His master's thesis, a study of Woodrow Wilson and the South, examined the neglected subject of political liberalism in the region. In the context of the late 1930s—a period when the South was attempting to shed its oligarchic past and embrace a new, progressive future—Arthur wanted to reinterpret the South's ideological roots. Ever optimistic, he believed in the existence of a southern liberal tradition that needed reclaiming.[23]

In his first year at the Institute for Research in Social Sciences at UNC, Arthur worked as Rupert Vance's research assistant. Vance, a sociologist and Odum protégé, arrived at UNC in 1926 and remained there for the next forty years. Like Odum, he was a student of southern social problems and an adherent of the Southern Regionalist approach to sociology, which asserted that social problems were best understood in the particular context of the region. Arthur worked with Vance, and even contemplated a dissertation that would borrow from Vance and Odum's regionalism and apply it to southern history.

In 1942, Arthur received a one-thousand-dollar fellowship from the Rosenwald Fund, a philanthropy involved for nearly twenty-five years in modernizing African American rural schools. In 1942–43, the year after he finished his master's thesis, Arthur applied his energies to researching and writing his dissertation, working at record speed. Completing a draft by February 1943, Arthur had essentially finished the thesis by the following summer.

Spending the summer and part of the fall of 1942 in Washington, Arthur discovered that Wilson's presidential papers—along with other relevant manuscript collections—had been evacuated to an "inland library" because of fears of military attack. These would be returned to the Library of Congress in 1944, though Arthur assumed that he would have no access for the duration of the war. During the summer of 1942, however, he secured permission to use the materials from Katherine Brand, curator of the Wilson collection, and from Edith Galt Wilson, Wilson's widow. Meanwhile, he interviewed such Wilson contemporaries as Oklahoma senator Thomas P. Gore, North Carolina senator Josiah W. Bailey, and Virginia senators Carter Glass and Harry F. Byrd. In North Carolina, he arranged interviews with others such as Progressive-era journalists Clarence H. Poe and Josephus Daniels. He continued his research during the fall of 1942, using Rosenwald money to visit Charlottesville and Richmond and to finish more newspaper research.[24]

Born on August 8, 1920, Arthur descended from German, Scotch-Irish, and English immigrants to the Shenandoah Valley of Virginia. Although there were slaveholders in his family lineage, most of his forbears were of modest means, members of the southern yeoman class. Arthur's ancestors lived in the same county for about 150 years, though during his father's generation the family spread into other parts of the South. Arthur's parents, John William and Helen Elizabeth Link, were both born and raised in Jefferson County, West Virginia. Located in the northern Shenandoah Valley, Jefferson County lay on the Potomac River, and its rich soil made the farmlands unusually productive. The first white settlers arrived in the region in the early eighteenth century, and Euro-American settlement was well under way by the 1730s. Into the nineteenth century, the commercial farming of the northern valley made Shepherdstown a prosperous market town.

My paternal grandparents—living in a community with relatively few new immigrants and a limited gene pool—were third cousins, both born within five miles of each other with the Link surname. John and Helen Link shared a common great-grandfather, but they came from very different experiences. Helen E. Link lived in a house in Shepherdstown that was two blocks from the town's main business district. She enjoyed reading and music, was the eldest of two daughters, and was educated and cultured. John W. Link, my grandfather, was born to a family of thirteen in a log cabin in the county, labored in a lime kiln and a barrel factory as a child, and worked his way through college. John was rough-hewn, with dark devils tormenting him. He trained for the ministry, yet he was ill-suited for that vocation. Undoubtedly, a hard childhood shaped John's contradictory personality: emotionally needy, he had great difficulty expressing emotion or in developing close personal relationships. Rarely reading books, John preferred fishing or building things to reflection or contemplation. He solved problems impulsively, acting rather than thinking. But John was also extraordinarily intelligent. He was especially clever with numbers, and in his elder years he used to amaze his grandchildren (one of whom became a math Ph.D. and later taught at the University of Virginia) with his computational and analytical ability. Late in life, he did the lion's share of research for and writing of a comprehensive family history that is a model of care and clarity.

When he was born, in the central Shenandoah Valley town of New Market, Arthur was described as "very peeked." His parents were concerned enough about his health to arrange for his baptism by a visiting clergyman in New Market the day after he was born.[25] Helen's maternal overprotectiveness focused especially on her children's health. John William, the eldest, had an acute case of rheumatic fever that resulted in what doctors called an "enlarged heart," and Helen worried constantly about his condition.[26] When Elinor, the youngest, was about three, she contracted a bad case of scarlet fever that spread to her kidneys and almost killed her. As an infant, Arthur was afflicted with a mysterious ailment that he always described as polio. The case remained unclear, but it appeared to have caused a spinal deformity that contributed to chronic back problems and numerous surgeries that began when he was in his mid-forties.[27]

In 1923, Arthur's family moved to Danville, Virginia, and four years later, to Mt. Pleasant, North Carolina, a small town of around one thousand residents that catered to local farming interests, especially cotton farmers.[28] The Link household in Mt. Pleasant was not a happy one, and, unlike Margaret, Arthur grew up in a severely troubled family. The household grew steadily after John and Helen were married, with the arrival of John William, Elizabeth, Arthur, and Elinor occurring in steady procession.

Years later, my mother admitted to my sister that Arthur hated his father, though he kept his contempt to himself. His feelings toward his father resulted from John's tyranny over the household. The eldest child, John William, was a homosexual with a tortured sexuality. He engaged in constant conflict with his father, rebelling against straight-laced southern Protestantism. John William goaded his father: on one occasion, he read the Koran at the dinner table. He took a kind of perverse delight in challenging his father and angering him. "My father would start chewing harder and louder," my father's younger sister, Elinor, remembered, and "breathing very hard, and we knew he was about to explode." John William would "just smile." Helen later remarked to Arthur that it "makes me very sad" to contemplate the animosity between John William and his father. "I wish that he could be large enough to forget some things and put away that terrible animosity that he harbors in his heart," she wrote. "I feel that it colors his whole outlook on life and he has let it assume entirely too much importance in his thinking." Yet she concluded: "Of one thing I am certain, and that is, that the best thing is for those two never to get to-gether," as John William's "whole personality changes when your Daddy comes around," something which she had "noticed . . . time and again."[29]

My grandfather beat Elizabeth, the second-born child, and the beatings went beyond the ordinary use of corporal discipline, even by contemporary standards. "Overbearing was a nice way to put it," Elinor remembered. Like the other Link children, Elizabeth hated her father; there was "not a lot of love lost between the two." Constantly critical, John often cruelly berated her and her abilities. As a teenager, Elizabeth, a great seamstress, once made a brown velvet dress with gold beads for a dance after her father gave her permission to attend. When she came downstairs to leave, her father stopped her. "Where do you think you're going?" he asked. "You said I could go to the dance," she responded. "No, I didn't tell you that. You're not going anywhere." She burst into tears and ran from the room.[30]

John succeeded in intimidating everyone in the family. Many nights, Elinor woke up hearing her parents argue. Recalling that her father could be sarcastic and cruel and "just cut you to ribbons," Elinor resented "everything that my father ever did to me—or to my mother." Elinor was especially fearful for the safety of her mother, whom she loved "beyond words." She recalled that when her mother took her to the first day of school, she threw a tantrum. Helen stayed with her all day because Elinor feared that if she returned home, her father would kill her. Her fears were allayed only after Helen went every day to school with her for a week. "That's how frightening the atmosphere was," she remembered. "He just scared the hell out of me." Frequently, the family sat and read in the family room and parlor. When John came in, a warning sign of bullying was if he put his hands in his pockets and started looking at his family. It was always better to stay out of his way, and it wasn't uncommon for all the children, one by one, to find an excuse to leave the room. The Link children were, remembered Elinor, "very clever about not being in his presence."[31]

After Arthur's birth in 1920 and Elinor's three years later, Helen became determined to protect her two youngest children from John. He might have been simply worn out with struggling with John William and Elizabeth; perhaps he mellowed a little with his younger children. John was "tired of beating everybody," Elinor recalled, "so he kind of ignored Arthur and me." Helen realized that she could have real influence, and better relationships, with her younger children, without having to worry about John. Arthur was fortunate, Elinor recalled, because Helen "had a lot to give, and he took it all in." Arthur and Helen shared many interests: music and reading were probably the most important. They also resembled each other in disposition, and Arthur shared her worldview. Like the rest of his siblings, he approached his father warily, learning to adapt by avoidance.[32]

When we were children, my brothers, my sister, and I encountered a kindly grandfather who liked to play word games, who took a strong interest in his grandchildren. My mother always said that Paw-Paw—which is what we called our grandfather—was a much better grandparent than a father, though we saw some hints of the tyrannical parent that he had been. I remember him in his eighties and nineties as a person of strong prejudices. He was anti-Semitic and racist, something we found shocking. I remember, as I grew older, Paw-Paw expressing curious theological views. He was a creationist, refusing to believe in the validity of evolution. Once, as a teenager, I challenged these views, and I remember my father providing some advice afterward. "Don't bother talking to Daddy about things like science and theology," he said. "It's nothing but a waste of time."

I never met either of my Douglas grandparents. My grandfather James McDowell Douglas died in June 1951, and my grandmother Anniebelle Munroe Douglas about a year later—two years before I was born. James was born in 1867 in Fairfield County, in Upcountry South Carolina, the fourth-born of nine children and the second son of James Douglas and Margaret McDowell Douglas. Remarkably, he remembered Union troops who continued to occupy the Upcountry during the Ku Klux Klan insurgency of the early 1870s. James's family came from devoutly Presbyterian and hardworking Scotch-Irish who arrived with the wave of eighteenth-century immigrants who peopled the Carolina backcountry.[33] My maternal grandmother, Anniebelle Munroe Douglas, was descended from the Highland Scots in North Carolina's Upper Cape Fear

Valley, northwest of Fayetteville, and tobacco planters in Southside Virginia. Like James, Anniebelle's parents were devout Presbyterians. Her father, Colin A. Munroe, like three of his brothers, was a Presbyterian minister. My mother was especially close to her father. Margaret saw James Douglas as a sort of kindred spirit, a person whom she described, as a twenty-four-year-old, as "an ideal father, counsellor, friend and companion to me in whatever I do."[34]

Teaching at Davidson for forty-three years, James became an institution at the college. When he died in June 1951, he was remembered in a faculty resolution as a teacher who imparted scientific concepts with "simplicity, clarity, and infinite patience." Many of his students went on to graduate work, but "none of them will ever forget his learning, his geniality, his sympathy." Widely read, James had a "deep interest in literature, especially in Shakespeare." In faculty meetings, he spoke only rarely, but when he did "his words were the words of wisdom." For James, "sanity—fine, rare, plain common sense—was one of his chief qualities."[35]

Born on July 22, 1918, just as World War I was ending, Margaret Douglas belonged to a tightly connected family that found its home, in the early twentieth century, in the little Piedmont college town of Davidson, North Carolina. For the most part, Margaret's antecedents farmed the South's four major crops: tobacco, cotton, rice, and indigo. Many of them were slaveholders, but they were also educators, ministers, and physicians, planters and entrepreneurs, what might be called part of a southern middle class. All of them were also a part of the Confederacy's rise and fall, and a number fought for the South during the Civil War.

As I was growing up, we gravitated toward the Douglas side of the family. The Douglases were warm, interested, intelligent, connected, and completely devoted to family. My mother had one sibling, John, who was three years older, and he lived most of his life in Charlotte. He had a vibrant spouse, Marjorie, who went to great pains to maintain family communication and to organize get-togethers, and who was wonderfully welcoming to children. Their three sons, even today, remain some of the closest family I have, people on whom you can count for support and encouragement. We enjoyed a bond with the Douglases because we shared so much time together. We spent summers in North Carolina, usually a full two months, driving down from New Jersey in late June and driving back just before Labor Day. Always part of that trip was a week in Charlotte and, often, another week at their cottage at the South Carolina beach. Sometimes the Douglases came north. In 1964, they spent a week with us in Princeton, and we went together to the New York World's Fair of that year. The three boys all stayed on a sleeping porch that was just outside of my room in the Princeton house.

My mother's extended family existed in an insulated cocoon that was defined by the town of Davidson and the institution of Davidson College. My grandfather, James Douglas, earned a Ph.D. from Johns Hopkins, but he undoubtedly belonged to a powerful southern Presbyterian culture that dominated the interior of the American South. Born in 1867, he came from a large family with scarce resources that managed to send all but one of his siblings to college. His older brother, John Leighton Douglas, taught mathematics at Davidson, while two of his sisters would live in town.

My mother grew up encircled by Douglases. Two of James's siblings, John and Catherine, along with Margaret's first cousin Grace James, lived in Davidson only a few doors east on Concord Road. John, a lifelong bachelor, was, according to Margaret's brother, John Munroe Douglas, "rather serious-minded," and Catherine a "pretty austere" woman who rarely laughed or smiled. John—known by my mother and her brother as "Der"—was the patriarch of the kinship network. John and Catherine both served as sibling leaders and dispensed advice and, when necessary, reproved their siblings. Once or twice a week, James, sometimes with John and Margaret in tow, walked to Der's house and talked for a few hours, discussing the news or telling stories about their youth.

In the world of Davidson, John and Margaret would listen in a corner, taking it all in. Margaret's aunt Margaret Douglas, who had left the Douglas nest in 1906 to become a Presbyterian missionary to Brazil, returned to Davidson on a furlough once every five years, and she stayed with John and Catherine. Two other brothers lived nearby: Robert, a lawyer in Chester, South Carolina, and Davison, a Presbyterian minister who became president of the University of South Carolina in 1926. My grandfather remained especially close to Davison; they shared a great sense of humor, and they enjoyed visits in which they exchanged stories and told jokes. In 1931, Davison's premature death, the result of a stroke and massive cerebral hemorrhage at the age of sixty-two, shook James.[36]

The town of Davidson, according to my uncle, ran "under the rules of the Presbyterian church," in which "what the Presbyterian church stood for, Davidson stood for." James served as a deacon (1912–20) and elder

(1920–51) of the Davidson College Presbyterian Church; the longtime minister Charlie Richards was married to his cousin. James and Annie-belle were often in charge of communion. Anniebelle would boil glasses, fill them with grape juice, and cut little squares of bread. All town residents attended church; among students, attendance was expected—and regularly taken. On the Sabbath, no activity was permitted aside from reading the Bible. John and Margaret could not read newspapers or the comics; James usually placed the Sunday paper on a bookcase, outside of the reach of the children.[37] North Carolina Presbyterians were theologically conservative, and Davidson divines strongly opposed modernism and the teaching of Darwinian evolution in the schools. In the 1920s, James Douglas and other Presbyterians enthusiastically greeted the new breed of popular evangelists such as Billy Sunday.[38]

Anniebelle and James married late in life, on May 27, 1909—he was forty-one; she was thirty-one. Quick-tempered and moody, Anniebelle found a good match in James Douglas. My mother often described her as "high-strung," and she remembered Anniebelle as moving quickly and impatiently, especially in the kitchen. Many years later, in an interview given when he was eighty-six years old, my mother's brother recalled that his mother was "moody" and "maybe had some depression." She had an easy relationship with her husband, even though she insisted on calling him "Dr. Douglas." James, who was "more placid," complemented the uneven edges of her personality. "Life's journey has been sweeter, fuller, and easier since you decided to share it with me," he wrote Anniebelle on Christmas 1919.[39]

Four years after Anniebelle and James were married, in April 1913, her uncle, John Peter Munroe, deeded the couple the North Carolina Medical College building in Davidson as a wedding present. Anniebelle and her uncle were close. She had worked as nurse, accountant, and housekeeper for her father's youngest brother. Born on March 29, 1857, John Peter graduated from Davidson in 1882 and studied medicine at the University of Virginia, where he received the M.D., first in his class, in 1885. In 1889, he became the Davidson College physician. Three years after taking over a small "medical department" at the college, John Peter obtained a charter for the North Carolina Medical College, and, in 1896, he constructed a three-story building across from campus.

John Peter was also an entrepreneur extraordinaire who was involved in running two banks, two cotton mills, a cotton oil mill, and drug store

Links: My Family in American History

in Davidson. As president of the Linden Cotton Mill, which he helped to organize, John Peter taught a Sunday school for the mill workers and even played the violin for them. At Davidson, he also served as athletic director, assisting the football coach, and often refereeing football games. While at the medical college, Anniebelle met James Douglas, and the relationship matured into a love match. When James proposed in early 1909, he asked John Peter for his approval. John Peter—whom Margaret and John called "Uncle Doctor"—remained a constant presence in the life of Anniebelle's family.

In 1911, John Peter moved the medical school to Charlotte so that it could be closer to the clinical facilities of a larger town. In 1910, Abraham Flexner's famous report, which was commissioned by the Rockefeller Foundation in order to upgrade American medical education, condemned the facilities of the North Carolina Medical College as "thoroughly wretched." A few years after, John Peter sold his control over the school to the Medical College of Virginia in Richmond, and the school came to an end.

Although he gave half of the old Davidson Medical College to the Douglases, John Peter retained the other half. For some time, he rented the adjoining eastern half of the building—known as the "Shaw House" because of its longtime tenant, college librarian Cornelia Shaw. James remained understandably anxious about the house's future. John Peter admitted that he had "numerous outstanding debts secured wholly or in part by my real estate," and there was always great uncertainty about John Peter's financial stability. John Munroe Douglas remembered John Peter as a wild speculator whose assets were constantly at risk.[40] Later, during the Depression, his house of cards collapsed; in 1938, broke and in bad health, Uncle Doctor moved back to Davidson and lived in Margaret's room. He died on October 14, 1940, with $61.36 in the bank, about $400 in assets, and numerous outstanding debts. After funeral expenses, John Peter's estate was worth $51.78.[41] In 1921, John Peter had agreed to sell the Shaw house to James and Anniebelle, and in 1928, they settled on a price of three thousand dollars. James paid him in installments, finally completing the transaction in 1932. The Douglases continued to rent the Shaw House portion of the old Medical College to relatives or other tenants.[42]

Although Anniebelle wanted to build her own house—and even kept notes about possible house designs—the old medical college served as a home for the Douglases for the next forty-two years.[43] Big and rambling, with a spacious backyard that housed chickens, a milk cow, and a vegetable garden, the house easily accommodated the family. Drafty in the winter, the house was heated by coal and kerosene stoves, and remained hot and stuffy in the summer. Certain parts of the house reminded young John of a college, he remembered. There were screw holes for benches and seats in floor, which was made of heart pine and hardwood. There were two finished, unheated rooms in the attic that John sometimes explored; one was an old anatomy lab, with the names of students written on the wall. Visitors came into a first-floor hallway that was unheated. On the right was a parlor, behind that a living room and study. On the other side was the dining room, and behind it the kitchen. Upstairs, a staircase led to a long hallway. In the front, on the left facing the street, was John's bedroom. Another large bedroom was his parents' room, heated by a Franklin stove. Halfway down the hall on the left-hand side was another bedroom, eventually occupied by Margaret. The family shared a single bathroom that was unheated except on Saturday, when it was heated for baths.[44]

James and Anniebelle's family grew slowly. Tragedy struck when their first child, whom they named James McDowell Douglas Jr., was born dead on December 1, 1912, because the umbilical cord had wrapped around his neck during childbirth. The death of the infant James was remembered in the family as a terrible blow to Anniebelle and James. Both were older parents: Anniebelle was thirty-five, James forty-five. Two years later, on December 21, 1914, John Munroe Douglas was born, and three and a half years after that, on July 22, 1918, my mother, Margaret McDowell Douglas, was born. At the time of her birth, her mother was forty-one and her father fifty.

Despite their differences, my parents both grew up in a world that was governed by well-defined rules and hierarchies. Across the North Carolina Piedmont, in towns like Davidson and Mt. Pleasant, cotton mills sprang up and produced a proletariat that lived apart from the town classes. Townsfolk viewed Piedmont mill workers with contempt. I remember vestiges of these sentiments in my parents' attitudes. Although both were classic racial liberals, neither cared much for the southern industrial working class, whom they considered ignorant, superstitious, and backward. My father even objected to the use of the word "overall" because it suggested the denim uniform that mill people wore. Both of my parents also lived in a world regimented by differences between men and women: women exercised authority in limited spheres, but were excluded from the main circles of social, economic, and political power. And the Carolina Piedmont was a place of strictly enforced racial injustice. The small towns that my parents grew up in nurtured contacts between whites and blacks of a kind that assured whites that "their blacks" were contented and happy under the Jim Crow system.

Davidson boasted two spinning mills south of town, across the railroad tracks. The white working-class population of mill workers inhabited a "mill hill" neighborhood; Davidson African Americans occupied a separate neighborhood. Merchants, professionals, and faculty lived east of the tracks, along Main Street, running north toward Iredell County and the nearby town of Mooresville, and south toward Charlotte, along Concord Road, which intersected with Main Street and ran east toward Cabarrus County. James belonged to the college and mercantile elite that ran the town. Within the bounds of this social system, James loved ordinary company, and he enjoyed speaking with different sorts of folk, including acquaintances from across the tracks and across racial lines. Davidson African Americans worked in a service capacity at the college, with many of the women working as domestics for the white townspeople. Even so, James was very careful to maintain the racial etiquette of never admitting African Americans through the front door.[45]

Situated in Cabarrus County, in the heart of the southern Piedmont region about thirty miles northeast of Charlotte, Mt. Pleasant was located in a large region that had experienced heavy German immigration in the decades before the American Revolution. The old Mt. Pleasant High School is now a middle school; a newer high school was constructed in the 1990s outside the town limits. Today, the town is little changed, with a population of 1,200 overwhelmingly composed of traditional, native-born, and white North Carolinians. Unlike much of the rest of the state, which has experienced a large infusion of Mexican and Central American immigrants, Mt. Pleasant possesses a small Latino population. Today, there is little cotton grown in the area, though the surrounding farms remain productive. Western and southern Cabarrus County has experienced a rapid transformation into an exurb of Greater Charlotte. Mt. Pleasant is located on the eastern side of Cabarrus, however, and the town has little economic activity. Most of the town is involved in service industries in nearby Concord, Kannapolis, and Charlotte.

In the 1920s and 1930s, Mt. Pleasant boasted two mills, a hosiery and a spinning mill, located at each end of town. Mt. Pleasant was acutely class-conscious, with an established town class that was linked to the landowning elite of Cabarrus County. Elinor recalled that her father used to preach that Mt. Pleasant was an "evil town." The town's Lutheran fathers sometimes slipped off to black neighborhoods for illicit sexual relationships, even while they maintained the appearance of propriety and piety. Beneath the veneer, Elinor said, "was all this filth going on," though "you never talked about anything."[46]

For both Margaret and Arthur, educational experiences became crucial. My mother had led a protected existence for all of her childhood and adolescence. She attended the all-male Davidson College under a special exception that permitted daughters of faculty to enroll during the cash-strapped years of the Depression. Under this arrangement, the girls were permitted to attend for a year or two and then transfer elsewhere. James and Anniebelle were committed to educating Margaret: when she left high school, James was sixty-seven years old, Anniebelle fifty-seven. James arranged that Margaret would skip one grade in elementary school, and she finished Davidson High School along with twenty-six of her classmates in May 1934, at the age of fifteen. During the following fall, she enrolled at Davidson along with fourteen other females out of a total student body of 674 students. Joining her were a handful of other town girls.[47]

After two years at Davidson, eighteen-year-old Margaret enrolled at Agnes Scott College in Decatur, Georgia, in September 1936. By the 1930s, Agnes Scott had become an intellectually rigorous liberal arts college dedicated, according to its catalogue, to offering "the very best educational advantages under positive Christian influences." It benefited from the largesse of local Atlanta families and the support of the Rockefellers' General Education Board. The campus grew in the early 1930s, and by the time Margaret arrived, its facilities had never been better. Among them was a new Gothic-style library, which opened the year that Margaret matriculated. With an emphasis on academics, the college also sought to "cultivate true womanliness, a womanliness which combines strength with gentleness and refinement." Enrolling nearly 500 students entering in September 1936—192 of whom were day students, 296 boarding students—the college occupied a secure financial position during the depths of the Depression.[48]

Before coming to Agnes Scott, Margaret had had only a few previous experiences outside her protected family cocoon. She lived at home during her years at Davidson, and her only experience away from home occurred during the summer of 1935, when she worked at the Massanetta Springs Presbyterian conference grounds, in the Shenandoah Valley, as a waitress.[49] In the fall of 1935, after a year at Davidson, Margaret's Davidson girlhood friend Giddy Erwin began at Agnes Scott, and Margaret visited her over Thanksgiving. Because her older brother, John, was enrolled at Duke Medical School, it was unlikely that the Douglases could afford the tuition, so when the college decided to provide a $250 scholarship, her decision to attend the school was sealed.[50]

At Agnes Scott, Margaret became immersed in the college's vibrant women's culture, which emphasized academic achievement and stressed careers in public service. The college opened Margaret up to an urban environment quite unlike anything she had previously experienced: although the Agnes Scott campus was itself sheltered, a nickel trolley took students to the heart of Atlanta. Agnes Scott also exposed Margaret to new ideas about her background. The Depression and New Deal had especially affected the South, and new ideas about social change were swirling around the region in the 1930s. Agnes Scott opened up new ways of viewing the South's social system.

Margaret roomed with Giddy Erwin, whose father taught English at Davidson.[51] Margaret soon embraced the intense student culture at Agnes Scott. Involved early on in the debating club, Pi Alpha Phi, she also participated in hiking and the Current History Forum. During her senior year, she became involved in the International Relations Club (IRC), which was funded by support from the Carnegie Foundation. The IRC merged with the Citizenship Club to form the Current History Forum, hosting discussions and speakers on current events. Especially important was the theme of peace, and the club joined with a national campus movement during the late 1930s to keep the United States out of the brewing European war.[52]

Though she was a woman in a male-dominated world, Margaret met the high expectations of the Douglases. She blossomed intellectually at Agnes Scott. Her two favorite teachers were Philip Davidson in American history and Arthur F. Raper in sociology. In 1941, Davidson, with a B.A.

from the University of Mississippi and a Ph.D. from the University of Chicago, would publish the influential *Propaganda and the American Revolution*, a revisionist account of Revolutionary ideology. Even more influential was Raper, a native North Carolinian who graduated from Chapel Hill, studied under the leading southern sociologist Howard W. Odum, and then went to work for the Commission on Interracial Cooperation in Atlanta in 1926. During Margaret's senior year, in 1938, the school yearbook was dedicated to Raper as a person "who lives by practical theories rather than as an advocate of theoretical practices." Raper was immersed in the network of liberals and race reformers. Serving as secretary of the Atlanta chapter of the Commission on Interracial Cooperation, he was an intimate of such Atlanta interracialists as Will W. Alexander and Clark Foreman. He also immersed his students in direct experiences with southern social problems. In October 1937, Raper took five automobiles filled with students and visited rural Tennessee to examine, firsthand, "the social problem of the intelligent use and conservation of natural resources of the United States." Margaret wasn't on the trip, but she was influenced by Raper's charm and ethos.[53]

Raper published at least two major studies of race, *The Tragedy of Lynching* (1934) and *Preface to Peasantry* (1936), which catalogued most of the instances of race-based vigilante violence that had occurred since the 1890s and outlined in vivid detail how the system of sharecropping oppressed white and black rural southerners. Under Raper, Margaret took a course in race relations that undoubtedly shook many of her assumptions about life in the South. Although the controversial Raper left Agnes Scott in 1938, Margaret was deeply influenced by his views on southern social problems.[54]

Academically, Margaret matured; with courses mostly in history and sociology, she also took four courses in education, evidently preparing for the possibility of teaching. In 1937–38, her final year at Agnes Scott, her courses in art history, Bible, history, sociology, and phys ed were all graded "merit," something equivalent to a "B" by Agnes Scott's standards.[55] For all graduating seniors, the faculty wrote assessments that were kept in a confidential file. Margaret's file included letters from two Davidson faculty, one from President Walter Lingle, the other from classics professor Ernest Beatty. Beatty described her as a "young woman of extraordinary social and religious culture" who had an "attractive personality" with "high spiritual aspirations and experience." Lingle wrote that, coming from a "family background noted for Christian culture," she possessed "good intellectual ability" and was a "young woman of high Christian character." The assessments by Agnes Scott faculty were more qualified. Philip Davidson said that she was "alert and easily trained." Arthur Raper described her as an "average student" who would do well as an elementary school teacher or as a "visitor to a social agency." Another history faculty member, Elizabeth Fuller Jackson, was even more frank. She noted that she had "excellent character," a "nice spirit about her work," and "poise and social adaptability." But Jackson also judged her a "fair student" whose work was "handicapped much more by training than ability" because she had learned to "rely too greatly on memory and not stimulated sufficiently in analysis."[56]

By the spring of 1938, facing graduation on June 5, Margaret pondered several possibilities. To an unusual degree for her time, Margaret's parents expressed confidence in her intellectual abilities. Her father (whose letters to Margaret included the affectionate salutations "My dear baby" or "My dear little girl") told her that he was proud of her "fine record" in which she was "getting better and better each quarter & that shows you are growing." "I always knew you had the 'stuff' in your head," he wrote.[57] As late as May 1938, however, Margaret had no idea what the future held in store for her. In the spring of her senior year, she tried to combine her new interest in sociology with her religious background, and she communicated with John L. Fairley, head of the Southern Presbyterians' publication board in Richmond, Virginia. Fairley's daughter, Mary Lillian (or "Pixie"), also attended Agnes Scott and was a lifelong friend. Margaret sought to explore future opportunities through this contact. Fairley promised a job for Margaret at least for the summer, working in social service with Presbyterians in North Carolina and Virginia. "I am delighted to know that you have a chance to get that position this summer," her father wrote, because it would be a "fine chance for you do some religious work and do some good in this world." But at the last minute the job fell through.[58] Her mother was, as always, reassuring: "I'm sure this disappointment in plans is Providential," she wrote, "& every thing will work out for the best."[59]

As it happened, things did work out for Margaret. At some point during 1938, Fairley came back to her and offered her a job as a proofreader for the Presbyterian publications board, and for the next three years she lived in Richmond, with Pixie as her roommate. Very little is known about these years. Living in the urban environment of Richmond likely deepened her interest in social action, in race relations, labor, and change in the South in a Christian, Social Gospel context. One of her coworkers working for the Presbyterians—and a feminist role model—was Nelle Katherine Morton. Born in 1905, Morton was in her late thirties when Margaret met her, with a career in teaching and religious education. In 1937, Morton became assistant director of youth work for the Board of Christian Education for the Southern Presbyterian church in Richmond.

Morton was an activist involved in the peace movement of the late 1930s, but especially important to her was the issue of racial justice. By the time Margaret met her, Morton had become an integrationist, and in 1945 she would serve in the Fellowship of Southern Churchmen, an important interracial, multifaith organization. Undoubtedly, Margaret absorbed new ideas about the inequity of white supremacy and, through Morton, participated in interracial gatherings, youth camps, and conferences that sought to contest segregation laws. Morton had a major influence on Margaret's decision to seek graduate training. But, like Morton, Margaret was always more interested in practical solutions of social problems than in abstract, academic inquiry.

Interested in the wider world, Margaret moved beyond the insular Davidson community. When she traveled with a friend by bus to New York City in July 1939, she wrote to her parents about experiencing urban life during a summer weekend. Visiting her friend Giddy, who worked in the New York Public Library after graduation from Agnes Scott, Margaret attended the New York World's Fair. Ironically, my father was working at the fair that summer, though the two did not meet. While in New York, Margaret visited Greenwich Village and was struck by its "careless-abandon" appearance. She also watched a show at Radio City Music Hall, where she saw the Rockettes perform and participated in a Saturday evening dance on the rooftop of the Hotel St. George in Brooklyn Heights. On a Sunday in New York, Margaret, Giddy, and their friends "broke the Sabbath open," she confessed to her parents, by spending the day at the World's Fair. "Circumstances sometimes have to govern cases," she assured her parents.[60]

Like many small-town North Carolina boys, seventeen-year-old Arthur, after graduation from high school, headed off to Chapel Hill for a college education at UNC. Leaving Mt. Pleasant, Arthur didn't look back. His hometown, he wrote in 1945, was "about the dullest place I know of."[61] Arthur vividly recalled how he first set foot on the Carolina campus. He remembered his sense of awe about the "grandeur and romance and glory of it," along with the "intellectual excitement of that place." UNC was experiencing a renaissance that began after World War I and brought some of the South's leading thinkers to Chapel Hill. "Traditions grow here with the ivy on the historic buildings and the moss on the ancient oaks," said the UNC yearbook of 1941, Arthur's senior year. "There is music in the air of the place."

The UNC campus was a veritable pressure cooker of free expression and ideas, and Arthur was struck by the "intellectual freedom" that contrasted so starkly with his boyhood. "Anything went," he recalled; "I mean it could be anything." Along with upper-class elite Carolinians, the campus also welcomed country boys from across the state—many of whom never made it past the first semester. Chapel Hill also enrolled a significant number of northeastern Jews who were excluded from Ivy League institutions. Especially under the university presidency of Frank Porter Graham, Chapel Hill, serving as the leading academic center of southern liberalism, welcomed divergent political views, and the campus housed Communists, Socialists, and other political minorities.

Arriving in September 1937, Arthur spent his first few days in Chapel Hill roaming the campus and looking at the UNC campus's buildings and admiring the many books in the university library. It was "like a banquet to me in those days," he remembered, and he was overcome by "the excitement of scholarly minds and bright people and bright undergraduate students."[62] Arthur worked his way through school. He was employed at the Campus Y as a typist; after a high school typing course, he had achieved speed and accuracy. In the 1950s and 1960s, we had several manual typewriters at home, and I remember watching as my father exhibited his blazing speed—more than 120 words a minute. While a UNC student, Arthur typed many theses and dissertations for extra cash. He also tutored football players for fifty cents an hour. Despite the demands of school and work, Arthur absorbed the rich student culture. He became involved in various campus activities, including the Y, the Dialectic Senate (known as the Di), and the Glee Club during his sophomore and junior years, singing baritone.[63]

At Carolina, Arthur learned new attitudes about race. The Campus Y, a center of UNC student culture, sponsored contacts between black and white students, something that was very adventurous for its day, though these meetings were careful not to violate racial taboos about interracial dining. Arthur was also exposed to the campus radicalism that appeared in the pacifism and left-wing politics in the late 1930s. One of the better-known radicals was Junius Scales, an acquaintance of Arthur's, a member of his class, and later a leader in the Communist Party. From an upper-class Greensboro family—his great-uncle, A. M. Scales, was governor of North Carolina—Scales became the only person tried and convicted in the United States for membership in the Communist Party. In his autobiography, Scales recalled numerous cross-racial contacts through his involvement in the American Student Union. He remembered that the experience of meeting with black students on an equal basis was "unbelievable." While a UNC undergraduate, Arthur traveled to the Blue Ridge Assembly, just east of Asheville, North Carolina, where interracial conferences brought together black and white students in strictly regulated environments. These were all limited steps, but they suggested important changes in racial attitudes among white southerners regarding segregation.[64]

Arthur remained loyal to UNC his whole life. He followed its sports teams, especially the football team, and he bled Carolina Blue. He liked to tell his sons and nephews that there was no point in attending an Ivy League institution when you could do just as well at UNC. Like most Carolina alums, he disliked Duke University, which, when he was a student, seemed to be home mostly to privileged Yankees. His anti-Duke feelings were half-serious but also visceral. In my family, the logical colleges to attend were, not surprisingly, either Davidson or Carolina: all four of Arthur's children attended one of those institutions. In 1968, my father and mother took my older brother Jimmy to visit Chapel Hill. We spent a full day touring the campus, and on the way out of town, going north, Jimmy suggested that we also visit Duke. My father's gaze stiffened. "No son of mine," he muttered, "will ever go to Duke." And none of us ever did.

For the first time, Arthur also traveled beyond North Carolina. In 1939 and 1940, New York City sponsored an international exposition, the New York World's Fair, on what had been a trash heap in Flushing Meadows, Queens. Emphasizing the future in the theme "The World of Tomorrow," the fair housed pavilions by countries and corporations and attracted more than 44 million visitors. The New York World's Fair attracted workers from the ranks of college students, and sometime in the spring of 1939, Arthur noticed an ad recruiting students to work at the fair. Arthur transported himself to New York by working as a baggage handler on a bus. At the fair he pushed visitors on wheeled carts and earned twenty-five dollars per week. Still, that summer my father came home early because, as he later said, he "got so homesick and hungry for watermelons, corn on the cob, and scuppernong grapes."[65]

In the male-dominated world of American higher education, women found a relatively hospitable environment at UNC. The first women enrolled in 1897, and in 1931 women began attending as transfers. There were a number of women on campus in the law school and graduate schools by 1941, when Margaret came to UNC. But even in Chapel Hill during the 1940s, according to one recollection, women operated in "a man's world."[66] A succession of female research assistants had already worked at Howard Odum's Institute. Many of them, including Guion Griffis Johnson, Harriet Herring, Julia Cherry Spruill, and Margaret Hagood, had gone on to distinguished academic careers.[67] When she joined their number, Margaret worked closely with Odum in Alumni Hall, where she found him personally engaging and academically impressive.

After only a year at UNC, Margaret enjoyed close association with Howard Odum, but she found him a mystery—courteous and gentlemanly but also strangely misogynistic. Margaret wasn't sure about her academic future, and she wanted some reassurance from Odum. With doubts brewing, Margaret met with Odum in August 1942, seeking his advice. She wondered what the alternatives were before her, especially whether Odum would support further graduate study by employing her at the IRSS.[68]

Margaret described her meeting with Odum in a letter to her parents. Typically, Odum's style was to challenge, prod, and even intervene in his students' lives. In this meeting, Odum tested Margaret's mettle by questioning her durability as a graduate student. She eagerly accepted the challenge. In "another bout with Odum," Margaret said, she acquitted herself well against the great UNC scholar. Deciding to take on Odum by "matching my wits with his," she described how, in standing up to him, she produced "the right reaction." Much of their exchange concerned whether Odum would support another year at UNC. Odum suggested that Margaret's father could continue paying for her education; she responded forcefully. "Listen, Dr. Odum," she recounted, "Father has given me enough education. I want to entirely support myself next year—without asking him for any help." With such "bland confidence that I surprised myself," Margaret told him that she could grade papers and even teach a social theory class. When he told her that he feared that she lacked "something dynamic I'm looking for, and I don't know what kind of worker you are," she got "mad." Though she "laughed as heartily as I could," beneath a polite veneer Margaret was seething. Odum, she told her parents, "doesn't care whether you're a student or a scholar," and everything came down to his "personal estimation of you, which isn't purely scientific." In Margaret's case, she believed that Odum had based his evaluation on an early impression. Now it was her turn to interrogate him. Did he have any evidence to support his impression? At this point, Odum backed down, apparently pleased by Margaret's forcefulness. He admitted that he had no factual basis for his views about her and informed Margaret that he would support her application for an assistantship.

Margaret found the interchange with Odum exhilarating. "Whether I get anything from him or not," she wrote about Odum, "I'm going to stick in there & really fight." As a young female scholar standing up to a leading academic, Margaret learned that sometimes assertiveness yielded results. She resented Odum's style, which involved "subjecting me to all this psycho-analysis and personal accusations." Margaret understood the politics of dealing with a powerful scholar in charge of her future, but she found Odum's condescension insulting. "Someday when I get to know Odum a little better," she wrote her parents, "I'm going to light into him for using that crude psychology in dealing with people."[69]

Growing up in the 1950s and 1960s, my siblings and I lived in the shadow of World War II. Most of our childhood friends had fathers, and sometimes mothers, who were veterans. That Arthur had not served in World War II seemed out of place. The explanation we heard was that he had attempted to enlist in the Navy after Pearl Harbor, but that a bout of infantile paralysis—polio—had medically disqualified him. Reluctantly, he said, he was unable to serve. The truth was more complicated. There is no evidence of an attempt at naval enlistment, though this is certainly possible. A letter from Arthur's brother John William in

January 1942, five weeks after Pearl Harbor, provides one suggestive clue. "How are you coming along with the draft business?" wrote John William, who was then music director at Dana College, a small Lutheran college in Blair, Nebraska. Many of the Dana students found deferments by enlisting in the naval and air reserve. Could Arthur do the same thing? Certainly, John William suggested, "a person with your education could get a job addressing letters."[70] "If your health is as poor as it seems to be," John William later wrote, "I hardly think you need to worry about the army."[71]

Certainly some of Arthur's friends were opposed to the war, and some were even active war resisters. During 1943 and 1944, Arthur's Chapel Hill friend and roommate Wesley Bagby, a fellow graduate student who would later receive a doctorate from Columbia and teach history for many years at West Virginia University, sought to avoid military service. Unlike Arthur, Bagby was openly pacifist. Even when the war ended in Europe, Bagby doubted the value of American intervention. "Where are the 'hosanna shouters' now who went to war to make a brave new world?" he wrote in June 1945. "In fighting for European civilization we have destroyed Europe," and in fighting "dictatorship we have made it possible for Europe to live safe under dictatorship for the next thirty years."[72] In 1943, Bagby applied for conscientious objector status, in what Arthur called a "truly sincere case of objection to military service." But Bagby's local draft board rejected his application, and he appealed. After investigating him for draft dodging—one FBI agent even interviewed Arthur about Bagby—the case against him was dismissed. Eventually, Bagby was granted conscientious objector status.[73]

On February 17, 1942, Arthur registered for the draft back home in Cabarrus County, but he received a high enough draft number to delay his induction. Arthur preferred to complete the Ph.D. In truth, there were few people less suited than Arthur to the physical and emotional demands of warfare. He abhorred violence of any kind, avoided physical exercise (aside from a vigorous walk), and believed that military hierarchy and authority were imbecilic. Although he toyed with the idea of alternative service, a medical deferment seemed the best way out. On August 11, 1942, he underwent a preliminary physical examination that uncovered a heart murmur "which I didn't know I had." Later, he added that the doctor had found a fast pulse and a "leaking heart."[74] The heart murmur, however, seems an unlikely component of Arthur's medical profile:

No other doctor, in any subsequent examination of Arthur (including a full-blown angiogram in 1982, a procedure that maps the heart and the circulatory system) would ever find anything but a completely healthy heart. Arthur continued to hope that the doctor's misdiagnosis—which he believed was real—would prevent his induction. On October 24, 1942, he reported that his heart problems, plus "very bad eyes," would likely lead to a 4-F classification, though the draft had "mysteriously left me thus suspended." Into the spring of 1943, Arthur wondered why the draft board was conscripting married men ahead of him, a development that he hoped meant that he had been deferred as a 4-F "or some similar class of undesirable character."[75]

In the spring of 1943, as the draft board moved toward induction, Arthur remained anxious about his draft status, an anxiety his parents shared. His brother John William had been drafted in late 1942, and by the spring of 1943 John William had volunteered, trained as a medic, and become a paratrooper. On April 23, 1943, he shipped out for duty in North Africa. His mother, Helen, was "simply petrified." Sometime in March 1943, Arthur received his induction notice. He was ordered to appear at Camp Croft, in Spartanburg, South Carolina, on April 27, 1943. "I knew this was bound to come, and yet I can't help but worry over it," his mother wrote. "I suppose it is best for you to have a show down with the army doctors because then no one can say anything about you and people certainly do criticize those who get out of going." Helen continued to worry about Arthur's fate. She was "hoping and praying that the army doctors reject you," she wrote in April 1943, "not because I don't want you to do your part, but because I am certain you are rendering more valuable service where you are." Arthur's father had a different set of perceptions. Probably retaining his ambivalence about an American war against the Germans, he admitted that Arthur was ill-suited for battle. "Your fine spirits were never intended to be steeped in bloodshed," Arthur's father wrote him. "I have ceased to see any lasting glory in War—men of peace are the glory men of the ages."[76]

By the spring of 1943, my father's hopes for deferment lay less with a defective heart than with spinal problems. Helen hopefully informed Arthur that an X-ray of his spine, taken six years earlier, revealed a curvature, and she urged him to seek a medical discharge on this basis. She urged him to find a "reliable doctor" to do an examination and not to rely on Army doctors. Helen reminded Arthur of the mysterious ailment that had afflicted him as an infant, which she believed was polio.[77] Arthur departed on an Army trailer from Concord to Camp Croft in a trip that he described as "rather gruesome." En route, the trailer broke down three times, while the passengers remained confined in hot quarters. Arthur found his compatriots to be "about the worst sample of human nature I have ever seen" and "true characters for sociological study." Once he arrived, he had a short medical examination and was classified 4-F because of a short left leg, an atrophic shoulder, and a bad curvature in his spine. Joining a busload of rejects en route back to Concord, Arthur was elated at his disqualification. This was "no more than I expected; but it does seem strange not to be in uniform these days."[78] Helen was even more relieved. "It is not necessary for me to tell you how thankful I am that you were rejected at Camp Croft," she wrote. Helen had been so worried that she could "neither eat nor sleep."[79]

Arthur's medical disqualification cleared the way for his continuing rise to academic stardom. There was little doubt that he wanted to avoid military service, and his 4-F classification was a great relief, although in the prowar atmosphere of World War II and its aftermath, this was a difficult thing for him to admit. I discovered his wartime struggle over the draft only when I explored his correspondence. I was surprised because his obvious reluctance to serve contrasted so sharply with what we had been told as children—and how we understood his role and contribution during the "Just War." But it is also true that not serving in the war made Arthur's professional advancement that much easier. Most of his peers came home in 1945 four years behind him. Just as they were reentering schools and colleges, he was assuming his first academic position.

In the fall of 1944, as the world war was moving toward conclusion, the South was battered by economic, social, and political change.
The wartime mobilization had brought most of the young males of the
region either under arms or to employment in war industries. The wartime boom ended the Depression but spurred unprecedented mobility as
millions migrated to urban areas, inside and outside the South, in search
of work. The construction and expansion of army bases, shipyards, and
airfields brought a new climate of change. White and black southerners
learned about the wider world in unprecedented ways.

Margaret's plans, like those of many women during the 1940s,
were changed by the war. Her relatives, including her brother and cousins, served overseas. Margaret's first cousin Colin Hudson, the son of her
mother's sister, Aunt Coline, worked in Washington as a physicist in the
Army's weapons program. The lives of many of Margaret's female friends
were turned upside down by the war. Some had hurried engagements
and marriages, and many more were working in war agencies across the
country and living in new places in eastern cities or on the Pacific Coast.

The necessities of the war prompted Margaret to move away from Chapel Hill.

In the spring of 1943, Margaret received a job offer. After the sudden departure of a faculty member at Queens College, a Presbyterian women's college in Charlotte, she was offered a job in March to fill in for the remaining two months of the spring semester. She hesitated, in part because taking the Queens job would interrupt her graduate study—she would have to rush to finish up her master's thesis—and also because Hunter Blakely, the Queens president, wanted her to teach not only sociology but economics. Although initially reluctant, Margaret accepted the job, receiving a crash course in economics from Clif Kreps, with whom she was still seriously involved.

Later in life, my mother's experience with Queens remained a family reference point. As children, we knew—and were proud of—Margaret's career as an academic sociologist. Like many other women of her social class and race, she relinquished her professional career to raise a family. Still, everyone who knew her realized Margaret's intellectual substance. Her teaching stint at Queens became a challenge that she eagerly accepted. Margaret arrived at Queens in April 1943 having to teach four classes: American government, introductory sociology, and two sections of economics. Not surprisingly, picking up these courses in the middle of the semester was difficult. Still, by the end of the semester, Margaret had adjusted to teaching—and to Queens.[1] By 1943, Queens had become the leading Presbyterian women's college of the Carolinas. Founded in 1857 as the Charlotte Female Institute, the school became the Seminary for Girls in 1891 and the Presbyterian Female College in 1896. Then, in 1914, the college renamed itself Queens College and moved from a location downtown to a 26-acre wooded campus in Charlotte's new, upscale suburban development of Myers Park. During the 1920s, the facilities and endowment grew significantly, and in 1930 it merged with Chicora College, a South Carolina Presbyterian women's college. The "Creed of a Queens Girl," which appeared in the student handbook of the 1940s, held that women students should be "adaptable, accepting with good faith the new and the difficult"; that they should exhibit "friendliness, tact, and sympathy"; that they should be "gentlewomen both on and off the campus"; and that they should strive toward "Christian womanhood." As was true at most mid-twentieth-century women's colleges, students followed a dress code on and off campus and were under strict rules in social inter-actions with males. As a Presbyterian college, Queens also required daily chapel exercises.[2]

Perhaps the main advantage of teaching at Queens for Margaret was the proximity to her aging parents. Her mother suffered a heart attack in the spring of 1943, and Margaret was able to visit her every day while she was in the hospital. Once Anniebelle returned home to Davidson, Marga-ret spent many weekends at home. During much of the summer of 1943, she looked after her parents and searched for a cook. The wartime labor shortage, she noted, had made African Americans' domestic service—in Davidson, as elsewhere in the small-town South—very scarce. For most middle-class white southerners, black domestic workers performed cook-ing and cleaning chores. Because of this arrangement, Margaret knew little about cooking. (Once Margaret married, in fact, the family legend is that my father taught her how to cook.)[3]

In the spring of 1943, Margaret took up residence in a Charlotte room-ing house two blocks from campus, on a tree-lined street in the heart of Myers Park, one of the city's premier neighborhoods. Her landlord, an elderly widow, became a good friend, and Margaret sometimes did gro-cery shopping and helped her evade the ration system for cigarettes. Her housemates, some of them fellow female faculty, were congenial. She played bridge, watched movies, listened to the radio, and talked with them in "bull sessions" that sometimes lasted late into the night. After one evening bridge marathon lasting three hours, Margaret pronounced herself "card drunk." She also attended church, when she could, at the nearby Second Presbyterian Church, pastored by the legendary Scottish preacher John A. Redhead.[4]

Margaret discovered strong women among the Queens faculty. She became good friends with Dorothy A. Rethlingshafer, who taught psy-chology and had completed a Ph.D. at UNC in 1938.[5] Another housemate, Hazel Barnes, whom Margaret described as "quite brilliant, a deep and sincere thinker," had a Ph.D. in philosophy and taught at Queens.[6] Mar-garet took full advantage of the amenities of Charlotte, where she heard speakers and singers such as journalist Norman Cousins, Wagnerian soprano Helen Traubel, the Austrian actress Marguerita Maria "Mady" Christians, and strategic airpower theorist Major Alexander P. de Sever-sky. She also became involved in organizations such as the Business and

Professional Women's Club, which sponsored speakers and discussions about public issues.[7]

Margaret took to teaching almost immediately and was successful enough for President Blakely to make her an assistant professor in the fall of 1944. In addition, Blakely urged her to return to obtain her Ph.D. and think about Queens as a long-term career.[8] Margaret was exhilarated by what must have been a stimulating environment. "The year's gone fast," she wrote at the end of the 1943–44 academic year, but there was "always something sort of exciting about what's opening up in the future."[9] She enjoyed the human contact and interaction, though Margaret wondered sometimes about what she called the "gruesome job" of awarding grades.[10]

Queens was, nonetheless, a pale reflection of the sort of women's education she had experienced at Agnes Scott. Margaret found the college's social restrictions confining, and she complained about the students' conservatism, especially on gender issues. In 1944–45, her final year of teaching, she served on a faculty committee that advised the student honor court. In her view, the women students were the severest enforcers of an unnecessarily rigid social code. In March 1945, the court considered the case of a girl who was charged with necking in public. The student had been reprimanded but continued to violate the rules; students were pressing for her suspension. Margaret disapproved of this sanction, which she considered too severe. "Students are more severe judges of their fellow-students in social conduct than faculty," she observed. "They always want the worst penalties imposed and therein lies the danger of student government." After the relative freedom that women enjoyed at Chapel Hill, Queens seemed a social throwback.[11]

Margaret saw her role to challenge the southern orthodoxies that ruled her students' lives. Her most satisfying moments, she reflected, occurred when the "light . . . dawns on some of my beginner students in the social sciences who get into concepts heretofore completely foreign to them."[12] During one of her classes in December 1944, she asked her students why women in the South seemed to have lower enlistment rates in the Women's Army Corps, the WACS, as compared to other regions of the country. The class then considered the differences between southern and northern women, but Margaret found their responses unsatisfactory. She spoke pointedly. Southern girls were "hidebound by tradition and prejudice," Margaret told the class. Strikingly to her, few took issue with her position, "but [they] saw no reason for making a change in this state of mind particularly."[13]

Without question, the war was changing life on the Queens campus. A rapid turnover of faculty and staff unsettled the college: a number of the male faculty were drafted for military service, while some of the female faculty were lured into war work, or married and left for other parts of the country. This simply mirrored Margaret's experience. She made many friends whose lives were in turmoil because of the war. Things were "in quite a mess" at Queens, Margaret wrote in September 1944, including shortages of classroom space and acute faculty turnover. To make matters worse, nerves were "on edge."[14] The students sensed the uncertainty of the future in the torrent of changes that came with the war. There was "nothing certain but uncertainty," the student newspaper, the *Queens Blues*, advised the graduating class of June 1944.[15]

Arthur, like Margaret, was swept up in the changes affecting North Carolina life during the 1940s. In February 1943, he received an offer to teach in the U.S. Army Air Corps pre-flight training program that had just begun on the N.C. State campus in Raleigh. The Army Air Corps—what later became the Air Force—was training thousands of pilots to fly in the Pacific and European air wars. In December 1942, a year after Pearl Harbor, the Army established the Army Specialized Training Program (ASTP) to expand rapidly its officer ranks. The ASTP program opened at college campuses around the United States and sought to compress a college education, along with technical training, into a year and a half course of study. The N.C. State program was desperate for teachers because of the outflow of men into military service; the graduate student ranks at UNC had been greatly thinned. James Patton, a UNC Ph.D. who taught at N.C. State and was running history ASTP instruction, hired UNC grad student Ben Wall to teach in the program. In February 1943, Wall ran into Arthur in front of the old engineering building on the Carolina campus. Arthur, he knew, was "always broke, we all were." Did Arthur want a job that paid two hundred dollars per month? he asked, realizing that this salary was a "king's ransom."[16]

Urged by both Odum and Green to take the job, Arthur accepted, explaining to the Rosenwald officials who were funding his graduate fellowship that this not only would give him teaching experience, but it represented a "clear opportunity to do service in the war effort." It was his "manifest duty to accept."[17] In his first full-fledged experience in college teaching, Arthur dove in enthusiastically. Teaching European history to Army Air Corps preflight cadets, most of whom lacked any college training, Arthur found the students generally intelligent and interested. By the summer of 1943, he was teaching American history to engineering students.[18] Boarding in Raleigh just a block north of the N.C. State campus, Arthur took full advantage of the urban environment.[19] While in Raleigh, he struck up new friendships. Sometime in the spring of 1943, he made an effort to seek out John Hope Franklin, who had just published his first book, *The Free Negro in North Carolina, 1790–1860*. Franklin had come to Raleigh while working on his dissertation, but discovered that the state archives' reading room was segregated. The archives staff provided space in the stacks for him to work—something of a backhanded privilege, since white researchers used the reading room.[20]

John Hope had been a Rosenwald Fellow a few years ahead of Arthur, and it's likely that they knew each other through that organization. Franklin had lived in North Carolina since the late 1930s, and he remained there after he received his Ph.D. in history at Harvard in 1941. He served on the faculty of St. Augustine's College in Raleigh, North Carolina, from 1939 until 1943; in 1941, he became the college's first faculty member to receive a doctorate. In the fall of 1943, Franklin joined North Carolina College for Negroes in Durham (later North Carolina Central University), where he would remain until 1947. John Hope's contact with white academics at UNC and Duke was limited to Howard Beale. They first met in 1940, and Beale became one of his most important white allies in North Carolina. UNC sociologists Guion and Guy Johnson also had Franklin over to their house in Chapel Hill in 1939.[21] But most white academics would have nothing to do socially with a black person, even an academic with the same credentials they had.[22]

Arthur had no inhibitions about associating with Franklin, and he swept aside the southern taboos about socializing with black people. No doubt Arthur recognized the quality of John Hope's mind, and he took the initiative and sought him out. "I have struck up a close friendship with Mr. John Hope Franklin, whom you know," Arthur wrote to Beale in May 1943. He described him as "really an interesting person and we have had quite a good time talking together."[23] The two men bonded intellectually and emotionally. John Hope later recalled that they became "friends at first sight."[24] In many respects, they were similar. Both were self-made, both had strong egos, and both were wonderful raconteurs who liked to hold forth and enjoyed the attention of others. John Hope and Arthur were both methodologically traditional, and they were devotees of the science of using documentary evidence and of the empiricism that dominated historical inquiry at mid-twentieth century. John Hope and Arthur were also intensely ambitious, and they probably sensed that each had a bright future ahead of him.

When he was in Chapel Hill, Arthur usually stopped by Durham: visiting in December 1944, he reported having lunch with Franklin and his wife, Aurelia. Franklin then took Arthur out to the North Carolina College in order to introduce him to James Shepard, the college's president.[25] Franklin and Arthur continued to correspond over the years, and John Hope spoke frankly about the inequities of the Jim Crow educational system. When, for example, Arthur asked about higher education opportunities for black people, Franklin reminded him that no black institutions granted the doctorate. At all-black institutions, "research and instructional facilities that are now available would make it a veritable farce." Over the years, they remained, according to Franklin, "very close friends despite the barriers that kept us apart."[26]

While in Raleigh, Arthur also became involved in a theatrical performance, a production of Mark Reed's 1936 romantic comedy *Petticoat Fever*. Arthur played Sir James Fenton, who was, in British parlance, an "upper-class twit." "I don't think I was born to be an actor," Arthur commented modestly to Green. But he noted that one advantage, as his friend and UNC classmate Carrington Gretter put it, was that since he was born in Virginia, "I would undoubtedly be a 'Virginia ham.'"[27] After rehearsals in October 1943, the play was performed in early November and was, according to Arthur, a "howling success." His mother insisted on seeing it. "Your memory is so good," she wrote, "I know you won't have any trouble learning the lines." The reviews in the *Raleigh News and Observer* were positive. "Top honors," the reviewer commented, should go to Arthur Link as "that stuffed shirt, Sir James Fenton"; he "was so stuffed that one would have liked to stick a pin in him."[28]

By early 1944, Arthur had become frustrated with the monotony of the ASTP program. "I tried to tell a Yankee class about the Old South," he wrote Fletcher Green in October 1943, but "they weren't very sympathetic and didn't seem to be interested." The cadets were smart enough, but the officers running the program provided them no time to read and reflect. The atmosphere of the ASTP was not conducive to study because the soldiers had to march and drill constantly, something that discouraged classroom involvement. The program, he concluded privately, was a failure.[29] By early 1944, the ASTP program had run out of steam and was shut down. The Army needed more manpower because of the forthcoming Normandy invasion, and the troops in ASTP programs were reassigned. Arthur was told that he no longer had a job.[30]

At some point during her relationship with Clif Kreps, Odum intervened with Margaret to offer her his usually inappropriate advice. "Margaret," he said, "you shouldn't be marrying Clif Kreps." Then he delivered the kicker: "Margaret, you should instead marry Arthur Link." My mother often told this story about Odum to illustrate his eccentricity, but, at the time, she surely saw this as an oddly inappropriate suggestion that reflected some of Odum's "crude psychology in dealing with people." But at some point during late 1943 or early 1944, the relationship with Clif Kreps soured, and the engagement was called off.

Part of what had happened to Margaret's relationship with Kreps was that he met another person: in 1944, he would marry Juanita Morris, a Kentuckian who graduated from Berea College and, along with Kreps, earned a Ph.D. in economics from Duke in 1948. Morris and Kreps met during the summer of 1943, when they both worked for the National War Labor Board as wage analysts in Atlanta. The friendship blossomed into a romance. Juanita Kreps later returned to Duke to the economics department and became the first female vice president at Duke, the first female member of the New York Stock Exchange, and, during the Carter administration, the first female secretary of commerce. In 1979, Clif Kreps shot himself in the mouth but survived the suicide attempt. Kreps, who was then Wachovia Professor of Banking at UNC, had had a distinguished career as an economist. Still, it seems likely that he suffered from some form of depression; before his suicide attempt, he had been hospitalized for psychiatric counseling at UNC hospital in Chapel Hill, and he was on leave from the hospital when he tried to kill himself.[31]

After Margaret's breakup with Kreps, Arthur was waiting in the wings. He first heard about the end of the relationship in February 1944, when his friend Carrington Gretter informed Arthur that he had seen Kreps, who told him that he was "all through" with Margaret.[32] With the way now clear, Arthur actively pursued my mother. Many years later, when I was about fifteen years old, we were driving from New Jersey to North Carolina, and my mother had fallen asleep in the back seat. While she was sleeping, I asked him a personal question: How had he met my mother? How had they become romantically involved? Sotto voce, he replied, "I got your mother on the rebound."

Margaret and Arthur had often talked during the 1941–42 year when they were together in Alumni Hall, but while she was involved with Kreps, the relationship remained platonic. When Margaret and Clif parted ways in the spring of 1943, Margaret saw the relationship with Arthur as an interesting friendship. "I enjoyed tremendously all the discussions which we had: religion, social questions, what-have-you," she wrote in March 1943, and she wished that those could continue.[33] Arthur remained very interested, more interested than she was at this point. "You know, Margaret, I think you're about the finest specimen of what a girl should be," he wrote to her in March 1943. "It's hard to make a statement like that without being suspected of having some ulterior motive. But I assure you that it was meant only as a sincere compliment and nothing else." He recalled "our little discussions" of 1941–42, "when we ranged over the problems of the world."[34] Although Margaret regarded Arthur as something of an oddity because of his social awkwardness, she was intrigued by him.

They shared a common religious background, though Arthur was often more sentimental in his faith. In 1943, he saw the popular movie *Song of Bernadette*, which starred Jennifer Jones in the title role (a role for which she won an Oscar). The story was a fictionalized and highly romanticized version of the life of Saint Bernadette Soubirous, who, in Lourdes, France, claimed to have seen the Virgin Mary in a vision in 1858. Bernadette was prosecuted by religious authorities; the film, based on a novel by Franz Werfel, depicted her as a mystic and romantic. Arthur, who pronounced *Song of Bernadette* "the finest movie I have ever seen," saw it twice and waxed eloquent about it to Margaret. Arthur was taken with the "simple, yet very beautiful, faith of the peasant girl" and her ability to "have faith in something good and fine," which was "about the most redeeming characteristic of man—that is, it is one of the few traits that distinguish him from other animals." Margaret responded less enthusiastically, and she was a little incredulous that Arthur had seen the movie more than once.

"I think I must be a good deal more mystical in my religious views than you," Arthur responded, "because I don't believe anyone who isn't something of a mystic could enjoy 'The Song of Bernadette' tremendously."[35]

At the same time, Arthur was a religious rationalist. He later observed that he agreed with Woodrow Wilson's views on faith and rationalism. For Wilson, he told an interviewer in the 1980s, "truth was a vital component of religion," and anything true was "from God." The truly religious were never afraid of following the truth, wherever it led: they "should not only accept it, but seek it, glorify it." In itself, the search for truth involved in scholarship and scientific inquiry "was a religious act."[36]

Arthur left Mt. Pleasant disgusted with Lutheranism, which he associated with parochialism, prejudice, and small-mindedness. He often liked to joke that he could always recognize a "Lutheran face"—long, solemn, and humorless—and Lutheranism to him represented hypocrisy and intellectual vacuity. Later in life, he often said that there was nothing less attractive in Christianity than excessive piety. According to a friend, Arthur was "contemptuous" of religious fundamentalism.[37] In July 1946, while in Washington, Arthur ran into an old Mt. Pleasant friend, the Rev. Roscoe C. Fisher, who had become a Lutheran minister. Roscoe, like many Lutheran ministers, was "unlettered, coarse, and unclerical."[38] Arthur thought little of Lutheran ministers' preaching abilities. He once wrote after hearing a disappointing sermon that the preacher was "pietistic" rather than "intellectual." Arthur was especially suspicious of thoughtless evangelicalism, whose "influence is usually unsalutary and serves only to excite the passions and intolerance of ignorant minds," particularly the "ministerial demagogues who left a great inheritance of intolerance and medieval superstition" among their uneducated followers by denying science and modernity.[39] Arthur noted that one of his favorite Bible verses was Acts 17:22, which included St. Paul's admonition to Athenians that "in all things you are too superstitious."[40]

While in Chapel Hill, Arthur attended Episcopal services. Through the war years, Arthur gravitated toward Episcopalianism, whose liturgy he described as the "summit of religious experience." "Nothing I know," Arthur wrote, "can remotely compare to it in its majesty, beauty, and compelling religious seriousness." As Arthur and Margaret approached marriage, they considered becoming Episcopalians, but he was increasingly attracted to the emphasis on high-quality, educated preaching emphasized by Presbyterians.[41]

Margaret was raised in a household in which Presbyterianism, and a strict adherence to its tenets, was a way of life. Though her parents were well-educated, they agreed with the southern Presbyterians' anti-Darwinian views during the evolution controversy of the 1920s. As Margaret left the Davidson cocoon, she questioned Presbyterian orthodoxy. She began testing the waters in her college years and, in conversations with her father, explored the limits of social Christianity. Like Arthur, she underwent a period of intense questioning in which she found modern southern Presbyterianism deficient. Where Arthur was most concerned about the intellectual vitality of faith and its viability in a modern world, Margaret wanted a religion that was more alive. She explored new approaches, finding especially appealing the social message of Christian writers such as the Methodist missionary and peace activist E. Stanley Jones, whose best-selling *The Christ of the Indian Road* (1925) described his many years as an evangelist in India.

The church, she believed, should engage with social problems, and what part of the country had bigger problems than the South? Margaret remained active in the YWCA all of her life, and while in Charlotte she worked with the local Y as an agency of social change. In July 1944, she heard a sermon by modernist Harry Emerson Fosdick, pastor of New York City's Riverside Church. Fosdick had been involved in a national fight against fundamentalism. In 1922, while pastor of New York's First Presbyterian Church, he delivered a sermon entitled "Shall the Fundamentalists Win?" In it, he presented a modernist, antifundamentalist position in American Protestantism in which he urged that the Bible be understood as a product of historical and cultural forces rather than the inerrant Word of God. In 1923, the General Assembly of the northern Presbyterian Church ordered a heresy investigation by a commission, and in 1924 he avoided censure by resigning. In 1930, Fosdick became pastor of the new Riverside Church, which opened that year and which John D. Rockefeller Jr. had financed in the Morningside Heights area in New York City.

Since Presbyterian fundamentalism was such an important part of Margaret's upbringing, listening approvingly to Fosdick represented a way of repudiating her heritage. In Fosdick's sermon, Margaret noted that he offered a "retrenchment of the Liberal position as he felt they haven't faced squarely up to issues but was no less severe in his hearty condemnation of 'fundamentalist, literal-minded Bible believers.'"

During the war, Fosdick also took the unpopular and what Margaret called the "rather difficult" position of pacifism. Although she thought his thinking "rather confused," she noted, "isn't all of ours?" Fosdick felt that Americans "should accept our full responsibility for inhuman deeds in this war and not feel that our noses are clean." "Of course he's right," she concluded, if "we still want to stop the enemy's technique of inhumanity to save our own skins."[42]

Although Presbyterians emphasized intellectual quality, she wrote Arthur, there remained a "sad deficiency at times and places in worship and also lack of social consciousness." Presbyterians, Margaret thought, instinctively sought to protect the status quo and were "pretty complacent and generally unaware."[43] Arthur agreed about Presbyterians' lack of social consciousness, but, he said, the "same indictment might be made of most of the Protestant churches." Roman Catholics, he added, despite all their "superstition and tom-foolery," had "always been the church of the people, and especially the lower classes in this country." Nonetheless, religion and a commitment to a modern version of Christianity constituted a common tie for Arthur and Margaret. They frequently shared religious and theological discussions in their correspondence after the spring of 1943.[44]

The war, of course, had steered Arthur and Margaret in different directions—she toward Charlotte, he toward Raleigh—but they maintained a growing correspondence, even during Margaret's relationship with Kreps. When Arthur left Chapel Hill for teaching in Raleigh in February 1943, Margaret commented that 408 Alumni Hall had "lost its air of industry and activity since you left—and [we] miss your inspiration!"[45] After Margaret left for Queens, the relationship survived, almost entirely, through letter writing, which often ranged over various topics. For the next two years, until their marriage in June 1945, they spent very little time together, and so the correspondence became, effectively, the only real means of communication in the evolution from friendship to romantic love. In this sense, my parents' exposure to each other was almost entirely supervised and appropriate. Their courtship-by-correspondence meant that their friendship became one of thoughts and ideas. Somehow in the two-year correspondence, between the spring of 1943 and the spring of 1945, Margaret came to regard Arthur as less the annoying, self-absorbed boor that he seemed to many of his peers. Perhaps, also, Arthur had changed, and had begun to find a person who could harness his demons and civilize him.

In my parents' correspondence, they discussed politics, but just as often they discussed literature and movies they had seen. Margaret didn't mind reading provocatively. In January 1944, she reported reading the iconoclastic Phillip Wylie's *Generation of Vipers* (1943), whose "vigorous impressions," she reported, "interest me very much." In early 1945, she read D. H. Lawrence's *Sons and Lovers*, which she concluded was not "too good."[46] Arthur didn't mind offering provocative comments; Margaret responded in kind. When he asserted that Americans were losing their intellectual vitality, she disagreed vigorously.[47] Commenting about a likely coal strike during the spring of 1943, he told her that Roosevelt's "chickens are just coming home to roost." Although he remained prolabor, Arthur asserted that FDR had granted "too much control to interest groups and hasn't reserved a sufficient and essential check for society in general." Labor leaders, he feared, had failed to live up to their responsibilities, and it was the duty of society to safeguard its own interests. We don't have Margaret's response, which was not preserved, but certainly she enjoyed the exchange.[48]

During their correspondence in the summer of 1943, Margaret remained unenthusiastic about war. She worried about her brother, John, a physician stationed with the Army medical corps in the Pacific, and her cousins Stokes and Colin Munroe, both with North Carolina's Thirty-eighth Evacuation Unit in North Africa. Although the Allied victory in the invasion of Sicily was exhilarating, she noted in July 1943, the press correspondents had been "really hilarious over the better-than-hoped-for turn of events." Ernie Pyle, whose reports were carried in the *Charlotte Observer*, always sent the message that the war was "one grand football game." She remained dubious that the war would be won without further bloodletting. "We Americans always get optimistic—at the first breath of victory!"[49]

Early on, Arthur was interested in accelerating the relationship beyond intellectual badminton. During the summer of 1943, Arthur pushed ahead. In July, Margaret invited him to come visit in Davidson, and Arthur responded immediately and arranged a quick trip in which he first met her parents.[50] During October, while Arthur was preparing for his Ph.D. exams, Margaret came from Charlotte to Chapel Hill, staying with old friends and watching a Duke–Carolina football game. Although Carolina lost the game to its hated rival, she commented that he had been "a grand host in every way."[51] The courting-by-correspondence continued during 1944. Interspersed were visits by Margaret, who rode the bus to Chapel Hill on a Saturday in January for an overnight visit. Arthur came over from Raleigh, and they had dinner together. In May 1944, he traveled to Charlotte from a research jaunt in Washington, and he stayed in a local hotel and visited with Margaret and her friends. Most of all, she seemed to value their good conversations when they were together.[52]

By the spring and summer of 1944, the courtship took a different turn. On April 7, for the time, Arthur daringly used the salutation, "My dear Margaret," and closed with the line: "Margaret, I think of you often."[53] He enjoyed her letters, written in her distinctive handwriting, he wrote to her later that month. "Honest," he wrote, "I do enjoy 'translating,' as you say, your letters. In fact, I love to get every one of them written in your distinctive way and read and reread them." Still, letters were a "poor substitute for personal relationships but in the absence of a better substitute I guess I will have to be satisfied."[54] Margaret reciprocated, though in a more cautious fashion. "Your expression of appreciation of our relationship was nice," she wrote, "and I do appreciate it." Arthur, she said, had expressed himself beautifully. Both of them, she thought, liked "so many of the same things," and she always enjoyed "our get-togethers—particularly the last one. We shall have to do it again—soon."[55]

In the spring of 1944, after a year's teaching at Queens, Margaret needed an intellectual refresher, and she went to Chapel Hill to meet with Howard Odum, who urged her to take summer classes at Columbia University.[56] Margaret spent six weeks in New York in July and August 1944. She stayed at the Parnassus Club, a women's boardinghouse located on West 115th Street, not far from the Columbia campus. Margaret enrolled in two courses, one on economics, the other on postwar reconstruction. Taking a train that left from the Concord, North Carolina, station, she traveled to Richmond and visited with her friend and mentor Nelle Morton, and she stopped off in Washington and stayed with an Agnes Scott friend. In Washington, Arthur and she met. "I want you to give me all the latest hot tips on New York," she wrote in anticipation.[57]

At Columbia, Margaret found her postwar reconstruction class especially stimulating. The instructor, who assigned Carl Becker's *How New Will the Better World Be?*, was a "healthy cynic" about Germany and believed that the country had been "coddled" after World War I. She seemed to agree with him that the Versailles Treaty had been insufficiently harsh.[58] Margaret loved Columbia. In her classes, she found the "same unhurried atmosphere as at U.N.C.," and, perhaps in contrast to Queens, the faculty were "truly scholars." A friend of hers who was taking a philosophy course described herself as "fascinated," and Margaret audited the class. The "slow and peaceful academic tempo" at Columbia contrasted with a "bustling city" in which everybody was "on the move" and in a hurry.[59]

In New York, Margaret enjoyed the city's amenities, visiting the Metropolitan Museum of Art, hearing the New York Philharmonic at Carnegie Hall, watching an ice show, and attending plays and musicals in the theater district, such as Rodgers and Hammerstein's *Oklahoma!* Margaret also took full advantage of the city's liberal Protestantism, attending Broadway Presbyterian, where she heard its pastor, John H. McComb; Madison Presbyterian, where she heard pacifist and fabled preacher George H. Buttrick; and Riverside Church, where she heard Social Gospeler Harry Emerson Fosdick. She also heard the great neo-orthodox theologian Reinhold Niebuhr speak one evening, and she described him as "good with 'plenty on the ball.'" One evening, she and her friends went out to LaGuardia Airport, ate at its Sky-Line Restaurant, and watched the planes take off and land. Early on, she visited International House, where Arthur would spend the next year, and found "terribly interesting people" there. Margaret was so busy that she worried that her pocketbook was "feeling strain," and she waited on tables at the Parnassus Club to help pay expenses.[60] As always, she reported about her diet of reading, which included Lillian Smith's *Strange Fruit* (1944), a novel about interracial love, religious fundamentalism, and class conflict in a small Georgia town, and Somerset Maugham's *Razor's Edge*. Fascinated with *Strange Fruit*—which because of its controversial themes was banned across the South and in much of the North—Margaret was disappointed in *Razor's Edge*.[61]

Margaret retained warm memories of her experiences in New York City during the summer of 1944, and in subsequent years she loved to return to the city.[62] Still, when she took a train out of New York and returned to Charlotte in mid-August, she declared herself "truly glad to get back to N.C." Perhaps she was "pretty sectional and local-minded": she liked the South "better than the North—after six weeks in the latter!" Although there were "loads of things to do up there which are fun and nice people, too—but we really live better, don't you think so?" She enjoyed shopping in Charlotte, where the store clerks were "in a better humor."[63]

While Margaret was in New York, Arthur returned to Chapel Hill to teach for two months in the Navy's V-12 program, which had begun a year earlier to train more than 1,300 recruits in college-level work. Taking a room in town, Arthur declared his return to "God's own country—yes, Chapel Hill." Arthur spent a languid six weeks in a hot North Carolina summer. He always loved fresh fruits and vegetables, and he wrote of the luscious and cheap cantaloupes, which were available for ninety cents a dozen. In the library, he put the finishing touches on a massive bibliography for his dissertation, spending a "hot afternoon" making bibliographic cards in the law library. For fun he played bridge in weekly student tournaments.

When Arthur returned to North Carolina, he found the UNC campus and history department severely depleted by the war. Chapel Hill was, however, less frenetic, and life was not "so rushed now," with plenty of housing and "practically no lines at the [Carolina] Inn cafeteria." There was now only a "skeleton department" at UNC: Green was gone on a year's leave to Harvard (which many believed would lead to an appointment there), George Mowry had joined the War Production Board, and Beale was gone on what seemed like a permanent leave. Later that summer, Mowry announced that he was moving to a teaching position at Mills College in Oakland, California. As Arthur observed, things at Carolina were in a "considerable mess." If Green left for Harvard permanently, he wrote, "won't our department be sort of shot through?" The university, against the wishes of faculty, had gone to a trimester system to accommodate the military training system.[64]

As early as the spring of 1944, with Kreps out of the way, Arthur pursued Margaret ever more ardently. In April, after he had seen her in Chapel Hill, he revealed himself to Carrington Gretter. He was now "more convinced than ever that I am very much in love with her." He believed that it was better to "make up one's mind—to be definitely sure—about a girl before one makes any commitments." Margaret was the one for him, he was sure. "I love to be around Margaret, to hear her talk, to look at her. I hate like hell to leave her." At the same time, he had "become rationally as well as emotionally convinced of my love," which was "all the more deep for that fact." "God and Margaret willing," he declared, "I'm going to marry her some day."[65]

Arthur waited for the best time to profess his love. In the spring, Margaret sent him her photograph, while in July he sent her one. He sent it on her birthday, July 22, but got the date wrong (he inscribed it, "To Margaret, on your birthday, July 18, 1944"). For years, the photograph hung in my parents' bedroom with the incorrect date, and when they had the photo reframed in the 1990s, my father changed the date to correct the error. In early July, Arthur wrote a letter announcing his love; the letter has not survived, though Margaret's response, on July 5, makes clear the outlines of what he said. "The sentiments of your letter," she wrote, "were quite a surprise to me." Margaret had little idea of how he felt until she received his letter. He was "so sure, so confident—and I do believe in and trust your expressed feelings." Although she was intrigued by Arthur, the idea of a romantic relationship was so "utterly new to me" that she was not ready to say that she loved him—"yet." "I'm not in love with anybody," but "that doesn't say I could never be in love with you." She was "not even in a position to define feelings until I have something to go on." Indeed, there were "definite potentialities for my loving you," above all a "sincerity of conviction which is so important to really stable love." Margaret felt that "we have something . . . which I value so very very much, but I can't know yet for my part if it's love." Time, she concluded, was "one important factor in determining what it will be."[66]

As Margaret and Arthur grew closer by means of their letter writing, their relationship began to solidify around an exchange of ideas. They were different personalities, but they shared many things. They both came from small towns imbued with the Protestant culture that dominated the lives of southern whites. But though firmly rooted in that culture, Margaret and Arthur were loosened from their moorings. Their lives differed from those of their parents and grandparents, and they had learned to question the traditional social and racial structure of the South. The advent of the war, and the rapid changes accompanying it, only further accelerated this process.

Many years later, Arthur told an interviewer for the *Philadelphia Enquirer* that he approached his doctoral work "entirely backwards."

Links: My Family in American History

Fearful of the draft, he had thrown himself into the research and writing of his dissertation, which examined Wilson, the South, and the presidential campaign of 1912. During 1942–43, the Rosenwald grant enabled him to travel widely, without taking courses, while the ASTP program took him away from UNC courses. So, although he lacked enough classes to graduate, he decided to move into his doctoral qualifying exams in the fall of 1943—taking the oral exam in October and the written exam in December.[67] The written/comprehensive exams were more of "an endurance contest than anything else," he observed after the fact. By December 1943, two years after he started the UNC graduate program, although Arthur had completed a version of his dissertation and his qualifying exams, he remained in the curious position of lacking enough courses to graduate.[68]

As early as November 1943, Arthur had already planned to abandon teaching in the military program in Raleigh, and he extended feelers to the Rosenwald Fund about a new, one-year fellowship that would free him up to finish his degree. Privately, in December 1943, Howard Odum, along with Rupert Vance, told Arthur that he would receive the fellowship.[69] Sometime during the fall of 1943, he learned that the Wilson Papers were being returned from their hiding place to the Library of Congress. Informed that he needed another year's worth of residency as a doctoral student along with coursework, Arthur decided to spend a year at Columbia University beginning in September 1944. Sure enough, official word arrived in April 1944 that the Rosenwald Fund had awarded him a $1,100 fellowship.[70] Arthur made arrangements to work at Columbia under historian Henry Steele Commager. He also applied and was admitted to the International House on the Upper West Side, near campus.[71] Arthur returned to his research with his usual intense energy. Over New Year's weekend 1944, he took a train to Washington and surveyed the Wilson Papers. In April and May, he spent a month in Princeton, doing research there and commuting to Trenton and New York City to read newspapers.[72]

In New York, Arthur took up residence on the fifth floor of International House, on the Upper West Side, only a few blocks from the Columbia campus. International House was constructed on Riverside Drive in 1924 with support from John D. Rockefeller Jr. Created to foster international exchange between students from all over the world, International House attracted an assortment of people, providing inexpensive and culturally enriching living experiences. Later on, other International Houses were established at the University of Chicago and the University of California, Berkeley. Arthur described International House as "a sort of modern Tower of Babel" where students "of all races, creeds, and nationalities . . . live together amicably."[73] Every Sunday, most of the house members ate dinner together and gathered in the house's auditorium to hear music or visiting speakers. In October, Arthur described a dinner that was followed by a piano recital by a Juilliard student. After that, the Indian nationalist Krishnalal Shridharani spoke. A poet and fiction writer, Shridharani was also a popularizer of Gandhian social activism through nonviolence. His *War without Violence* (1939) gathered a wide American audience, especially among peace and civil rights activists. Arthur left intrigued with Shridharani's plea for Indian independence. Margaret had heard Shridharani speak during her summer class on postwar reconstruction at Columbia; she was equally fascinated with his critique of British imperialism and racism.[74]

By the fall of 1944, Arthur was already boasting a productive record. In 1944, he published articles in the *Southwestern Historical Quarterly* and the *Journal of Southern History*, and in 1945–46 in the *American Historical Review*, the *North Carolina Historical Review*, the *Georgia Historical Quarterly*, the *East Tennessee Historical Society Publications*, the *North Carolina Historical Review*, and *Agricultural History*. The years 1947 and 1948 yielded four more articles. Meanwhile, he reluctantly completed his course requirements. Arriving in New York in September 1944, he registered for courses at Columbia on modern Britain, with John Bartlet Brebner, and Soviet Russia, with George Vernadsky, along with a year-long research seminar with Henry Steele Commager.[75]

Arthur was annoyed with having to take all these courses, especially his Russian history course. Fifty-seven years old in 1944, Vernadsky, according to Arthur, was an "old gentleman" and "quite dull" and his course "really asinine." "What with a hot room and two hours of droning," he complained, "it all gets pretty boring."[76] Arthur saw little of the American historian Allan Nevins, whom he described as a "typical Babbitt type of business man, self-made." Arthur enjoyed Brebner's modern British history course more, but the main reason for his presence at Columbia, he believed, was the opportunity to work with Commager. On the faculty at Columbia since 1936, Commager, an American intellectual and cultural historian, was legendary as a demanding yet invigorating teacher of graduate students. A snappy dresser, Commager often appeared in class in colorful attire. For one class, he wore a brown suit, brown shirt, and yellow tie. Commager was reputedly the "toughest man in the department," according to Arthur, though he found him "very stimulating and helpful." Commager became a mentor.[77]

Arthur was already well along toward completing his dissertation when he arrived in New York. In November 1944, he finished a draft that he sent along to Green, who was spending the year as a visiting faculty member at Harvard, and he was done with the dissertation by early 1945. Arthur intended to use the year at Columbia to write his first book, an initial volume in a larger biographical project on Woodrow Wilson. Whether he had in mind the five-volume work that he wrote between 1947 and 1965 remains unclear. In 1944–45, Arthur wanted to write a study of the early Wilson's concept of political economy: only later would he see himself as a Wilson biographer. Whatever his intentions, Arthur's subsequent career as a historian would be defined by his decision to write this book. He began as a skeptic of the worshipful approach of previous historians, such as Wilson's authorized biographer, Ray Stannard Baker. Years later, ironically, Arthur himself would often be accused of a similar worshipfulness. "I'm afraid you're becoming hypercritical of Wilsonian principles and I shall be very disillusioned when I read your book!" Margaret teased Arthur in late October 1944. If it was the historical truth he was seeking—and she was sure it was—"I suppose you can't help it. But it does seem strange that you're bringing the great god Wilson down from his pinnacle."[78]

Within about a month of his arrival in New York, Arthur had completed a draft of a first chapter of the new book and presented it to the Columbia seminar. The hard-to-please Commager liked Arthur's work and was encouraging.[79] "I must be getting some sort of literary style!" he wrote excitedly after receiving Commager's comments.[80] Simultaneously completing his dissertation and beginning a new book, Arthur worked at a feverish pace. In libraries in New York, Princeton, Trenton, Newark, New Haven, and Washington, he read more than three hundred newspapers, working twelve- to fourteen-hour days in what Margaret would call the "ditch-digging" of research, on the two-year period covering Wilson's governorship of New Jersey (1910–12) and the presidential campaign of

1912.[81] "You're going to have an Encyclopedia Britannica by the time you finish with Wilson!" Margaret wrote in November 1944. "There'll be little left to know."[82]

During the winter and spring of 1945, Arthur expressed new worries about his draft status, as Congress threatened to conscript 4-Fs and require national alternative service. Congress had discussed the issue for about a year, without taking action. Then, in January 1945, the House of Representatives passed the May-Bailey Bill, which addressed the dire labor shortages by conscripting noncombatants. For Arthur, conscription and national service created a "terrible state of confusion." "I am awfully unnerved about the uncertainty of the whole business," he wrote to Margaret. Congress would almost certainly enact 4-F work legislation, he wrote. "The first problem," he wrote, was "how will it affect me?" A second problem, he wrote, was how to "put myself to be of more service to the country." For him, the solution was to avoid waiting on conscription. While in Washington in January 1945, he visited the offices of the Fair Employment Practices Committee (FEPC) and met with the assistant director of field operations, who told Arthur of a vacancy in their Dallas office in about three months. However, he feared that working with the FEPC would undermine his professional advancement. Should Arthur pursue the FEPC job, he asked Margaret, or should he stay put and await further development? If he took the FEPC job, should he take time in Washington to try to finish his research? If he concentrated on seeking a teaching job, would that be consistent with his duty to country?[83]

In the end, Arthur's anxieties about labor conscription subsided after he learned that his draft board had little need for war-industry labor. After a moment of panic, he concluded to Margaret that "it might be better after all's said and done for me just to stick by my guns and await developments." If he was conscripted, he would go, but in the meantime he would proceed full steam ahead. Soon, the collapse of Germany's offensive capabilities and the looming end of the European war, which would come in May 1945, ended the possibility of national service.[84]

Absorbed in her Queens teaching, Margaret grew more involved in wartime Charlotte. Although she lived a few blocks from campus, she regularly rode the bus to the downtown district. By 1945, she was complaining about frequent breakdowns and a scarcity of buses and repair parts.[85] Margaret was strongly pro-union, and she approvingly reported that one of her former fellow grad students at Chapel Hill was now working for the National War Labor Board and was associated with CIO organizing activities. In early 1945, she attended her first American Association of University Professors (AAUP) meeting at Queens. Margaret had previously ignored the organization, but when she discovered that it functioned as a labor union she became more interested. The Queens AAUP chapter, though not especially strong, offered "one means of teacher protection, and I think every teacher should join."[86]

During her first year at Queens, in 1943, Margaret took her sociology classes to juvenile court in downtown Charlotte.[87] In April 1944, after her government class visited the courtroom, she wrote that her students "got pretty depressed (and so did I) at some of the cases presented, but that's what goes on in court life." She described Judge F. Marion Redd as a "fine person in many ways," but she criticized the absence of "more scientific methods" in his evaluation of evidence.[88] After her sociology class visited court in November 1944, she wrote that the students had found it "terrifically depressing" to observe "some of the specimens" appearing in court.[89]

As she had in Richmond and Chapel Hill, Margaret remained active in the YWCA, an important women's activist organization in the twentieth-century South. When the Queens chapter secretary came under fire for administrative incompetence, Margaret attempted to mediate.[90] At the campus Y, she spoke about war work and postwar reconstruction. Margaret introduced her Y students to a war production plant in Charlotte, and in May 1944 she helped to establish a recreation program, with swimming and bridge tables, for female workers. A story about her activities even appeared in the evening *Charlotte News*.[91] During the presidential campaign of 1944, Margaret participated in a voter education project organized by a local women's club, and she spoke to working white women. At one talk, after only fifteen women showed up, Margaret complained that the lack of interest in voting among Charlotte women was "appalling."[92]

Margaret realized that the most pressing home-front issue for southerners was race. She first seriously confronted segregation's injustice while she was a student at Agnes Scott, and her interest grew during her years in Richmond and Chapel Hill. When Gunnar Myrdal's classic study of race in the United States, *An American Dilemma*, appeared in 1944, she read it and wanted to know Arthur's opinion. "I've seen so many comments on it, pro and con, mostly con," she wrote. "How do you react towards it?"[93] Arthur eagerly read the book, pronouncing it "really a remarkable study" that offered a "good summary and synthesis of practically all existing knowledge about the Negro problem."[94]

Myrdal's prediction of changes in southern apartheid were heartening, but they also indicated a restiveness among African Americans, an unwillingness to wait for incremental change. Such unrest became especially evident during the war years. In Charlotte, as in other parts of the urban South, black bus riders challenged Jim Crow. In October 1944, Margaret described an incident on the bus when a black woman refused to relinquish her seat, as was the custom, and move to the rear. Instead, the black woman was "openly antagonistic, declaring her rights, etc." After the bus driver lost his temper and struck the woman, other black passengers objected, and the woman kept her seat. The driver telephoned local police to meet the bus at a later stop, and a police force escorted the bus through town. From the "standpoint of justice," Margaret concluded, the law "should have protected the negro girl." She doubted that the driver was prosecuted.[95]

At Queens, Margaret continued her participation in interracial organizations. While the campus Y was one important organization, she also invited officials from the Commission on Interracial Cooperation (CIC) to speak to her sociology class. Organized in 1919, the CIC, based in Atlanta, brought together white liberals and African American leaders in an effort to soften and eventually end segregation. The CIC advocated "interracialism"—the enhancement of contacts between southern white and southern black leadership through organizations and meetings. At this point in its history, the CIC stopped short of favoring integration. But because the organization advocated racial justice, it represented the prevailing mainstream of southern white liberalism.

Margaret was already thoroughly schooled in interracialism. She made a point of attending interracial gatherings in Charlotte, such as the visit of Allan Knight Chalmers, a Scottish liberal white pastor of Broadway Tabernacle Church in New York. Chalmers served as chair of the Scottsboro Defense Committee, president of the NAACP Legal Defense Fund, and treasurer of the NAACP. The gathering at Charlotte to hear Chalmers attracted an audience that was half white and half black. He "certainly spoke from his heart, and is very sincere in his convictions," Margaret recounted. According to Chalmers, while the war was "one of the simplest social problems," the most complex problems revolved around racial justice.[96] Later, in March 1945, Margaret attended a play put on by the local NAACP chapter at the all-black Johnson C. Smith College. Entitled *A Black Woman in White*, the play, written by a Smith English professor, told the story of a black woman doctor. Although it was "filled naturally with a lot of N.A.A.C.P. propaganda," Margaret wrote, she thought it was a good play.[97]

The contacts with the all-black Johnson C. Smith College faculty formed an important part of Margaret's participation in CIC-style interracialism. In March 1944, she appeared in Charlotte on a panel with the registrar of Johnson C. Smith.[98] The following fall, in November 1944, Margaret helped to organize a joint Queens/Johnson C. Smith interracial meeting. Remarkably, Queens president Blakely approved of the meeting and even wrote to North Carolina College president James Shepherd to urge a follow-up meeting. Margaret and other interracialists were amazed at Blakely's response; they had assumed that he was conservative about matters of race.[99] The Smith participants were a "fairly alert bunch," she wrote, and "I hope we're really getting something started to be continued."[100]

Margaret also participated in other interracial groups. In Chapel Hill, she attended the First Presbyterian Church, whose controversial pastor, Charles M. Jones, was a founding member of the Fellowship of Southern Churchmen (FSC). Her friend Nelle Morton joined Jones at the Chapel Hill church in 1945 as his director of religious education and later become executive secretary of the FSC. Margaret predicted that Jones and Morton would work well together. Arriving in Chapel Hill in 1941 from churches in Keswick, Virginia, and Brevard, North Carolina, Jones forthrightly opposed segregation, and for most of his career was the object of segregationists' wrath.[101]

In November 1944, Margaret attended a conference of white and black interracialists that local Quakers had organized in Greensboro. The meeting was held at Bennett College, an African American women's college, and hosted speakers such as black sociologist Ira de A. Reid of Atlanta University and the FSC's Jones. Margaret also met Bennett College president David Jones, a prominent African American educator. She was favorably impressed. Reid reminded Margaret of Arthur Raper, she wrote, "in encouraging the discarding of prejudices, etc." Jones, meanwhile, provided a closing message that, Margaret wrote, "really packed a wallop."

Margaret detected that Jones had accelerated his assault on Jim Crow, and he was "hailed as quite a hero and pioneer in the field of race relations at an interracial conference!"[102]

By the fall of 1944, Charlie Jones had already acquired what Arthur called the "literal martyrdom" for civil rights activists. He was also theologically adventurous—especially so for the usually conservative Presbyterians. Margaret heard him deliver a sermon entitled "Who Art in Heaven" in which he argued that heaven and hell were "simply a state of mind." Arthur, who had already heard a number of Jones's sermons, agreed with Margaret. "If one follows him in theology," he wrote to Margaret, "he is liable to be led right out of orthodox Christianity—and in a hurry, too!"[103] In the summer of 1944, some of Jones's opponents in the Chapel Hill church, questioning his positions on race, began a campaign to oust him. This occurred while Arthur was teaching in the V-12 program at Chapel Hill during the summer of 1944; he described a "furor" that was the product of a "few persons who are quite vociferous."[104] Later, in the fall of 1945, another group—which included Arthur's old friend Carrington Gretter—submitted a petition demanding Jones's firing. When Arthur learned of Carrington's participation, he wrote to him expressing his "sense of deep shame" about such "intolerance" and "ignorance." The anti-Jones campaign seemed, he thought, a "lack of real Christianity." How could this act of intolerance have occurred in Chapel Hill? The rest of the nation, Arthur told Carrington, looked to UNC for progressive race policies. He hoped that Carrington "would be fighting one hundred percent to preserve the community's and the University's integrity."[105]

Although perhaps not an orthodox liberal, Arthur was unqualified in his opposition to bigotry. In the 1960s, Davidson College—where my elder brother Stan was attending—was reconsidering its present policy to tenure only Christians to its faculty. Arthur wrote a long letter to Davidson's president. Not only was the policy wrong, he predicted that it would ultimately stand in the way of Davidson becoming a nationally ranked liberal arts college. Later, after I had graduated from Davidson, the issue became a full-blown national controversy. In May 1977, the college withdrew a job offer to a Jewish faculty member at Swarthmore because of its "Christian tenure policy." The job offer, made in February 1977, was the first instance in which a Jewish faculty member would be hired, but when the faculty member, Ronald Linden, refused to accept the tenure policy, the college withdrew the offer. After a storm of controversy, Davidson redrafted its policy to provide a nondiscriminatory hiring policy. The controversy even received attention in the *New York Times*. Only recently did the college change its policy that required trustees to be Christian, and this occurred over the protests of many Davidson alums and supporters.[106]

In the 1940s, Arthur was, however, less an activist than a skeptic about the impending civil rights revolution. He wondered if white southerners could ever be persuaded to change their system of racial apartheid. "I sometimes think we are merely scratching the surface of the problem," he wrote in early 1945, "when we do things like having inter-racial meetings, etc., but I suppose they are part and parcel of the tremendous re-education of the South which is one of the prerequisites of progress in the matter."[107] The issue of race, he wrote in 1948, profoundly divided the country and made the South a "unique and separate region with a unique way of life." Conflict, even civil war, loomed over the question of integration. The reality, Arthur believed, was that the white South had never accepted what he called the "American democratic tradition—when Negroes are concerned." A race war, involving "one of the worst slaughters in our history," might come in response to federal orders to desegregate public schools. Arthur could imagine what might happen if integrated transportation were required by federal edict. "I am talking about the real South," he wrote, "not the college students and teachers, the liberal clergymen, or the editors. Even the liberal minority tends to be slow and enormously cautious."[108] While in Washington during a research trip in the spring of 1944, Arthur spoke with E. B. Trimble of the University of Kentucky, who was working for the Fair Employment Practices Committee (FEPC), charged with enforcing nondiscriminatory employment in war contracts. Trimble expressed a "pretty discouraging" view about the situation, Arthur wrote, which did not "make a pretty story." He agreed with Trimble's conclusion that "the South won't give the Negro justice and that Northern Negro leadership is demanding more than it can get at the moment."[109]

Arthur was irritated after reading Sidney and Beatrice Webb's *Soviet Communism*, which suggested the Left's naïve views about human nature and its tendency to view things through rose-colored glasses. Students in the graduate history club at Columbia read Howard Fast's *Freedom Road*, a work of historical fiction that suggested the possibilities of biracial cooperation during Reconstruction. The book, Arthur thought, was "pretty terrible." Although some of Columbia's Marxists admired the work, he noted that the "sanest person present" at the club meeting was a black woman from South Carolina who was skeptical about simple solutions.[110] Fast was a "pretty good writer but a terrible historian," Arthur concluded.[111]

Margaret read *Freedom Road* a few months later, and she and her Queens colleagues were more attracted to Fast's ideas. Her colleagues judged the book as "graphic and good." Margaret was initially attracted to Fast's message of biracial cooperation and coalition building. But she soon deferred to Arthur's expertise. Fast's spirit "might have been good," but she admitted that it was "very bad to use an historical novel as a substitute for history." Perhaps *Freedom Road*, Arthur suggested, was more a case of Fast's wishful thinking about the possibility of biracial coalitions. Her friends were surprised at Arthur's reaction. Several of the faculty members were "much upset" by Arthur's assertions about its historical inaccuracy, and they asked Margaret for details. Arthur wrote back emphatically. "Tell your friends," he wrote, "that *Freedom Road* was built around a historical absurdity: the idea of the possibility of cooperation between poor whites and Negroes during Reconstruction." Even in the South of the 1940s, Arthur asserted, it was nearly impossible to achieve interracial unity among white workers and Africans. "I wish what he wrote had been true. But it wasn't." Fast was "nothing less than a colossal liar."[112]

Though thoroughly in sympathy with the end of Jim Crow, Arthur was often bemused by interactions between white and black people. Taking a train north to New York in the spring of 1944, he described how a black passenger fell asleep on his shoulder. "Sounds as though you're practicing brotherhood!" Margaret observed.[113] While in New York City in May 1944, Arthur took the wrong subway and found himself "deep in Harlem." As the only white person within sight, he was fascinated by the all-black world. He was taken with what he called exotic "magic stores" that sold herbal remedies, books of magic, exotic idols, and abundant spiritual advice. Finding all of this "literally true, and . . . rather shocking," he promised to return for further anthropological investigation.[114]

During the autumn of 1944, Arthur befriended a black minister from Texas, Mr. Fuller, who was enrolled in Commager's seminar. Arthur described to Margaret how Fuller dressed elaborately in the robes of a Catholic or Episcopal priest and wore a cross around his neck, with a collar and bib. Asked if he was Episcopalian or Catholic, Fuller responded that he was neither: to Arthur's surprise, he was a Baptist. Fuller wore a bib and collar, he said, because a "minister should dress to look like a minister." Arthur tutored Fuller a little in French and helped him with his seminar paper, and they ate dinner and socialized together. Fuller told him what all white southerners loved to hear. "You are from the South," Arthur reported him as saying, "and you understand the negro much better than northerners." Fuller was Arthur's first Columbia friend.[115]

But Fuller turned out to be a bit of a problem. When he had Arthur read a draft of his seminar paper, Arthur called it "perfectly atrocious." Fuller was "about the most fitful student I have ever seen, and completely incompetent," Arthur concluded. "He doesn't know as much about American history and research methods as you or I did when we were freshmen—and that's the God's truth." Arthur found too much preaching and moralizing in his writing—mostly because Fuller was aggressively opposed to slavery as "that sum of all villainies"—and Arthur, ever the scientific historian, advised him to avoid offering an opinion or judgment of his own. Fuller took Arthur's criticism well, or so he believed: "I know it must have been a blow when I told him, in effect, that he should throw all he had written in the waste basket."[116] Arthur's attempt to tutor Fuller for his French exam—which he was required to pass for the doctorate—was equally frustrating. Fuller studied hard, but was hopeless at verb tenses and got "snarled" on grammar. Later, Arthur derisively described Fuller as his "star French pupil." In April, he reported "another discouraging lesson with Mr. Fuller, whose chief difficulty is he doesn't study and lacks imagination. Only two more lessons, I suppose before he fails the examination."[117] When Fuller participated in Commager's seminar in the spring of 1945, it was a disaster. Each time that he presented his ideas, Arthur wrote, "all of the rest of the students, including myself, nearly have convulsions from keeping from laughing."[118]

NEW YORK

3

In the fall of 1944, when Franklin D. Roosevelt ran for his fourth and last term as president against New York Republican governor Thomas Dewey, Arthur and Margaret differed about the election. Arthur was a loyal New Dealer, and, for the most part, a strong Roosevelt supporter. In April 1945, when Roosevelt died of a massive cerebral hemorrhage, Arthur described FDR as a "great man in many respects" who would eventually occupy a place among "the greatest of presidents." Roosevelt had the "foresight and vision to realize that we could not exist in a world dominated by Nazi tyranny, and that was a great deal more than most of us realized before 1941."[1]

Still, there were many things that troubled Arthur about Roosevelt. A committed internationalist, Arthur believed that there would be no lasting peace if Americans regarded their adversaries as "perverse and evil." "It can't be—never has been—done." It was difficult, he believed, to find a moral, philosophical, or religious justification for war. Waging war contradicted his own religious convictions, he wrote in early 1944, but in the struggle against the Axis powers he had accepted its utter necessity and the imperative to win. Life did not always present a choice between absolute evil and absolute good. Arthur acknowledged the need to choose between the lesser of evils in the war and postwar reconstruction. The "only justification" for fighting was the possibility of building an effective international organization to prevent war. Arthur favored Allied postwar occupation of Germany and the reconstruction of its economy, accompanied by the establishment of a representative, democratic government. He opposed reparations and a punitive peace, though he favored war crimes trials. Still, he noted that Germans could insist that American bombers who terrorized civilians should also appear before the same court. For Arthur, the two standards governing future action were Christianity and democracy.[2] Not surprisingly, Arthur was appalled, in September 1944, when Secretary of the Treasury Henry T. Morgenthau announced at the Quebec Conference a plan to dismember and deindustrialize Germany after the war. "I am consoling myself that no one will take it seriously," Arthur wrote, "and have been encouraged by the almost unanimous opposition of newspaper editorials." He regarded the Morgenthau Plan as "preposterous, evil and imperialistic."[3]

As Roosevelt's fourth presidential campaign approached in 1944, Arthur expressed some momentary doubts. He thought little of the Democratic political establishment in North Carolina. Clyde Hoey, who was elected governor in 1936 and U.S. senator in 1944, cut "quite a ridiculous figure," with "his long hair and vacuum brain capacity." "I wish we had a Fulbright or a Hill!" he exclaimed, referring to Arkansas senatorial candidate J. William Fulbright and Alabama senator J. Lister Hill.[4] Although he told Margaret that he was "strictly neutral" in the contest between FDR and Thomas Dewey, his Republican opponent, he remained "suspicious of what the Republican party will do once it gets into power." He predicted that the election would be a "toss-up."[5]

Margaret remained less enthusiastic. Her doubts about Roosevelt reflected her discouragement about his domestic policies and his desertion of his progressive coalition. In the spring of 1943, she looked on in dismay as Roosevelt seemed to abandon the New Deal in order to galvanize a coalition in support of his war policies and postwar internationalism. FDR must have felt "like a defeated man," she wrote, after losing his domestic reform program to congressional conservatives.[6] Revolting against the Democratic orthodoxy in North Carolina, during the May 1944 Democratic primary, she supported the gubernatorial candidacy of Ralph McDonald, an insurgent challenger of the Democratic establishment's candidate, R. Gregg Cherry. McDonald, who had taken on the political machine in the 1936 gubernatorial contest, lost in a bitter primary battle. Margaret was an avid McDonald supporter, attending a rally in downtown Charlotte on the eve of the election. She was shocked to discover, however, that most of her students remained Cherry supporters: she took a poll in her political science class and discovered that no one supported McDonald. Remarkably, Margaret forgot to register to vote, missed the deadline, and did not cast a ballot. She reported that she debated with her father, a Cherry supporter, but was "most distressed" about not being able to "kill father's Cherry vote—and he's glad!"[7]

Though pacifist in leanings and unenthusiastic about the war, Margaret believed that Germany should be punished. She did not share what she called Arthur's "tolerant and kindly feelings towards Germany." "I'm rather inclined to think we were suckers before and hope won't be again," she declared. "It's true that there's a strong hate-the-militarism-of-Germany propaganda campaign—but I can't see that it isn't good."[8] She and Arthur had other differences about postwar reconstruction. She described his views as "more optimistic and humanitarian," though she thought that the two of them shared some views. Although she lacked "any blue-printed plan of reconstruction for a new and better world," she hoped that "we won't repeat many of the same mistakes."[9]

When Dewey opposed Roosevelt, Margaret moved toward bolting the Democratic ranks. In September 1944, she told Arthur that she was "steadily swinging to Dewey." She criticized both campaigns for emphasizing "political repartee" rather than "real issues." Roosevelt, she believed, held no monopoly over representing the common man.[10] Margaret found Dewey's challenge appealing in the one-party world of North Carolina politics; she thought that the Roosevelt White House was a tired presidency, bereft of ideas. She believed that Charlotte, and North Carolina, would support Roosevelt, despite some support in the Myers Park neighborhood for Dewey. She remained sympathetic toward Wendell Willkie, the GOP's presidential candidate in 1940, and she regarded his death on October 8, 1944, during the middle of the presidential campaign, as a "real loss," though she noted that both sides showed "utter disrespect of his death." Politics, she mused, "doesn't respect life or death."[11] Margaret declared that she preferred Socialist Norman Thomas over Roosevelt.[12] Arthur teased her by wondering, late in the campaign, whether her "Dewey agitation" had much of a chance in "good old Democratic N.C."[13]

On election night, Arthur attended a party held by his friend Lefty Meisen, a Columbia alum who had attended graduate school with him at UNC. With plenty of beer to drink, Meisen's party was "very interesting." All the local Democrats were happy the morning after; even Commager was "feeling 'chipper.'" FDR's victory, Arthur wrote, meant that Democrats would be held responsible for making the peace. Wondering whether the Republicans were now extinct, he believed that unless the party realized that the "Ice Age is over, they are doomed to continual defeat." "Oh, excuse me!" he teased. "I forgot you were for Dewey!"[14] Margaret followed the election with her housemates on Queens Road. Mrs. Murphy, their landlady, was a strong Roosevelt supporter, but the residents were otherwise split.[15] On election eve, Margaret and three of her friends gathered for dinner and a sleepover while they stayed up late listening on the radio to the election returns, celebrating the election with a bottle of Portuguese wine. Three of the women were Dewey supporters, two of them from Pennsylvania; Margaret was the only traditional Democrat, and the northerners were all Republican (though none of them was especially conservative). The women agreed that the losing side would buy dinner. "I think I know who'll foot the dinner bill," Margaret mused. Later, she reported that the group had had a "wonderful time."[16]

During his year at Columbia and in New York City, Arthur had, in contrast to Margaret, a more limited social life. He interacted with fellow graduate students and International House tenants, often playing bridge and chess with them. Complaining about the quality of the bridge players, Arthur met his match in the house's chess players. John Dunba, an International House resident, provided a challenging opponent, and Arthur found that the Haitians living nearby were skillful players. "I can beat all of them but one," he wrote with his usual braggadocio.[17] Arthur was quite taken with his black neighbors; this was, no doubt, the first time that he had ever seen anyone from Haiti. He described how he lived next door to a Haitian who spoke beautiful French and only a little English. Arthur, who always fashioned himself an able French speaker, enjoyed the opportunity to improve his conversational skills. Another neighbor, from Mexico, proved good enough to beat Arthur at chess, while still another hallmate was a Methodist minister who had been interned for two years while a missionary in Japan.[18]

Like other smokers in wartime New York, Arthur improvised in order to find a regular supply of cigarettes. Wartime rationing caused constant shortages; he would later have Margaret send him her ration. During his year in New York, he discovered a little cigar shop near the New York Public Library that sold cigarettes every day from 12:30 p.m. to 5:00 p.m. He managed to get a pack a day by waiting in line for five minutes, though frequently in weather that wasn't "exactly warm." "Only confirmed smokers," he wrote, understood "why an otherwise sane and rational person would do such a thing."[19]

Arthur's most difficult adjustment to New York City was the harsh winter. "The weather here has maintained its dreadful status," he complained in November 1944. "It gets cold (and they tell me seriously that we haven't seen anything yet) and a terrific wind blows. And the colder it gets the harder the wind blows. I just hope I can last out the winter!"[20] The weather did indeed worsen; the winter of 1944–45 was a cold one. On January 11, 1945, a few days after Arthur returned from Christmas holidays, temperatures hovered around zero, with strong winds. Describing "great cakes of ice" floating in the Hudson, he wrote that it was "really painful to be outside." Things did not seem to improve much, as a deep freeze then gripped the city. "Now I know what long underwear is for!" he wrote Margaret.[21] Walking from Columbia's library to International House, the wind blew Arthur "so fiercely" that he was forced to grab onto posts and fences to keep his balance. It was "so cold it really hurt."[22] "It simply gets cold . . . and stays cold," he complained to Margaret in February 1945. In contrast, the milder North Carolina winters were always relieved by periods of springlike weather.[23]

Although Arthur commented that, for most graduate students, "poverty is a severe mistress and conspires with one's own conscience to make them study," he took full advantage of the city, developing a lifelong love of New York.[24] In 1944, his sister Elinor moved to New York to pursue training at the Manhattan School of Music. He saw her regularly. Arthur was hopelessly romantic about movies: in January 1945, he went to see William Wyler's film production of Emily Bronte's *Wuthering Heights* (1939) for the fourth time, pronouncing it "that greatest of all love stories in movies."[25] Arthur also explored the working-class sections of town, though he often disdained urban life. "Have you ever been in the working districts of New York and seen how the other half lives?" Arthur asked Margaret in January 1945. Working in the New York Public Library Annex on Twenty-fifth Street, in the heart of the garment district, Arthur frequented working-class cafeterias. "What an education it is to see the poor, miserably poor, people who eat in them." They were "worse in appearance than our Southern sharecroppers, sort of like the folks on Tobacco Road."[26] His fascination with working-class culture in New York City formed an important motif of his year in the city. Once, in March 1945, he visited Union Square, which was known as a left-wing center, to have dinner at Bonat's, a French restaurant on West Thirty-first Street. He also watched *We Will Come Back*, a Russian film about anti-German guerilla warfare in the Soviet Union. Arthur described the theater as a "real working-class place," and in its lobby a man was selling the Communist Party's publication, the *Daily Worker*, with a "large display of cheap radical literature."[27]

Sometimes, Arthur observed the Sabbath. A Sunday in February 1945 offers an example. "What a lovely Sunday this has been for me!" he wrote Margaret. Starting the day with church and communion, at 12:30 he joined a group of three fellow students on Forty-third Street. He and his compatriots lunched at a German American restaurant on Forty-seventh Street, where they dined on *hasenpfeffer*, or rabbit. He described it as "all right, but not too delicious." Then, Arthur and a male friend strolled down Fifth Avenue to St. Patrick's Cathedral. Afterward, they walked to Central Park and spent an hour and a half at the park's zoo. That night, after dinner at International House, Arthur attended a performance of the Broadway musical *Carmen Jones*, a stage version of the opera *Carmen* with an all-black cast. He declared it "superb," although he complained about women sitting behind who ate candy and spoke with a Brooklyn accent throughout the performance.[28]

Arthur's most significant experience in New York City was his discovery of opera. On December 2, 1944, his brother John William was in town, and John William and Elinor joined him at the Metropolitan Opera—Arthur's first opera. John William bought tickets at the last minute, but he secured good seats to a performance of *La Traviata*, with Licia Albanese singing Violetta and Charles Kullman singing Alfredo. In December, he bought tickets for Richard Wagner's *Götterdämmerung*, which featured Helen Traubel as Brünhilde and Lauritz Melchior as Siegfried. Arthur fell in love. The performance was on December 8, 1944, and he started with seats located high in the balcony. Once the performance began, he moved to the orchestra seats and stood behind that section. "I leaned against a railing and the opera was so magnificent," he wrote, that he "wasn't conscious of physical existence." The opera was a "terrific emotional experience, and the singing was the very best I have ever heard." He was now hooked on opera—in a way, perhaps, that only opera fans can understand.[29]

It was during his year in New York City that Arthur became a dedicated opera fan. On January 26, he attended Verdi's *Il Trovatore* with a Muslim neighbor from International House (whom he called "my Mohammedan friend"), and they waited an hour and a quarter and "almost froze" in order to get a standing-room position.[30] The next night, January 27, he saw Charles Gounod's *Faust* with his sister Elinor. He proclaimed, with his usual hyperbole, that it was "truly the greatest musical experience in my life." With *Il Trovatore* and *Faust*, Arthur discovered the advantage of standing room at the Met. Those standing were positioned immediately behind the best seats in the orchestra level, but they paid only about a third of what orchestra seats cost. For only $1.50, Arthur saw the "finest opera I have yet seen." The music, he reflected, was "so wonderful you don't think of getting tired." In the future, he went about an hour before the performance and stood in line. "Then if you're early and lucky you get a place on the railing." For both *Il Trovatore* and *Faust*, he managed to get "elbow room on the rail, and that was a lot of help."[31]

Arthur's battery of operas resulted in a love affair with Wagner. On February 2, after he had seen *Tristan und Isolde*, Arthur declared that he had "really lived, musically speaking, and that all other musical experiences must be anti-climactic." Arthur and two friends from International House got in line at 5:00 p.m. for the 7:30 opera, and they secured places on the rail. It was, he wrote, "almost as good as sitting down—and the music carried us so far away from reality that we didn't think of getting tired—not until it was all over." The four-hour opera was "simply out of this world." He especially enjoyed the love duet and when Isolde sang the Liebestod in the final act.[32]

Arthur became a regular at the Met throughout the remainder of the 1945 season. On February 7, he saw Verdi's *Rigoletto*; the following week, he watched Wagner's *Siegfried*, with top Wagnerians Melchior, Traubel, Kerstin Thorborg, and Norman Cordon. On February 23, he got in the standing-room line and saw *Lohengrin*. On March 7, he heard *Carmen*, a performance he called "just about perfect." Arthur's opera obsession soon became a Wagnerian obsession. On March 17, he stood two hours in line to get standing room to see a "truly great" performance of *Die Walküre*— with singing by Melchior, Astrid Varnay, Thorborg, Herbert Janssen, and

Emanuel List, the "greatest aggregation of musical talent on the stage I have ever seen, or expect to see." This was the first time that he had seen the complete Ring cycle, which he called the "greatest artistic creation of man's genius." Arthur noted that one of his friends had seen the Ring through five separate times, "so I feel I have a lot yet to learn." The Wagner operas only seemed to get better. After a March 22 performance of *Die Meistersinger* for which he secured a center balcony seat, he wrote Margaret immediately before going to bed. "Like all of Wagner's operas I have seen it was quite wonderful," he declared. "The last act was especially beautiful and I don't think I shall ever forget the scene." The culmination of his operatic experience was Wagner's *Parsifal*, which he saw on March 28, 1945. "I know that I have raved about a number of operas," he wrote when he returned from the five-hour performance, "but this was simply the most wonderful of them all. It is inconceivable that the mind of a man could give birth to such beauty, power, and grandeur. I don't know when I have been so deeply moved, for it was a deep religious experience for me, too. How I wish you could have been with me tonight, my love!"

Arthur closed the opera season with Richard Strauss's comic *Der Rosenkavalier*, which he described as a "delightful comedy of manners about early 18th century Austria" with some "truly glorious music." In all, Arthur's opera experiences had been transformative. "It has been quite a winter for me and I think that the things I shall remember longest and appreciate the most were the operas I saw. Certainly my musical horizon has been considerably broadened."[33] In all, in the space of three months, Arthur had seen fifteen operas, eight of them by Wagner.[34]

Arthur remained an opera lover for the rest of his life. I attended my first opera in March 1992, when he took me to see an evening performance of *Parsifal* with Siegfried Jerusalem singing the title role, Waltraud Meier singing the role of Kundry, and James Levine directing. It was one of the more memorable experiences of my life, and I began to understand my father's obsession. After my mother's death in 1996, though debilitated from lung cancer, he insisted on keeping his season tickets at the Met and making the ever-harder trip to New York. My brother Stan took him up to New York City several times and would help him down the aisle to his seat.

Although Margaret had refused to reciprocate in Arthur's profession of love in July 1944, she did not discourage him. He took that as a positive sign. Gradually, however, she became more overtly affectionate. Absence also made her heart grow fonder: Margaret seemed to regard Arthur's love as more valuable when he was in New York. "I do miss you very much and the fact that we aren't closer together," she wrote in late September 1944, after he had moved. "I often think of things I want to talk with you about."[35] In November, Arthur responded with ever more ardent expressions. "If I could see you tonight I would say, 'I love you Margaret, I love you more than anyone in the world.' But since I can't see you except by imagination I will let this second-best method do for now."[36] Anticipating a trip to North Carolina that he eventually had to cancel, he noted that it would not be long before he headed southward to see Margaret. "Do you know, I realize, being away from you, how very much I need your love and affection," he wrote. "I need someone I can completely confide in—as I can in you—whom I can tell of my ambitions and hopes and who won't think me crazy."[37]

By Christmas 1944, Margaret was giving Arthur more positive signals. She conferred with her father, ever her best adviser, about Arthur. The Douglases had met Arthur in the summer of 1943, and he was an instant hit. James Douglas, in particular, saw a great deal of potential in him, and he believed that Arthur would be a good match for his daughter. "Keep your eye on that young man—he is going to really be something," James told his daughter. Arthur was worth a second look, he suggested. James had become impressed with him despite his rough edges. He privately told his son, John, that a man of Arthur's stature "needed to work" on his clothes and grooming.

Sometime during the fall of 1944, Margaret decided to accept Arthur's profession of love. On December 1, she wrote: "I don't know that you're thinking of me unless you tell me, so I always like to hear."[38] In response, Arthur pushed matters further. In December 1944, during his meeting with Fletcher Green in Cambridge, Green asked Arthur if he was making any progress in his pursuit of Margaret. "I told him I thought I was," he slyly wrote her. "Was I being too optimistic?" "I think you gave Mr. Green a correct report on your progress—not too optimistic at all," Margaret wrote back several days later.[39]

Arthur and Margaret agreed to a reunion in Davidson over Christmas 1944, and it was there that Arthur proposed. There is no written description of how Arthur proposed marriage, but on a balmy Christmas Day in North Carolina, he visited Davidson, popped the question, and Margaret accepted.[40] Because of Green's insistence that Arthur add another chapter to his dissertation, his Christmas vacation was cut short, and he spent weeks in Washington doing more research. Margaret, writing to him in Washington, wistfully remembered how they had sat next to the Christmas tree while he proposed. She "so hated" to see the tree come down after the holidays, but "down it had to come." She wondered where "we'll be dressing a Christmas tree next year, sweet?" Although the war in Europe—then in the throes of the massive German counterattack at the Battle of the Bulge—looked "gloomy," Margaret announced that she looked forward to the start of 1945 because it meant the "beginning of us together."[41] "We can't expect freedom from uncertainties when nobody else has it," Margaret wrote. "And our love is the most all-important certainty."[42] When her father drove Margaret back to return to teaching at Queens, she announced that she was "having terrible difficulty in putting my feet on the ground!"[43]

Arthur was equally giddy, and described to a friend his engagement as "quite a coup."[44] "My girl was just as I had hoped and, as you know, we are engaged," he informed Fletcher Green.[45] To Margaret, Arthur was effusive. "I am writing you New Year's eve, my sweet," Arthur wrote from Washington. "Being away from you now has only one redeeming feature and that is that it reminds me that we shall never again be separated at this time. Do you think of me often? I think of you always. Happy New Year!"[46] "I've been thinking about you all day," he wrote her on January 10, on his return to New York City. On the way back, while sleeping on the train, he dreamed about her. "I do love you immensely. With what we've got, don't you think we can go a long way together? I am sure we can and go hand in hand."[47]

Early on, they considered church membership, an important part of their life together. When Arthur went to New York, John Link had advised his son, "Remember to attend a Lutheran Church."[48] But Arthur had long ago rejected his father's Lutheranism and in Chapel Hill had attended an Episcopal church. Margaret was willing to follow him toward Episcopalianism, she said, but her church preference was Presbyterian because of her "constant association" with that denomination. Nonetheless, she wanted to be in the same church as he was, so she was willing to become Episcopalian. The matter of church membership was put aside for the moment in their correspondence, but Arthur gradually warmed to the idea of becoming a Presbyterian. After their marriage, he would become an enthusiastic Presbyterian churchman.[49]

Arthur and Margaret's correspondence intensified: they wrote every day, or, if they didn't, apologized for not doing so. The language was ornate, a little Victorian, but also ardent. "Sweetheart, did you know that I love you so much?" Margaret wrote. "Wish you were here tonight I would tell you with more meaning!"[50] "Please remember," Arthur told Margaret in February, "that you are the mainspring of my happiness and that I love you so much that only you and I know the dimensions of our love."[51] Arthur complained if her letters did not arrive daily; she apologized if she missed a day. "Will you forgive me?" she asked when she did not write one day.[52] Sometimes a day would arrive with no letter, to Arthur's disappointment; other days, more than one would arrive, to his delight. On a January day when two letters came in the mail, he wrote that he "enjoyed every word of them."[53] As the weekend mail service resumed, Arthur eagerly anticipated the arrival of several of Margaret's letters, which were "always the best features of Mondays for me."[54]

The correspondence solidified an important element in their relationship: Arthur was emotionally needy, and Margaret could provide loving care. Margaret worried about Arthur's obsessive attention to work and his tendency to exhaust himself in frenetic bouts of energy. After their engagement, she told him he was "working entirely too hard and going at things too intensely." She could sense that "between the lines that tremendous amount of intense research is taking its toll on you, so take it easy for awhile." She was worried that overwork was "pulling you down." "I think you need me to make you let up," she wrote, but she urged him to "please do it without me."[55]

Arthur's family pattern, with an abusive father and an overprotective mother, meant that love was often expressed in the emotional veil that his mother spread over him. Often this veil, which shielded Arthur from his father, was related to his constitution—and the need to protect it. Arthur expected the women in his life to protect him by protecting his health. Margaret, for her part, was drawn to caregiving. She took a constant interest in people, but during the course of her life she was attracted to emotionally needy, usually neurotically needy, men and women. Arthur was, in many ways, an emotional project who would fulfill Margaret's need to express love through caring.

The author and his mother in August 1973 at the family gathering place in Montreat, North Carolina. I was twenty years old, and Margaret was fifty-five.

Arthur speaking at West Point in the early 1970s.

Arthur at the Mercer Street kitchen table reading the *New York Times*. One of Arthur's favorite activities was to hold forth at the kitchen table; mornings almost always included bacon, eggs, and a dose of the *Times*.

PRESBYTERIAN LIFE

March 1, 1963

Historian Arthur Link (above) describes the faith of Woodrow Wilson, page 8

● From the Mountain to the Multitude by John A. Mackay
● The Boundless Love of Dolly Melville
● My Life Behind Bamboo Bars, Part II

Arthur on the cover of *Presbyterian Life,* March 1963. Though raised Lutheran, Arthur became a dedicated Presbyterian once he married my mother. He was very active both in his church and in the national church affairs. Unlike most academics, he considered his religious beliefs as central to his system of thinking.

Arthur in his Firestone Library office at Princeton in the late 1980s, as he was nearing completion of his lifelong work, *The Papers of Woodrow Wilson.*

Margaret, about 1980.

Helen Elizabeth Link, Arthur's mother (*top row, third from left*), about 1910. Helen taught school before she married John William Link on June 11, 1913. The school was located in Uvilla, not far from her hometown of Shepherdstown, West Virginia.

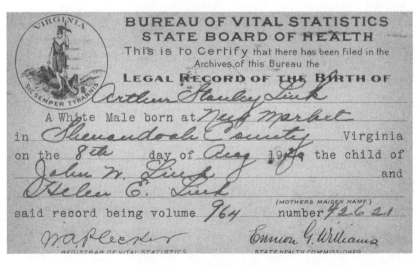

Arthur's birth certificate, August 1920. Arthur's mother, Helen, worried constantly about his health and had him baptized only days after his birth in New Market, Virginia.

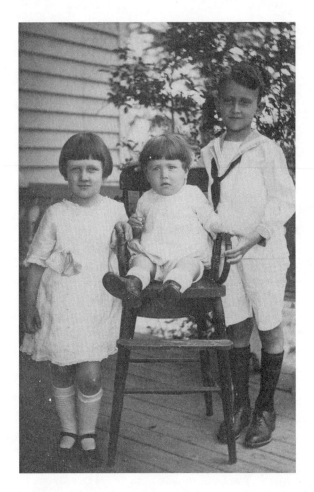

Arthur and his siblings, about 1922. *From left*: Elizabeth, Arthur, John William. Arthur's younger sister, Elinor, was born in 1923.

John William Link, my grandfather, about 1918, when he was around thirty-three years old. John served as a World War I chaplain and is shown here in uniform.

The North Carolina Medical College, about 1900. The college was owned by my mother's great-uncle John Peter Munroe, who moved it to Charlotte in 1907. When my maternal grandparents married, John Peter gave them half of the building, a duplex, as a "bridal present." Later, my grandparents bought the other half of the duplex from John Peter, known affectionately in the family as "Uncle Doctor." My mother grew up in the house, a large, rambling Victorian located across the street from Davidson College. It was torn down in 1971. Courtesy of Davidson College Archives.

My mother's father, James McDowell Douglas. A longtime physics professor at Davidson College, James was perhaps my mother's closest friend. He was fifty years old when Margaret was born in 1918, and he remembered the presence of Union troops in Reconstruction South Carolina, where he grew up.

My mother's parents, James and Anniebelle Munroe Douglas, in the 1940s.

My mother, Margaret Douglas, in
the early 1920s in Davidson.

My mother's first memory, at three years old, was of the Chambers Building, the
main building at Davidson College, burning to the ground on November 28, 1921.
"Old Chambers" contained seventy-two dormitory rooms (including one occupied by
Woodrow Wilson when he attended Davidson during the 1873–74 school year), three
laboratories, five classrooms, and a commencement hall. The building rose three
stories and 95 feet high and extended 280 feet wide; it was constructed of red brick
and gray stone, with four massive columns adorning the front of the building and a
cupola on top. This photo was taken after the event, from which the college recovered during the 1920s. Courtesy of Davidson College Archives.

Margaret, late 1930s.

Arthur, about the time he started as
an undergraduate at the University of
North Carolina, September 1937.

Arthur as a college junior in the
UNC yearbook, *Yackety-Yak*.

Howard W. Odum, sociologist and leading Chapel Hill academic, sponsored work by both my parents. Odum also gave them both advice about romantic relationships. Courtesy of the University of North Carolina Library.

John Hope Franklin, sometime in the 1940s. Courtesy of Duke University Library.

Fletcher M. Green, historian of the South and a leading figure at UNC. Arthur worked under Green as an undergraduate and a graduate student.

Margaret (*far left*) returning as a senior to Agnes Scott College, in Decatur, Georgia, in the fall of 1937. Agnes Scott was Margaret's first exposure to the world beyond Davidson, and the college had a great effect on her. The photo comes from an unknown newspaper clipping.

John Hope and Aurelia Franklin during their first visit to England in 1951. The Franklins were among my parents' oldest and dearest friends. Courtesy of Duke University Library.

Margaret's engagement picture, early 1945.

Margaret's wedding picture. Arthur and Margaret were married in Davidson on June 2, 1945.

Joseph R. Strayer, longtime historian and chairman of the history department at Princeton University. Strayer hired Arthur at Princeton in 1945 and served as a supporter and mentor for many years thereafter. Courtesy of Princeton University.

Margaret with my brother Stan, about 1948.

James Douglas with my brother Stan, probably 1947, in Princeton.

Arthur and Stan, about 1948.

The first house my parents owned in Princeton, at 66 Cedar Lane, about a mile east of campus. The house was completed in 1948, but my father accepted a job offer at Northwestern University in 1949.

Cedar Lane house in 2010.

Our house in Evanston on Orrington Avenue. My family spent eleven happy years in this house. My father kept an office on the third floor and looked over the children as they played below.

Arthur in his home office in Evanston. Arthur was known throughout his career for his prodigious and productive work habits.

Greetings from the McGoverns

George McGovern and his family after his election to Congress in 1958. McGovern was Arthur's first doctoral student at Northwestern, and the two remained lifelong friends.

Arthur and Margaret visiting Lookout Mountain, Tennessee, during the summer of 1956.

The Link family at Oxford, December 1958. *From left*: Peggy, Jimmy, Stan, Bill, with my parents in the back row. The four children are wearing their English school uniforms.

Ortrun Lenz, punting on the Cam in the summer of 1958. Ortrun, a German who served as an au pair, became an integral part of the family during the year in England.

Bill, Peggy, and Jimmy posing in lederhosen during the summer of 1959, when we spent a month at a Bavarian pension. To my far left is Angelica, a German girl I befriended at the pension.

The house on Mercer Street in 2009. I lived here from first grade through high school. The house was owned by the university and rented to my family at a discounted rate—a condition of Arthur's move to Princeton in 1960.

Mercer Street, located just off Princeton's main business district, was about 200 yards from the university campus.

Arthur and Margaret on a cruise to the Bahamas, 1961. My father's great passion in life was traveling, especially on cruise ships.

The author on his tricycle about the time that we moved to Princeton in 1960.

Sheldon House, which was located two doors down Mercer Street from our house, in a photo taken in 2009. The house was floated by barge from Northampton, Massachusetts, in the nineteenth century. In the 1960s, the university owned it and rented it to single faculty.

The old Witherspoon School, where I spent sixth grade. Begun as the only segregated black school in Princeton, by the 1950s it had become the Princeton Borough's junior high school. After I completed sixth grade, the school, located in the heart of Princeton's historical African American neighborhood, became a nursing home. It was recently converted into condominiums. (Photo taken in 2010.)

Arthur and the staff of *The Papers of Woodrow Wilson*, mid-1960s. *To Arthur's left*: John Wells Davidson; *to his right*: David W. Hirst. Courtesy of Princeton University.

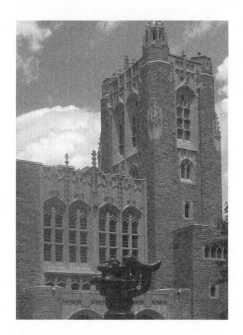

Firestone Library, Princeton, in 2009. When Arthur moved to Princeton in 1960, the university provided ample office space in the library to house the Wilson Papers project.

My parents with Eleanor and George McGovern, July 1983. Margaret was holding our eldest daughter, Percy, then only a few months old.

The author as a high school junior, fall 1970.

Arthur in the late 1980s.

She took a constant interest in his health, and Arthur was happy to provide details of any illnesses or afflictions. "I forgot to tell you in my last letter about the miracle that happened to me," he wrote Margaret in March 1945. "Night before last, as you will remember, I had a very bad cold and felt rather miserable. I went to bed and when I got up my cold was practically gone. I still have a slight stuffiness in my head, but I have felt fine yesterday and today."[56] Arthur provided clinical detail, sometimes too graphically: "When I have a cold my sinus tubes get awfully bloody. Recently I have been discharging quantities of blood along with the mucous matter."[57]

During the early months of 1945, an "epidemic of engagements" broke out among Margaret's Chapel Hill friends, including four former UNC classmates.[58] In the correspondence that followed, Margaret and Arthur began wedding planning. In February, Margaret submitted her resignation to Queens president Blakely; like many women of that era giving up their careers upon marriage, she did so with little apparent regret. They planned for a small wedding in Davidson to take place on June 15, once Arthur had finished his time in New York and had completed the doctorate. Eventually, Arthur decided to have his old friend and college roommate Lew Williams serve as best man, while he asked his brother John William to play organ and his sister Elinor to sing. (John William, in character, refused, though Elinor agreed.) In addition, Margaret wanted to have only her first cousin Mary McCann Hudson as an attendant, and she hoped that her brother, John, would somehow be able to return from the Pacific for the wedding.

Like most couples during World War II, Arthur and Margaret made their marriage preparations hastily. After her Christmas engagement, Margaret returned to Charlotte and went shopping for a wedding dress. She also began investigating china and silver, discovering that the war had caused acute shortages in both.[59] Margaret also arranged for an official engagement portrait. At Arthur's suggestion, for the first time in adulthood she abandoned what he called "those old hair pins that always get in my way" and let her hair down. "I am experimenting on which is best before I see you, sweet!" she wrote. Margaret's official engagement portrait was in Arthur's hands by the third week of February. He was delighted, proclaiming the picture to be "the best of you I have ever seen."

"It looks exactly like you, only not as beautiful as you really are, my dearest. Pictures somehow can't portray one's own intimate experiences with a person quite adequately—and that is a part of beauty, too. But I love it very much because it is you."[60]

For Arthur, there was the matter of the engagement ring. He was without much money; he even had some trouble finding a New York bank to cash his Rosenwald Fund checks. For a while Arthur sent the checks to a friend, who cashed them and returned a money order to him.[61] He wanted to provide a nice diamond for Margaret. En route back to Washington and New York in January 1945, he stopped in Charles Town, and his Uncle Adam, his father's younger brother who ran a general merchandising business, agreed to find him a ring at cost.[62] Diamonds were in short supply, but Uncle Adam found a single blue-white diamond set in a yellow gold mounting.[63] Arthur arranged a payment plan with his uncle.[64] On January 22, the engagement ring, along with a gold wedding band, arrived in New York. Afraid that he might lose both rings, he sent them by overnight express to Margaret.[65] She was ecstatic when they arrived. "Such a very exciting day!" Margaret exclaimed, and she had a visiting friend there with her to "squeal with me."[66] Arthur was equally delighted. "I could tell from your letter that you were thrilled and excited and very pleased—and I'm very happy, too. I thought you would like them, especially the diamond which I think is the prettiest of its size I have ever seen. Now, do you know what my dearest wish is? It is to see you with the engagement ring on. I'm also anxiously awaiting the day when I can slip the wedding ring on your finger and say, 'With this ring I do thee wed,' or words to that effect."[67]

Margaret showed off the rings to family and friends during the following weeks. In late January, her mother was "crazy to see the ring," and she went with Margaret to the Charlotte jeweler to have the engagement ring sized. "Mother thought it to be quite as beautiful as I had described it—a perfect stone."[68] Once the jeweler returned the ring, she showed it off to friends and family. The diamond was "beautiful in different lights," she told Arthur in early February 1945, and she had "such a good time trying it in all kinds of lights to see the blue and gold lights in it." Margaret immediately showed what she called "my rock" to Queens president Blakely, her Davidson friend Elizabeth Shewmake, her aunt Mary Stokes, and her uncle Stokes Munroe. Back in Davidson, she showed the ring off to her aunt Agnes and her cousin Grace James. "My diamond looks so pretty tonight," she wrote Arthur. "I have such a good time gazing at it. Wish you were here, sweet, to look at it with me. I should like to look at you, too."[69]

Arthur paid for the ring through creative financing. His father offered some advice, which, as usual, Arthur ignored. John offered to split the cost with Arthur, an offer that Arthur, determined never to accept a penny from his father, rejected. But John insisted that Arthur should "settle with Uncle Adam," who was a sharp businessman who rarely left much money on the table. In addition, John—of all people—offered advice on how to remain happily married. Marriage, he advised, was the "first and all important clause in the sentence of great living." "Do not fear to make known your circumstances to your future helpmeet—she will understand," John Link wrote in January 1945. Somehow, about a month after he got the rings, Arthur scraped together enough money to send a check to Adam.[70]

Arthur paid for the rings by taking on a part-time job in New York at a cafeteria on the Upper West Side, a job where he worked during March and April 1945. Arthur always told his children that he paid for the ring by "scrubbing floors," but none of us realized that meant work in New York City. "Today I joined the ranks of the proletariat," he wrote to Margaret in early March, claiming to have become "a member of the great working class." Working from noon to 2:00 p.m. Mondays through Fridays (later, he would work from 5:30 p.m. to 9:30 p.m.) and Saturdays from 8:30 a.m. to 1:30 p.m., Arthur received lunch and $1.75 a day. On his first day, he reported that he enjoyed his work, which, "thank goodness, requires little mental effort." He stacked dishes, and the job gave him "just the right amount of physical exercise." The surroundings were bright and clean, the hours good for his schedule, and his coworkers were mostly "awfully nice" middle-aged women. He predicted that he could pay for the ring and save perhaps one hundred dollars for the wedding and honeymoon.[71]

Arthur found the work interesting, and, as usual, he applied a sort of anthropological lens to his environment. His supervisor at the cafeteria was a friendly, elderly Canadian, while the servers on the cafeteria line were German and Irish. The Irish, he observed, were "often quite ignorant and dumb, but they have a good sense of humor."[72] In March, he described how his Irish coworkers "were on a rampage because it was St. Patrick's day." They were fiercely anti-English, and one of them, he wrote, launched into a "tirade" about Great Britain. The United States had joined World

War II, she declared, "just to save England's skin, and that we ought to quit." He concluded that his coworkers were "really very unintelligent."[73]

Arthur and Margaret remained separated during most of the winter and spring of 1945. Margaret planned a trip to New York to see Arthur during the Queens spring break in March. In February, the college canceled the spring break at the urging of war authorities intent on reducing travel during a time of fuel shortages. "That certainly throws a bombshell into our nicely laid plans," Margaret wrote glumly, "but there doesn't seem to be anything to do but wait until June till we can see each other."[74] Arthur was profoundly disappointed. "I can see the reason for cancelling spring holidays," he wrote, "but it hits awfully hard just the same. You know how awfully much I have looked forward to your coming up. I've just lived from day to day, waiting for you. And now this happens!" Arthur offered to come to Charlotte, but he had no money. Still, it was "simply ridiculous to think that we can wait until June to see each other." He urged Margaret to see if she could rearrange her teaching schedule to make for a long weekend so that they could talk over their wedding plans and he could feel her "warm embrace." "We certainly picked a fine time to become engaged, didn't we, honey, with me here way in New York and you in Charlotte! But even at this distance, it's the most wonderful thing I have ever known."[75]

Despite a furor at Queens over the canceled holiday, Margaret faced social censure at Queens if she skipped classes: "The one thing most greatly condemned at Queens is teachers taking any time off—particularly for pleasure!" There were, she thought, "definite advantages in being a student—I wish teachers had a cut system!" She felt "considerably fenced in by the whole situation at this point."[76] Queens had some difficulty enforcing these policies. Although Blakely promised to provide an extra day for the Easter weekend, he prohibited faculty travel. Despite these pressures, Margaret decided to go up to New York in early April. Traveling on the *Southerner*, the train that ran from New Orleans to New York, she planned to leave Charlotte on Thursday, April 5, arriving in New York City at 7:00 a.m. the next morning. "I'm so excited over seeing you," she wrote Arthur.

Throwing caution to the wind, Margaret decided not to inform the Queens authorities until after her trip. "It's so wonderful to think about seeing you, my sweet—I hope nothing happens to blow the trip up—We'll have to keep our fingers crossed!"[77] Margaret was so excited about the trip, she told Arthur, that "I'm sure I'll be completely no good for teaching till April 5th. The combination of spring weather and seeing you is too much. The least of my interests at this point is teaching. You're a demoralizing influence, darling!" Arthur bought Margaret's return ticket on the *Southerner*, but informed her sheepishly that he needed a money order from her to pay for it as soon as possible.[78] When Margaret suggested that she might want to see some Broadway shows, Arthur told her that he also wanted their limited time together free. He preferred attending matinees to keep the evenings without obligations. "Really, honey, I would prefer to go to a Saturday matinee and keep Friday and Saturday evenings free," he wrote. "You're going to be here such a short time I can't bear to think of looking at actors or actresses most of the time and not you."[79] "We shall certainly not spend all our time 'looking at actors and actresses,'" Margaret assured him. "We shall spend a long time looking at each other!"[80]

The reunion in New York—the only time that they would see each other before their wedding in June 1945—was a great success. Arthur and Margaret saw William Berney and Howard Richardson's *The Dark of the Moon*, a Broadway romantic tragedy that was just beginning a two-year run on the New York stage. But otherwise they did little but try to make up for the past three months of separation. Richardson had been on the UNC campus as a participant in the Carolina Playmakers, and Arthur described the production as "Playmaker stuff glorified." Two of his old female acquaintances from Chapel Hill were in the cast.[81] When Margaret left, Arthur was gloomy. "I couldn't express in words—and I can't in writing—how much seeing you has meant. I think you know, though. Couldn't you tell by the way I looked? I have looked forward to the past three days for months, and now they are gone. And two months now stand between us. But we both have plenty to do, and let's hope the time goes by rapidly." Margaret was more cheery and, as usual, related her experiences to the experiences of those around her. On her return trip on the *Southerner*, she sat next to a merchant marine sailor on his way to Atlanta who was "geared up" on Seagram's Scotch whiskey, and who felt that the "only way to stand the trip was to continue feeling no pain—so he had come well fortified." She found him amusing. She was able to sleep, despite a woman across from her who spotted a rat and became hysterical. Margaret wrote to Arthur on her return: "We have certainly stored up some New York memories, haven't we? We shall have to revisit it often—as we can afford!"[82]

       After his engagement to Margaret in Christmas 1944, Arthur bore down on the reality of becoming a professional historian. Soon after he returned to Columbia in January 1945, he had completed the extra chapter that Fletcher Green had required, and in mid-February, Green approved the dissertation.[83] After completing the exams for his Columbia courses in January, Arthur, unburdened by any further course work except for Commager's seminar, turned the remainder of his attention to writing his book on Wilson, which by early 1945 he was calling a "partial biography" entitled *The Road to the White House*. Having already drafted three chapters by the end of 1944, Arthur moved forward rapidly. Working in newspaper collections and manuscript materials in New York and New Jersey, he wrote ferociously during the winter of 1945.[84]

By June 1945, Arthur had completed eight of fifteen chapters, about 450 pages of text, and he had also begun shopping the book to publishers. Short of money, he calculated that an advance would put him in much better position. "My, but it would be nice to get, say, $500.00 advance royalties," Arthur mused to Margaret. "Our financial worries would be over, at least for the time being." In November 1944, he heard from an editor at A. A. Knopf, and in January 1945, Arthur sent three chapters and an outline. But he had little hope for Knopf, and the response was a decisive "no."[85] Arthur then tried Farrar and Rinehart but encountered little interest. Describing his experience with trade publishers as "pretty discouraging," he wrote a friend that finding a commercial publisher for a scholarly book, even about Woodrow Wilson, was "an impossibility these days."[86]

Getting nowhere with commercial presses, Arthur decided to write to Princeton University Press director Datus C. Smith Jr. On one of his earlier trips to Princeton, Arthur had met Smith, who expressed interest in his work. In mid-April 1945, Arthur sent him the first six chapters. Reading them within two weeks, Smith wrote back enthusiastically. Although he admitted that he was "no scholar and not even a sound judge of someone else's scholarship," Smith described himself as a layperson who had read deeply in Wilson biographical materials. "I am absolutely fascinated by what you have written." He promised to send the chapters out for scholarly review, but he emphasized his "tremendous enthusiasm" and his "great hope" that Princeton would publish his book.[87] After Arthur continued another year of writing and revision, Princeton offered him a contract. In March 1946, Smith proclaimed it "the best book written on Woodrow Wilson."[88] *The Road to the White House* appeared in 1947, but not until Arthur completed much more research and revision. Smith had sent a rough version of the manuscript out for review in the summer of 1945, and a critical report had come back. Arthur's manuscript was "undigested," the anonymous reviewer concluded, and it did not do full justice to Wilson. But with revisions, the critic predicted, *The Road to the White House* could become a "lively and controversial book." Smith dismissed the review, urging Arthur to proceed with his revisions. The book would become the first of Arthur's five biographical volumes that Princeton published over the next two decades, dealing with Wilson's life until 1917.[89]

As his time at Columbia was coming to an end in May 1945, Arthur faced uncertain prospects. His UNC mentors thought highly of him; friends in Chapel Hill reported that both Ray Newsome and Hugh Lefler had declared Arthur "the finest graduate student in history they had ever had." But any possibility of employment at Carolina, he was told, was hopeless. Arthur extended feelers to James Patton at N.C. State, but he was unencouraging. He considered seeking fellowships and applied for support from the Social Science Research Council (SSRC) to provide some time in Washington. He and Margaret explored the limited housing options in Washington, but the SSRC application was eventually turned down.[90]

During the winter and spring of 1945, Arthur kept Margaret apprised of his job search. Any employment "will affect you just as much as me," he wrote, "and I want to get your frank opinion beforehand, so if I have to act quickly I will already know what you think." Margaret's response was unequivocal: she would go anywhere with him.[91] "I would like nothing better than to get into a good university," he wrote to a UNC professor, "where a young man is encouraged to do research and writing."[92] A flurry of job possibilities opened up in the spring of 1945, though few seemed to lead anywhere. In January, February, and March, there were reports of jobs at Michigan State, the University of Washington, Swarthmore College, and Rollins College. Arthur wrote to all of these departments, but with no result.[93] Margaret urged him to calm down: "you leave me breathless hopping from Michigan to Washington!" she wrote. She urged him not to rush into anything; "we don't have to grab desperately at any straw."[94] Although no jobs materialized, Arthur maintained his usual optimism. In March, he predicted a rush to the colleges and universities if the war ended by summer, and, in that event, he would have his choice of jobs.[95]

By April 1945, Arthur's analysis of the situation proved correct. His earlier dealings with Datus Smith and Princeton University Press bore further fruit after Smith urged Princeton's history department chair, Joseph R. Strayer, to take a look at Arthur. On April 20, Smith wrote to Arthur and urged him to write to Strayer, and Arthur responded immediately. On April 26, Strayer asked for his credentials, and Arthur arranged for Commager, Green, Patton, Newsome, and Vance to write on his behalf. Arthur then visited Princeton for an interview. As a result of two previous research trips, in May and October 1944, Arthur was already familiar with Princeton. During his May visit, he was entranced by the university and town. "I am already charmed by the outward appearances of the place," he wrote Margaret. "The town itself is a typical college or university town and is very much like Chapel Hill. It has a very friendly atmosphere."[96] In October, he spent more time in the Wilson materials at Princeton, where he became fascinated by Wilson's presidency of the university.[97] The prospect of a job at Princeton excited Arthur's professional ambition. Getting the job was something "I had never dreamed of," he wrote Fletcher Green, "and the chances are that I won't get it after all."[98] It was "hard to keep from getting excited" about this job because Princeton "would be just about my first choice were I able to choose where I was going." "I thought especially of you today," he gushed to Margaret, "how much you would love Princeton (it's very much like Chapel Hill) and how much I wanted the job for your sake. Let us pray it will turn out that way!"[99]

There's little record that Arthur prepared extensively for his Princeton interview, though Ray Newsome provided advice in correspondence about how to act during his visit.[100] Arthur described the interview, which occurred on May 11, 1945, in a letter to Margaret. Datus Smith hosted him in the morning; during the afternoon, he visited the history department offices in Dickinson Hall. "I was in a highly nervous [state] by the time of the interview," Arthur wrote, "and probably showed it the first five minutes. I was put on display before the entire department, Mr.

Links: My Family in American History

Strayer acting as master of ceremonies as one man would drop in another would go out." Arthur was interviewed for about an hour and a half, as various faculty wandered in and out, discussing "various topics, nothing particular—just making conversation generally." Finally, Strayer "got down to brass tacks and talked business." Princeton's job was an instructorship in American history, he told Arthur, and it paid at least $2,200 and perhaps $2,400. The job had a future: if Arthur worked out, Strayer promised to promote him. He talked to Arthur mostly "in the future tense (not conditional)—such as 'You will find it hard to get an apartment,' or 'You will have a twelve-hour load.'" The job would begin on July 1; Arthur wondered whether he could do everything and still get married before the middle of June. He also worried that the Princeton job might make a honeymoon impossible. Arthur found Strayer "certainly encouraging in every respect," and he promised to reach a decision within a week. Although things looked "a little brighter," he told Margaret not to "count on it yet and don't allow yourself to believe I have the job until I get the formal offer in black and white."[101]

While he waited to hear from Strayer, other possibilities emerged. On May 13, Commager privately informed him that he was under consideration for a position in Columbia College, the university's undergraduate division. The next day, he had lunch with the faculty as part of an interview. On May 15, he visited Sarah Lawrence, a woman's college in Bronxville, New York, and met with the president, dean, and members of the social science department. Arthur found the college intriguing, and he described the faculty as "top-notch" and "very congenial." He found the president, Constance Warren, "cordiality personified." This might be a "pleasant experience for a year," he wrote.[102] Although offers would eventually come from both Columbia and Sarah Lawrence, he was sold on Princeton. "All things being equal, I think I would take the Princeton job if it were offered to me," he wrote Margaret. "Promotions are so much faster there, and I like the town of Princeton so much better than New York. Anyway, it is rather flattering, this whole business—and much more than I deserve."[103]

On May 15, while Arthur was visiting Sarah Lawrence, Strayer made the offer. As promised, Strayer came through with a good salary of $2,400. He also promised to help with the search for housing; Princeton's housing crunch during the war was especially acute. Arthur and Margaret would have to relocate quickly, by July 1, which would necessitate speeding up their wedding and honeymoon. Strayer's letter arrived on May 16, and Arthur immediately called Margaret—the first person he spoke with about the Princeton offer. Long-distance telephone calls in those days were extremely rare, and Arthur was amazed at the rapidity with which the connection to Margaret went through. It took the operator only three or four seconds, "much quicker than I could make a call to a person here in the city." Margaret, very excited, tried unsuccessfully to reach Arthur's parents, though she was able to get through to her parents in Davidson. Princeton, she told Arthur, would be "delightful—and I'm looking forward to it." Arthur considered the $2,400 annual salary a princely figure, though he asked Margaret: "Do you think we can live on it?" After discussing the offer with Commager and Bart Brebner, Arthur accepted the Princeton job. He was "elated beyond measure," he wrote. "What a wonderful year this has been for me," Arthur wrote to Margaret. "Surely my cup runneth over! I am truly grateful to God for all these blessings, and, above all, for you, my sweet."[104]

In the summer of 1945, as the European war ended and the Pacific war was coming to a brutal close, Arthur and Margaret were married and entered into a different phase of life. Hired at Princeton, Arthur and his new wife began a new life in the North, away from friends and family. Like so many war-era contemporaries, they were southern expatriates who left their native region as a result of the tumultuous changes that had transformed the United States during the war years. Margaret and Arthur both became part of a new and different generation in their families. Their ancestors had lived in Virginia and the Carolinas since the end of the eighteenth century; breaking out of this enclave, Arthur and Margaret would live outside the South for the next forty-seven years. Though they traveled north unhesitatingly—like other southern migrants who left the familiarity of their home—and often questioned southern practices and cultural values, they nonetheless considered themselves southerners.

Arthur and Margaret's marriage marked a distinct departure for them. They had discovered each other in Chapel Hill, but their relationship was founded on an intense letter-writing experience. In fact, they had spent very little time with each other in the two years since Margaret's departure for Queens in the spring of 1943. Margaret's acceptance of Arthur's proposal meant that she would relinquish her academic career. This decision was not unusual for women of her generation, many of whom chose marriage over career. But it is also true that Margaret had long been frustrated with the student culture at Queens, and was ready to move on to a more interesting intellectual environment.

Margaret and Arthur's marriage brought together complementary personalities: Margaret's compassion for people and her caretaking instincts, combined with Arthur's neediness, bound them together in a marriage of mutual dependency. Marriage meant departure in another sense. Within weeks of their wedding, Margaret and Arthur would leave North Carolina for life outside the South, and a new world of future promise.

PRINCETON

4

Arthur and Margaret were married in Davidson on June 2, 1945, in circumstances that were more hurried than originally anticipated. In May, Margaret received the good news that her brother, John, was returning on a leave that would put him in North Carolina, and, in order to accommodate his schedule, the wedding was moved up from mid-June. During May, Arthur worked hard to make progress on research and writing. Margaret, meanwhile, eagerly anticipated the wedding, and saw relatives and friends throughout the month. Wedding presents flowed in. The Douglases gave the couple a chest of silver; John gave them a sterling after-dinner coffee service set. When one of Margaret's Queens students gave them an ashtray, she quipped: "I think I shall have to take up smoking in self-defense!"[1]

Arthur planned to return to Mt. Pleasant only a week before the wedding, and his graduation from UNC would occur on May 25. He telegraphed Margaret that the new wedding date suited him. "It's all very sudden, darling, but wonderful nevertheless," he wrote, though he worried about a honeymoon. They had made no arrangements, but he explained that he needed to return to Chapel Hill for his dissertation defense on June 15. Having not yet heard about the Princeton job—he would in the next few days—he worried. "If the Princeton job comes through I will have to try and find a place for us. Oh, Lord, preserve me!" These last two weeks in New York were "going to be pretty heavy ones," he wrote. Margaret sent out wedding invitations on May 12. "There it is down in black and white," she wrote, "so I guess we will be tied together—for better or worse, honey, very shortly."[2] On May 26, "excited and supremely happy," Arthur packed up and left International House and New York City for North Carolina, where he arrived the following morning. En route, he came down with what he called a "good case" of the flu and "a bad cold besides." Margaret traveled to Mt. Pleasant and spent the day with Arthur on May 27, but he was not well enough to go to Davidson for two more days. He and Margaret remained there, taking part in a round of parties and teas, until Saturday, June 2, when the wedding was scheduled.[3]

The marriage ceremony took place in the evening. Arthur later related that he was "pretty shaky" several hours beforehand, and during the ceremony his knees trembled "uncontrollably." But, he reported, "we got the proper words spoken and apparently everything was quite legal."[4] The ceremony at the Davidson College Presbyterian Church occurred against a screen of white roses and cathedral tapers. Appropriately, the organist, Davidson College music professor James Christian Pfohl, played music from Wagner's *Lohengrin* and *Meistersinger*, with Mendelssohn's march from *A Midsummer's Night's Dream* as a recessional. Elinor sang three songs, "O Promise Me," "O Perfect Love," and "Because." Her father gave Margaret away, Arthur's friend from UNC, Lew Williams, served as best man, and Margaret's first cousin Mary McCann Hudson was maid of honor. The ushers included Margaret's brother, John, her first cousin Colin Munroe, Arthur's friend from N.C. State and an assistant dean of students Fitzhugh Dade, and UNC grad student Buck Yearns. The ceremony was followed by a reception across the street at the Douglas home, which was decorated with white roses and greenery.

A good number of Arthur and Margaret's families attended the wedding. The Douglas clan was all present: Margaret's cousin Grace James, who lived in Davidson, and her aunt Agnes Douglas, who, according to the *Charlotte Observer* account, "presided over the punch bowl." The South Carolina branch of the family was also there: her first cousins Elizabeth Douglas Josey and Margaret Douglas Woods, daughters of Uncle Davison, and her aunt Coline, among others. From Chapel Hill, Jo Bone, Margaret's friend from grad school, also attended.[5] "Married life," Arthur declared, was "more than folks ever said it was," and his wedding was "the greatest event in my life—that ceremony on June second—and I feel that I am just beginning to live."[6]

At the last minute, Arthur and Margaret decided to spend their honeymoon in western North Carolina, in the Presbyterian conference grounds in Montreat. Located seventeen miles east of Asheville, Montreat was taken over by Presbyterians in the early 1900s, and by World War I they had subdivided the cove into plots and cottages. Montreat also had plenty of boardinghouses that were maintained for church groups and for visitors seeking to escape the summer heat. It remains delightfully temperate most of the time, and the evenings usually bring in cool evening air. My mother began visiting Montreat with her family in the 1920s, when her family would pack up a large steamer trunk and make the long drive from Davidson. Usually the Douglases stayed in the North Carolina Home, a boardinghouse run by the North Carolina Presbyterian Synod. Arthur had never visited Montreat, but he hated the summer Carolina heat and humidity, and eagerly agreed to a honeymoon there.

Without question, the honeymoon was a low-cost operation. John Douglas put the newlyweds on the bus, which they rode up to the station in the town of Black Mountain, about a mile south of Montreat. Margaret and Arthur stayed at the Montreat conference center's main lodging spot, Assembly Inn, a large stone building that overlooks the center of the valley. Arthur immediately fell in love with what he described in June 1945 as its "very cool weather and grandeur of the mountains and natural scenery."[7] Montreat would always occupy a special place in their hearts. Arthur recalled growing up in Mt. Pleasant during the heat waves of the 1930s, in a house that lacked even a single fan. During the 1950s, Arthur began the practice of making a Montreat trip a ritual part of the summer visit to North Carolina. My first trip to Montreat took place when I was less than a year old in July and August 1955, and nearly all summers thereafter involved a visit there, in one form or another. That summer and subsequent summers, Arthur and Margaret rented cottages in various locations around the Montreat Valley surrounding Flat Rock Creek. Arthur loved the cool climate—and just the simple fact of sleeping under blankets in July and August. Beginning in the summer of 1955, Arthur wrote for several hours a day at the small archives that housed the records of the southern Presbyterian church—what was called the Historical Foundation—where, he told Howard Beale, "the only noise I heard was the sound of a mountain stream nearby."[8]

In 1964, Arthur bought a small lot on Montreat's Louisiana Road from Anniebelle's younger sister, Aunt Coline, just up the mountain from where, for two summers in the early 1960s, the family had rented a cottage owned by a local Presbyterian minister. Aunt Coline, who lived in Greenville, South Carolina, had bought the lot years earlier, hoping to construct a family gathering place, but she had never gotten around to it. Her son Colin Hudson married Martha, who was from Weaverville, near Asheville, and Weaverville had become the Hudson gathering place. In the summer of 1963, as we were having lunch with Aunt Coline, Arthur acted impulsively but decisively. Would she consider selling that lot to him? With equal impulsiveness, Aunt Coline agreed to sell on the spot, and they came to terms. Construction on the house began in the spring of 1964, and it was ready by the late summer of that year.

In 1945, while on their Montreat honeymoon, Arthur brought his work with him; his workaholic habits would never leave him. With his Ph.D. exams coming up on June 15, he explained to Margaret, "I will need to study very hard. . . . I have already begun to review, but there is so much more that has to be done. I'm sure you'll understand."[9] After about a week in Montreat, the couple returned to Mt. Pleasant for a few days. After that, things were in a whirl. On June 11, Arthur went to Chapel Hill to put the finishing touches on his dissertation and to conduct his doctoral defense four days later, while Margaret returned to Davidson to be with family and to prepare for their move to Princeton. After Margaret joined him to spend the weekend of June 15 in Chapel Hill, they spent the next week in Davidson to continue packing. Then, on June 25, Arthur took part in UNC's graduation—using a cap and gown borrowed from James Patton—with Arthur's parents present. That night, Margaret and Arthur boarded the train from Raleigh for Princeton and made the big move north.[10]

Before they left, one of their first social calls as a married couple was to visit John Hope Franklin and his wife, Aurelia. Arthur had invited the Franklins to the wedding, but John Hope felt uncomfortable. "I didn't think that this was any place for me to go to a wedding," Franklin recalled, "at a small college, where I didn't know anybody, nobody knew or cared about me." John Hope made an excuse, but the "real reason" for not coming was that he realized that he would be the only African American attending, and he was uncertain whether the white attendees would be "as cordial and friendly as Arthur was." Politely declining the invitation,

John Hope urged Arthur to visit while he was in Chapel Hill for his doctoral defense, "so that the two of you can spend a *long* time with us." But Arthur, as John Hope later recalled, was "simply flabbergasted that I didn't show up," and during his visit to Chapel Hill for his doctoral exam, Arthur and Margaret came to Durham for lunch. As Franklin recalled, Arthur said: "Since we're going to be friends for life, we are going to start today. You have to know Margaret, because she's a member of the team." John Hope later wrote that Margaret was a "charming and lovely person and is entirely worthy of the bright future that lies ahead of the both of you." The fact that this sort of treatment came from a younger white scholar—rather than older white mentors—made Arthur a "most remarkable combination of friend" and was "more than I could take in."[11]

The Links' arrival in Princeton on June 26 launched a new phase in their lives. For the most part, Margaret went from being a fully employed woman with a career to living an existence focused on home and family. Over the next two decades, their family would grow: my eldest brother, Arthur S. Link Jr. (Stan), was born on November 2, 1946; followed by James (Jimmy) Douglas Link on April 20, 1950; Margaret (Peggy), August 30, 1951; and me, August 18, 1954. The growing family totally occupied my mother's life. In 1945–46, their first year in Princeton, Margaret was employed by the Office of Population Research, which had been established ten years earlier at Princeton under Frank W. Notestein. She worked under Wilbert E. Moore, a demographer and sociologist, and the office focused on data-gathering relating to social problems. Once Margaret was in the late stages of pregnancy with my brother Stan, like many other educated professional women, she relinquished her career and never worked full-time again.

I don't think that Margaret ever regretted this decision. Most women of her class and upbringing returned to the home with the end of World War II, and not to do so was unusual. Still, there was certainly something of an adjustment and perhaps a tinge of regret. In future years, Margaret remained an insistent believer that women should seek careers. She encouraged my sister to avoid marriage until she was absolutely sure of herself, and, as a result, my sister didn't marry until the age of forty-two. Margaret also believed in family and children, but she always was at least a little restless with the role. Nonetheless, she plunged into domestic life when she and Arthur moved to Princeton. After their arrival in July 1945, Arthur and Margaret established temporary quarters by subletting an apartment at 7 Cleveland Lane, a few blocks north of campus. These living quarters were not easy to find: when Arthur scouted out housing in May 1945, he complained to Margaret that the housing shortage in Princeton was "even worse than in New York."[12] They celebrated Margaret's twenty-seventh birthday on Cleveland Lane with a cake that Arthur baked and decorated with candles. After a highball before dinner, they opened presents, and it was a "truly happy occasion for her." "Margaret and I do love each other enormously and are supremely happy," he reported to a friend. "It is certainly true that the joy of being loved by a wonderful girl and sharing her intimate companionship is the finest thing in life."[13]

After the summer at Cleveland Lane, the Links moved to a more spacious, furnished four-room apartment west of campus at 75 Patton Avenue, where they remained for the next three years. Arthur described the apartment as in "pretty bad shape, so we painted the woodwork in the livingroom and bedroom, and the landlady kindly had the rooms papered." Once their things were arranged, "it looked swell," "small and cozy." The apartment was upstairs, and below lived P. J. Conkright and his wife, and they and the Links socialized. Conkright was the award-winning book designer at the Princeton Press, and he and his wife introduced Margaret and Arthur around. On a fall evening in 1945, they went on a canoeing expedition with the Conkrights and friends on Carnegie Lake, which extended four miles along the east side of the campus and town.[14]

The arrival of Margaret and Arthur's first child was an important family event—the first grandchild for Margaret's parents and the first grandson for Arthur's parents. After discovering that she was pregnant in the spring of 1946, Margaret decided to spend much of the summer with her family in Davidson, while Arthur conducted research in Washington. There was much speculation about the baby's gender. In Davidson, Margaret saw an elderly black woman who used to nurse her. Was Margaret "right proud" of the baby she was carrying? she asked. Margaret told her that she was. The black woman predicted that the baby would be a boy since she was carrying it on her hips. Where would she carry the baby if she were female? Margaret asked. "On your stomach," the woman said, "and it be lighter." Margaret was unable to "tell the difference—stomach or hips," but she knew that she was "daily protruding, some days by jerks." Her stomach, she wrote Arthur in August, had "shot straight out," and he would "see great changes" when he next saw her.[15]

Margaret's pregnancy was uneventful, lasting through most of her summer in Davidson and then into the fall of 1946. Arthur was scheduled to give a paper at the Southern Historical Association meeting in early November 1946, and he traveled to Birmingham, Alabama, taking a twenty-six-hour train ride from Princeton. Margaret seemed to have some unease about his departure, and when he left she burst into tears. She had experienced another bout of tears about two weeks earlier, when she thought that she had broken their new pressure cooker. On October 30, Margaret wrote a letter that arrived ahead of him in Birmingham. "I do apologize for the tears," she wrote. "I hope it doesn't make you feel very uncomfortable, and I'm sorry my emotions take such disgustingly genuine form!"[16]

While Arthur was at the Birmingham meeting, Margaret was undergoing the last stages of her pregnancy. Arthur would miss the births of his first two sons because he was working. He fought a constant struggle between his love for Margaret and his family and his work. Most of the time, his work won out. On Halloween, Princeton had some late fall warm weather, with the thermometer reaching 80 degrees. Margaret was exhausted and a little demoralized. It had become "harder for me to get around," she complained to her parents; a nerve in her leg "makes me walk like a cripple and walking is pretty painful." "I'm trying to lay in as much as I can," she wrote, "for I never know when the call to the hospital is coming."[17] The "call to the hospital" came all too soon: while Arthur was still in Birmingham, their first son, Arthur Stanley Link Jr.— eventually known as Stanley—was born on November 2, 1946, weighing eight pounds, six ounces. Margaret had a relatively easy time—Arthur described her situation as "about as perfect as it could possibly be"—with active labor of about two hours. As was common in post–World War II childbirth, she was given gas to dull the pain. In a last-minute "unnecessary extravagance" for which she later felt guilty, she ordered a private room; one of the faculty wives told her, while visiting, that she only had had a semi-private room. After Stanley's birth, she was moved into a corner room with five windows and a telephone. The total hospital bill came to fifty-five dollars.[18]

Margaret stayed in Princeton Hospital for ten days, and in the meantime Arthur immediately returned from Birmingham by plane. Once home, he was restless. "He doesn't like living alone," she wrote her parents, "and spends all of his free time at the hospital."[19] When Margaret and Stanley came home to the apartment, she commented that the "young master of the house" had returned, and he was the "young master of the house indeed." The Patton Avenue apartment was "now all his and we love being his slaves."[20] The Links had arranged for Helen to come to Princeton to help for about two weeks. According to family lore, after her arrival at Patton Avenue, Helen took matters immediately in hand. The household was chaotic: Stanley was a challenging baby who cried a good deal. Arthur and Margaret fretted about the newborn's welfare. When Helen walked in, she announced: "There's nothing wrong with that baby. He's just hungry." In her time in Princeton, Helen did not hesitate to provide advice and observation, telling Margaret that Stanley was an "ugly" baby—something that she would say later about my older sister, Peggy, when she was infant. Despite Helen's advice to feed Stanley, John predicted within a few months that he would be a "buster of a lad" and "should play foot ball—tackle." John thought that Stanley took after both of his football-playing grandfathers. He warned, more seriously, that "you feed little Arthur too much" and that he was "too fat"; his weight would "wear out Margaret." Although Margaret regarded Helen's presence as a "grand help," she disagreed with her assessment of his looks. To Arthur and Margaret, "it has never entered our heads that he wasn't beautiful. We just sit and admire him! We have thought him beautiful since the day he was born—and are so proud of what we produced."[21]

Helen's help and love for the young family, as always, revolved around food. Helen arrived in Princeton with a large supply of food, butter and margarine, beef, and a slaughtered chicken—all from North Carolina. While she was visiting, she prepared two gallons of mincemeat, plus two of her fruitcakes, to leave for the Christmas holidays. The baby's Link grandparents were always ready to provide advice, whether welcome or not; the Douglases were more tactful. When Stanley was born, Paw-Paw had urged my parents to name him Arthur Douglas Link; Arthur and Margaret preferred to make him a junior. Later, when Elinor named her son Douglas—he went by Doug—Helen commented to Margaret: "I can't imagine Elinor giving her baby your name, Margaret, though I think it's a beautiful one. It was the one I wanted Stanley to have." Later, when I was born, John advised my parents to name me Jacob, a suggestion they quickly and perhaps fortunately rejected.[22]

In the first few months of his life, Margaret and Arthur called Stanley "Junior," or "Little Arthur," but by the time he was two months old he had become "Stanley." Later, he would rename himself "Stan." I was always "Billy" to my family; like Stanley, I remain so within my immediate family circle, though by elementary school I had become "Bill." Stanley was a demanding baby, especially about his food. Margaret briefly experimented with breast-feeding, but when she encountered difficulty, like most mothers of this era, she was encouraged to move into formula feeding. "He does like to eat," Margaret wrote her parents. "He *demands* his food at least every 3 hours." For him, crying always meant, "Give me food."[23] He was a less talented sleeper: "Arthur likes food too well to sleep the nite thru—He wakes at least twice," downing five ounces of milk "without batting an eye every 3 hours and asks for more!"[24] His wakefulness continued into toddlerhood, and Stanley remained demanding and sometimes imperious. During summers in Davidson, Stan spent time with his mother's first cousin Grace James, who lived in the other side of the duplex in the Davidson house. An early riser, Stanley would often pop over and wake Grace up. She subsequently loved to tell plenty of Stanley stories; Grace would impersonate him with a deep, authoritative voice. While in Davidson, she nicknamed him "General Link," according to Margaret, "because of the way he shouts his orders around to all of his retinue."[25] In the summer of 1948, Stan, a little less than two years old, started to call his mother "Margaret"—something his father became very concerned about.[26] At Davidson, Stanley, as the only grandchild, received inordinate attention from the Douglases, so much so that Arthur commented in August 1948 that it might "go hard with him to lose at one fell stroke such a company of admirers and servants." As he grew a little older, he had the run of the Davidson campus, though sometimes his mother worried about the possibility that he might contract polio as epidemics raged in the late 1940s and early 1950s.[27]

Almost immediately after arriving at Princeton in July 1945, Arthur threw himself into his work in his new office at 108 Dickinson

Hall, which was equipped with a desk, bookcase, maps, lamps, and eight chairs for students—all luxuries that he had never enjoyed. Like most American campuses, Princeton University remained on a war footing, and Arthur was contracted to teach Army students during the summer of 1945. About two weeks after their arrival in Princeton, Arthur told his friend Joe Steelman that a newspaper strike in New York was "something of a relief" because it meant more time for work, especially the dose of reading that he needed to complete for teaching. As it turned out, the Army ended its program at Princeton, which provided Arthur plenty of time to keep up his writing and revision on *The Road to the White House*. His setup at Princeton had given Arthur "a great amount of free time to do my own work and doing it I am!" he wrote. He and Margaret, he wrote, were enjoying Princeton "immensely—enjoying this truly beautiful town, the people, and the University."[28]

Under the university presidency of Woodrow Wilson, Princeton in 1905 had adopted the preceptorial system, in which students were taught in common lectures delivered by senior professors but then were instructed in breakout groups—precepts—by the faculty. All faculty were expected to precept, but the university had long hired instructors to help out with the preceptorial load. Instructors were at the bottom of the heap, and, as part of their apprenticeship, they never taught their own courses, which were under the control of the senior faculty. Strayer had made clear to Arthur that he might be promoted, but Arthur was not able to teach his own course for the first few years on the faculty.

Soon after his Princeton appointment, Arthur renewed ties with Howard Beale, with whom relations had been distant since Arthur began graduate school in 1941. Beale initiated a correspondence, and Arthur responded. In September 1945, Beale visited Princeton and spent the night with Arthur and Margaret in their Patton Avenue apartment. The visit was cordial and warm. "Despite all his work and travels," Arthur observed, "which have been quite stupendous, he looks better than I have ever seen him look. We had a really interesting time and enjoyed having them down." Beale's efforts during the war had yielded "some very creditable work . . . , work that was distasteful and without pay, but that was terribly important nonetheless." Beale had "his faults, but I am inclined to think more and more highly of him all the time." Although Beale had given Arthur a "raw deal" as a graduate student, "no man is perfect, and I am sure his intentions are very excellent." Arthur and Margaret reciprocated in December 1945 with an equally cordial visit to the Beales' apartment in New York City.[29]

By 1946, Arthur had changed his opinion about Beale. He was "pretty broad-minded and pleasant to deal with," he now thought, and he had "come to like him very much since the beginning of the war and have found that most of what people say about him isn't true."[30] In 1945–46, Arthur sent him a draft of his first book, *Wilson: The Road to the White House*, and Beale read it, and reread subsequent drafts, with extraordinary care, providing long critiques. When the book was published, Arthur warmly acknowledged his help. After Beale's death in 1960, Arthur concluded, in a letter to historian Merle Curti, that there was a "considerable element of tragedy in this unfinished career" and in his "seeming inability so to organize his energies and time as to press on ahead at an earlier stage in his life." Arthur acknowledged that Beale's "greatest contribution" was his mentoring of students and his "extraordinary high standards" and his unwillingness to be "satisfied with inferior work."[31]

After he finished *The Road to the White House*, Arthur considered writing a book that would examine social tensions and conflicts in the South during the 1920s and focus on the anti-evolution controversy and the election of 1928.[32] During the summer of 1946, he took up residence in Washington to research the subject. Still, it remained clear that his career path was leading toward a lifetime as a Wilson biographer. In the summer of 1946, Henry Commager began a New American Nation series, published by Harper and Row, that sought to produce multiple volumes on periods of American history. Commager asked Arthur to write the volume on the Wilson period, and he readily agreed. *Woodrow Wilson and the Progressive Era* was eventually published in 1954 as one of the first volumes of a thirty-nine-volume series. It provided an outline of Arthur's subsequent biographical volumes on Wilson that appeared between 1956 and 1965.[33]

While *The Road to the White House* was in the final stages of preparation in the spring of 1946, Datus Smith suggested that Arthur publish a new edition of Wilson's letters. Later, between 1960 and 1994, he would devote the last two-thirds of his professional career to editing a comprehensive sixty-nine-volume edition of Wilson's papers. In 1946, neither Smith nor Arthur then had any such project in mind: rather, they were contemplating a ten-volume selected edition. While in Washington, however, a roadblock suddenly appeared. Katherine Brand had been the longtime curator of the Wilson Papers at the Manuscripts Division of the Library of Congress. With the blessing of Wilson's widow, Edith Galt Wilson, Brand controlled access to the collection. In late June 1946, when Arthur visited Brand, she suddenly announced her intention to edit a collection of Wilson's letters. The young scholar was shocked. "Wasn't it strange the way Miss Brand acted!" he wrote Margaret. "I wonder if she could suspect that we have any such project in mind; if so, she is psychic, because I said absolutely nothing, even by way of intimation." Margaret reacted angrily. This meant, she feared, that "9/10 of the job will be done by you, with 1/10 of the credit." It was a "bad situation with Sister Brand holding the keys to the gate of your most needed possession," and she advised that he "get out of this project" and work on his own on "something else." Why should he "be a slave for Miss Brand and work for her advancement?" Margaret would "certainly pray over the matter," she told Arthur, "but I must say that I'm not in a praying mood at this point. My feelings are anything but charitable and kind towards certain parties. It makes me madder when I think this was your original idea in the first place." Arthur shared her concerns, though he teased her that "I nearly burned my hand when I picked up the first page of your letter today; it really was hot!" He wrote to Joe Strayer in late July, asking whether he thought he could write a volume for Commager's New American Nation series and also edit a volume with Brand. Strayer was more concerned about the editing project: "editing never pays for the time spent," he advised. But he thought the two projects together made sense.

Worried about working with Brand, a formidable woman twenty years his senior, Arthur wrote Datus Smith. But Smith's response was to urge Arthur to work with Brand. Whether his name came first or last made little difference, Smith advised. "In general, I think a name with a guttural ending is better at the end than one with a dental sound," though he was "entirely happy to flip a coin." Smith's response notwithstanding, nothing came of the project, no doubt because of Arthur's concerns about becoming Brand's junior partner.[34]

As was true of most newlyweds, there were many adjustments in Margaret's and Arthur's lives. Margaret had never cooked much; in the Douglas household, African American domestic workers did the cooking and cleaning. Arthur, whose family had always done their own cooking and who had spent time in the kitchen since boyhood, promised to teach her. Gradually, she acquired domestic skills. In the first year or two of marriage, they lived on a small academic salary during a period of rising prices. In April 1947, Arthur declared that he would either have to teach summer school "or sell bibles" to make ends meet. "The present cost of living has really got us where it hurts."[35] Food prices, Margaret complained to her parents in the fall of 1946, were "very unstable now," and they "jump up & down every day—and you can't tell what's happening." She managed a food budget of forty-five dollars per month, and she reported that her home management was "improving somewhat" since she was spending less on food in 1946 than a year earlier. It helped to "have a little experience in housekeeping," and there were many corners that could be cut. Arthur laughed at her "obvious delight when we receive dinner invitations—because it reduces our board bill!"[36]

Margaret adapted to a domestic lifestyle without servants. "You would be amazed to see how I am out-Yankeeing the Yankees in the housework and manual labor I do!" Margaret wrote her parents in late 1946. She reported that she did "every bit of washing & ironing (except sheets) including Arthur's shirts." Even then, however, Arthur continued to do the sweeping of the apartment because there were not "enough hours in the day to get around to doing that!"[37] Helen Link worried about Margaret's household abilities, and in a letter not long after they moved to Princeton, she wrote assuringly that she was "sure Margaret is enjoying cooking and keeping house and I know you all are having a grand time together." She did offer some matrimonial advice to Arthur: "Margaret is a grand person and I hope you will never cease to appreciate her." Perhaps thinking of her own marriage, Helen wrote: "Appreciation and consideration mean so very much in one's life."[38]

Arthur remained a dynamo in his work. It was said that he was the only Princeton history department faculty member who was seen in the library on Sunday afternoons—all the more surprising since he was a regular churchgoer.[39] After his first year of teaching at Princeton, during summers he worked in Washington at the Library of Congress, usually taking a room somewhere on Capitol Hill. Margaret, meanwhile, spent much of her summers with her aging parents in Davidson. Arthur and Margaret's separations, during the early years of marriage, were difficult. In Princeton, Margaret found adjustment to the university and town culture hard. She had realized before marriage that Arthur worked relentlessly, and her father advised her after their wedding to "be careful of Arthur's time, for he is a young man with a future."[40] Margaret decided, early on, that Arthur was a prodigious talent who needed special handling. When he came home one day and commented that he'd read that some types of foods increased brain power, Margaret's response, only half-joking, was he didn't need "*increased* brainpower" because it was "all I can do to keep up with the brain energy you have." Another time, they saw a friend of Arthur's who was working on a book, and Arthur asked him whether he'd finished. "Heavens, no," was the response. "I think I'm doing well to be halfway done. I'm no Arthur Link!"[41]

Margaret worried about Arthur's pace and intensity. She urged him to rest for fifteen or twenty minutes a day, and she fretted that he worked too hard at the expense of his health. Arthur went into his university office every day from 8:30 to 6:00, then often returned in the evenings for more work or campus events. In October 1946, Margaret wrote her parents that Arthur was exhausted and had "just about reached the limit of his endurance." She had "never seen him so whipped," and she worried that he was "going to drop in his tracks if he doesn't slack up." On another occasion, she confided to her parents about Arthur's work habits, commenting that he "works terribly hard." Even Strayer warned Arthur that "he'd better ease up" and that he was "going too hard." Margaret urged him to get regular exercise, "for he works his brain so hard!" Arthur came home for lunch—a habit he adhered to his whole life—so he walked to and from campus twice a day. Margaret urged Arthur to take time off, but he rarely went on vacations without bringing along work. He worked "nearly all his waking hours—nights too," Margaret told her parents in October 1947. She realized that Arthur was "so happy when mentally active," she wrote in a futile attempt to get him to take a vacation in the summer of 1946, "but darling will you promise me not to work as hard and long as you have all summer? And can't you take a little vacation?"[42]

Though she rarely admitted it to Arthur, Margaret suffered from loneliness, especially once she quit her job at the Office of Population Research—and even more after Stanley was born. No doubt the adjustment from the world of teaching at Queens to a Princeton apartment with a baby was a shock to her. Because Arthur spent so much time working in his university office, she told her parents, she was "alone much of the time and apply myself alternately to domestic activities, reading, and walking." Margaret anticipated Arthur's return for lunch and dinner every evening.

His lunches at home provided "me a chance to see him (as well as saves us money!)." Pregnant during the fall of 1946, Margaret expected that Arthur would be home more frequently and "keep me company (plenty of it, I'm sure!) during the day." Arthur was not only absent during the day, he traveled a good deal in the early years of his marriage. From 1945 on, every summer was spent in the archives. Until the death of her father in July 1951, Margaret spent a month or two in Davidson while Arthur spent hot summers researching at the Library of Congress in Washington.[43]

During summer separations, Arthur and Margaret corresponded regularly, and their letter writing reveals an evolving partnership. When he was back in Princeton without her, Arthur complained that the Patton Avenue apartment was "absolutely and completely lifeless without you." It was "nothing but walls, floors, furniture, etc., and that is all—nothing to look forward to coming home to. That is really the *truth*. It just isn't a home without you."[44] Arthur's devotion to his marriage approached a religious belief. His love for Margaret was "something you can't express by saying or writing," he explained to her. "You just know it and feel it, don't you. It is like one's belief in God; it gives meaning and purpose to life."[45] He was not so much lucky in having Margaret, he wrote another time. "Blessed is what I really mean."[46]

Arthur's belief in marriage was quite genuine. One of the few things he admired about his parents' marriage was their loyalty to each other. Although he acknowledged that they both suffered from a bad match—especially his mother—he admired their perseverance. Arthur had little comprehension of adultery. He once told me, with some admiration, that Princeton's dean of the faculty, J. Douglas Brown, had informed him, when he first came to Princeton, that if any faculty member were found guilty of impropriety, he would be gone within twenty-four hours. Arthur's old-fashioned attitudes persisted even into the libertine culture of the 1970s and 1980s, after which, to a certain extent, things came full circle. Catherine Clinton, a historian of the U.S. South who was among the first generation of female graduate students at Princeton in the 1970s, described a highly misogynist culture at Princeton. The university was, she recalled, the "last plantation." The history department had only two tenured female faculty members, and women graduate students were sometimes exposed to sexual harassment. Arthur's "great moral fiber" combined with the ambiguities of the sexual revolution produced a certain cluelessness. When Clinton explained to Arthur the possibility of sexual dalliances between female grad students and married faculty at Princeton, he was dumbfounded. "Well, it is already against the rules of the college," Arthur told her. "It violates the ethics of the university. It's adultery."[47]

Arthur and Margaret were both people who never used curse words, and they corrected their children vigorously when they did. My mother's worst curse was the exclamation, "Damnation!"—always reserved for especially frustrating situations. My father would occasionally use words such as "damn" or "shit," but only rarely. They were both especially opposed to taking the Lord's name in vain; I never heard either utter the phrase "Goddamn." My brother Stan recalled coming home as a boy and testing out the use of four-letter words. He was quickly reprimanded—and perhaps even whipped. I remember at least once having my mouth washed out with soap after uttering a curse word. My parents would resort to corporal discipline, though never enough to inflict more than emotional pain. Arthur would sometimes, with a dramatic flourish, yank out his belt—as a soldier might pull out his sword in hand-to-hand combat—but the whippings were not anything that came close to abuse. My offenses were usually minor, to be sure. By the time I was ten or eleven, however, I had come to regard whippings as something of a joke because of their ineffectual nature. At that point, Arthur gave up the exercise.

In the 1940s, Arthur's absences were very difficult for Margaret. "I have been haunting the mails literally," she wrote him while he was in Washington in late June 1946. She became "so homesick" for Arthur after he left her that she burst into tears and had a "terrific impulse to get on the next train and follow you to Washington." Every separation became "progressively harder, my darling, because we grow so much closer together," and she felt "more and more lost without you." Though his departure often brought tears, Margaret was analytical, even clinical, in understanding her feelings, and the following morning "felt better," and she decided "I shouldn't act so emotionally immature."[48] While in Davidson, Margaret's father observed that she had become "more homesick for Arthur than you've ever been before—which I didn't deny!" "I do miss you and want to be with you so much, my darling. I can't become acclimated to separation!"[49]

Margaret found the early years of motherhood in Princeton isolating. When Stanley was a little more than a month old, she complained to her parents that the baby had been "rather fretful all day today—demanding his bottle every 2 hrs and then not drinking all of it." She wished that babies could speak "so you could know what they wanted instead of having to guess from the tone of their cries!" "It really takes patience to be a parent," Margaret admitted, "and sometimes I wonder if I have it—more and more I marvel that you all survived 2 of us." When Arthur canceled a research trip to South Carolina just before Christmas 1946, she admitted that she was "quite relieved" because she "rather dreaded being alone with the baby even for 2 nights."[50] In early 1947, she wrote that she was in "virtual hibernation," as Arthur did all of the food shopping and she stayed home with the baby. She planned to get out for a meeting of the Instructors' Wives Club; Arthur would watch Stanley. "I hope he'll get along O.K.," she wrote her parents, "for he isn't too used to doing things for the little boy." Arthur hated to change diapers, and he "always uses every excuse to avoid doing it! . . . I suppose this is the age that little babies most of all belong to their mothers. The father's part comes later on."[51]

Margaret had few diversions. She attended some meetings of Princeton faculty wives and, as had been true in North Carolina, became involved in the local YWCA. In October 1947, she was elected to the Y's executive board, a responsibility that she described as "glad to be able to do" because it gave her "an outside interest which I certainly welcome." Later, she became the Y treasurer.[52] Some years later, in the 1960s, my mother continued her involvement in the Y when it went through a turbulent period of desegregation. Margaret led the way toward more fully integrating the organization, and she remembered with some frustration the sort of muted racism that she encountered among her Princeton contemporaries—many of whom, she believed, had condescending attitudes about the racism of southern whites.

Arthur enjoyed two other diversions from his work. He was a ferocious house cleaner, and during the early years in Princeton took full responsibility for keeping the Patton Avenue apartment clean. "No matter how tired he is from his University work," Margaret commented to her parents, "he will come in and regularly turn the apartment upside down cleaning it and scrubbing floors." Nor did he mind housework, "for he always does it voluntarily—I never ask him—and he says it's good exercise for him." At the same time, he also prepared and maintained a large garden during the spring and summer of 1947.[53] During the spring, he came home early to prepare the soil for the plot, which measured 30 by 50 feet, and he planted black-eyed peas (after obtaining seeds from Davidson, since no one in Princeton had heard of them), broccoli, carrots, cabbage, corn, tomatoes, and beans. In July, he could proudly report to Margaret that his garden was the "finest in Princeton."[54]

Princeton was not an especially friendly college town. From the 1800s onward, there were two Princetons: the borough, which included the university and the town center, and the township, which included what was originally the rural outskirts and later became the more affluent, suburban side of Princeton. The town possessed a strict class and racial structure, with an Italian and African American working class separated from campus, while neighborhoods on the northwest side of town housed spacious homes, even mansions. Princeton's black community, well established by the early nineteenth century, was concentrated on the north side of town, along Witherspoon Street as it snakes through town. Paul Robeson, who spent part of his childhood in Princeton, recalled that the town was "for all the world like any small town in the Deep South." "Bourbon and Banker were one in Princeton, and there the decaying smell of the plantation Big House was blended with the crisper smell of the Countinghouse." "The theology was Calvin," according to Robeson, "the religion—cash." Rich Princeton was all white; African Americans, as domestics, cooks, waiters, and caretakers, "were there to do the work."[55]

Two centers of the black community were the old Witherspoon School, which housed elementary and junior high grades, and the Witherspoon Presbyterian Church, organized in the mid-1800s when the First Presbyterian Church decided to exclude black members. Across from the Witherspoon Church was the Princeton Cemetery, which was segregated into white and black portions, with separate entrance gates from its earliest existence. The Princeton Borough's school system was segregated, and, until World War I, black students had to travel to Trenton to attend high school (by the 1920s they were permitted to attend Princeton High School). In 1947, facing a statewide mandate to desegregate schools, the schools adopted what became known as the "Princeton Plan." It provided that black and white students would attend elementary school at Nassau Street School, and then move to the old Witherspoon School during sixth to eighth grades. Princeton High School united students from the borough and township.[56]

We moved to Princeton from Evanston in September 1960; I remember

Princeton as an unfriendly place. I attended Nassau Street School, located in an aging building on the east side of Nassau Street, from first to fifth grade. My first friends were black children—the first time that I had had much exposure to a multiracial environment, after the lily-white existence in Evanston. I remember, a few months into my first grade at Nassau Street, being chased by an African American girl, Milly Brooks, who caught me and kissed me on the lips. My first male friend at Nassau Street School was Kim Craig, and I used to go to his house in Princeton's African American neighborhood to play. In sixth grade I moved on to the old Witherspoon School in the heart of Princeton's traditionally black neighborhood, but, in 1966, Princeton opened a new school building, the John Witherspoon School, for the borough's grades kindergarten through eighth. In 1967, the borough and township school systems merged, after a fight in which some township parents opposed the change because of overt fears about racial mixing. In the fall of 1967, I attended my third junior high school, the Valley Road School, on the north end of Witherspoon Street. When the borough and township kids merged, it was immediately apparent to me that there was a class and racial divide in Princeton: borough children were poorer, their schools a step behind the newer and more affluent township schools. The adjustment in eighth grade wasn't easy.

Growing up a block away from the university, I regarded the campus as my backyard, but I never felt especially welcome. The university's police force, the notorious proctors, were trained especially to look out for "townies" in order to prevent their entrance to university facilities, such as the student center or the Dillon Gym. Football games, where I sold programs, communicated the elitism of the institution, and in the mid-1960s, the alumni seemed to exude class hierarchy. The annual alumni reunions, held just before commencement in June, were an occasion of extravagant partying and, in the 1960s and 1970s, represented a challenge for townie kids to crash. My friends and I became experts at forging the identification badges that gained admission to any of the reunion events.

When my parents moved to Princeton in the 1940s, the university had a different culture and mission than did the University of North Carolina. Princeton was a single-sex institution, a private university with a history of catering to the northeastern elite and, like other Ivy League institutions, with a history of excluding Jews and minorities. Norman Cantor, who arrived on campus as a graduate student in 1951, described it as "small and bucolic in a well-trimmed way; it was like living on a golf course."[57] The student body was dominated by its undergraduates, and its teaching mission during the 1940s focused on educating elite gentlemen, many of whom came from the South. Teaching graduate students was considered extra work that was apart from the university's undergraduate mission, and the faculty, until the 1940s, was dominated by undergraduate teachers. The history department during the 1940s was very hierarchical and very patriarchal, and its culture combined, according to one historian, "hierarchy and a touch of intellectual snobbery." Strayer ran the department with an iron hand, and he expected fealty from younger faculty, who were expected to be seen and not heard in departmental affairs. Still, Arthur felt a sense of loyalty to Strayer, whom he described as "one of the straightest and best fellows I have ever known."[58]

The atmosphere at Princeton was especially hard "on intelligent and well-educated faculty wives," according to Cantor. The women faced a "stultifying Princeton environment."[59] Certainly Margaret's experience confirmed Cantor's observation. She often recounted the story of her first departmental cocktail party, which occurred sometime during the autumn of 1945. She appeared in a bright red cocktail dress—perfectly appropriate in the South, but socially awkward in the stuffy Princeton atmosphere—and when she entered the room, she discovered that everyone, men and women, was dressed in tweed. Even more shocking to her—and telling—was that the men and women stood separated on either side of the room.

Once pregnant with her first child, in the spring of 1946, Margaret became especially restive. "I am still terribly anxious to get down south to live particularly with a family coming on to raise," she told her parents. She had not "even implied this to Arthur," she wrote, and she asked them to promise to tear up her letter—a promise, happily, that my grandparents didn't keep. Margaret missed southern accents and southern food. She described to her parents how she and Arthur ate a "delicious southern meal"—of rice and gravy, pickled peaches, peas, asparagus, roast lamb, hot rolls, salad, relish, jelly, celery, olives, and coconut—at the home of a couple from Georgia whom they knew from Princeton's Second Presbyterian Church, which they attended. Although Arthur obtained "such a tremendous amount of satisfaction and pleasure out of his teaching experience and writing here that I don't want to make him dissatisfied," Margaret admitted privately that she was not "terribly satisfied with the idea of living with these damn Yankees the rest of my life!" Her hope was that they would stay in Princeton for a few years, and after Arthur's reputation was secured, they might move south. "I think he definitely has the stuff—providence permitting him to develop it—and right now he's better off here than anywhere—as far as his career is concerned."

Nonetheless, in this very candid letter, Margaret described the situation in the department. Princeton, she wrote, had a "rigid caste system in academic ranks," and, as an instructor, Arthur was a second-class citizen. "It's like the army," she told her parents, with instructors like enlisted men, and "officers' rating begin[ning] with assistant professors and above." The Princeton faculty remained "very conscious of rank." She often wondered "why they don't wear bars to designate rank as the Army does!" Fundamentally, Margaret liked Princeton—"as well as any place above the Mason-Dixon line, I guess," but she was "just . . . terribly fed up with the people & place sometimes." She did not want Arthur to know the extent of her unhappiness; "it would make him unhappy and he would think immediately he should get another job." That summer, she hoped to accompany Arthur on a research trip to Washington, and she would look forward to being with friends there who were *"southern and therefore human. I'll be glad to get away from Yankee land for three months!"*[60]

Even while Margaret and Arthur felt alienated as southerners in the North, they had left behind traditions and practices of the past. When Margaret was in Davidson in June 1946, she complained about hearing the "most amazing political opinions" from a Davidson neighbor "till I didn't know how much longer I could stomach it, altho I did hold my peace and said not a word." The woman claimed that President Harry Truman was "an agent of the CIO," and she believed that the "only man with any sense in Washington" was conservative Virginia senator Harry F. Byrd. Her neighbor's attitudes, Margaret believed, were a "bundle of prejudices" that typified "the worst in Southern reaction."[61] Later that summer, Margaret attended what she called a "very insipid hen party with much conversation as times were so hard now . . . that you couldn't get a thing to eat or a negro to cook it for you." Margaret wondered, with plenty of land in the back of their house, why these people "don't grow something on it." The discussion at the gathering also focused on how a Davidson veteran was marrying an Australian woman whom he had met abroad; the women wondered why he wasn't marrying someone local. Margaret thought all of this was "a little nauseating."[62]

Arthur shared Margaret's disdain for the postwar southern white backlash. When he visited Margaret in Davidson in July 1946, he was forced to listen to the antediluvian racial attitudes of her first cousin Stokes Munroe Jr. Although he was a "fine generous" person who "would do anything to help someone who needed help," Stokes was "the perfect, arch-type of southern fascist." This was true in Stokes's attitudes about labor, civil rights, and his own profession of medicine. Arthur wondered if there was something "dreadfully wrong" with an educational system that allowed Stokes "to get through with such ideas as a Negro should not make as much money as a white man, for example." Margaret didn't disagree with Arthur's characterization of Stokes's "extremely reaction-ary" attitudes—and those of his wife, Martha, too—but she explained it as the product of "conditioning by Charlotte society rather than the edu-cation either have been subjected to." Doctors, alas, possessed "the most regressive social views—no matter how much they may help and desire to help people they stand rigorously against progressivism general[ly]."[63]

As a professional historian, Arthur was forced to face the depressing reality of race in southern politics. Although he believed that Harry Tru-man had served as president with "great courage and wisdom," he be-lieved that his civil rights positions didn't go far enough, and he won-dered why conservative white southerners were "getting so excited about it."[64] In July 1946, after Georgian Eugene Talmadge, a vicious race-baiter, defeated challenger James V. Carmichael in a hotly contested primary that was dominated by Talmadge's racial appeals, Arthur was despon-dent. "I have been dejected today by the results of the Georgia primary," he wrote Margaret. He wrote that it was "inconceivable . . . that the people of any state could vote for such a mountebank of race hatred and bitterness." Now, Arthur feared, Talmadge would "really run amuck, so just watch him and the Klan, which is sure to grow and flourish under his leadership." Nothing so dreadful as Talmadge's nomination had hap-pened in domestic politics in years, and it was worse still because these were such "critical times in the realm of racial tension and conflict."[65] Re-searching the southern newspaper press in search of white liberals dur-ing the 1920s, Arthur was astounded. The "appalling thing," he wrote, was that no southern editor of that era "refused to raise the old white supremacy issue." This remained true of them during the 1940s: southern liberal newspaper editors failed to confront the race issue.[66]

Despite some ambivalence about the white South, both Margaret and Arthur always felt strong ties to Chapel Hill. In October 1946, Arthur came home on a Saturday afternoon. "We're going to the Princeton-Rutgers game with President Frank Graham & wife," Arthur announced. Margaret thought he was kidding, but Graham was in Princeton to receive an honorary degree as part of Princeton's bicentennial celebration. After Arthur ran into him on campus, Graham invited the Links to come to the game with him and his wife, Marian. Arthur knew Graham, as did many Carolina students, because of his Sunday evening open houses, when he invited any students to come by the president's home in Chapel Hill. Graham was known for his photographic memory for people, and he immediately recognized Arthur. After he told Graham who Margaret was, Graham said that he remembered her, identifying her as the daughter of a Davidson professor. Margaret reported to her parents that the visit with the Grahams was "grand," and she described Marian Graham as "quite beautiful and charming and good fun." They concluded by walking the Grahams from Palmer Stadium to the president's house, Prospect.[67]

While on his Washington research trips, Arthur frequently visited with John Hope and Aurelia Franklin. John Hope had moved to Howard University in 1946, and often, during that summer and subsequent summers, the Franklins had him out to dinner, or he and John Hope would meet for lunch. In November 1947, Arthur stopped by Washington en route to the Southern Historical Association meeting in Savannah to see the Franklins' "beautiful and properly furnished" home in an "exclusive Negro section," and Aurelia prepared a supper of T-bone steak and french fries. They listened to John Hope's new Magnavox and "sampled sparingly" from his White Horse scotch.[68] About a year later, in July 1948, Arthur spoke before John Hope's class at Howard and reported that his visit "seemed to go over awfully well." Washington remained a very segregated place in the 1940s and 1950s, so Arthur and John Hope had a limited choice of integrated restaurants that was confined to Union Station, the lunchroom of the Supreme Court building, and the Methodist Building on Second Street.[69]

Arthur and John Hope kept up a close correspondence and relationship during the coming decades, even after Arthur and Margaret moved to Evanston. John Hope and Aurelia moved to Brooklyn College in 1956, and then to the University of Chicago in 1964. "Your little visit was very delightful, the only hitch being its brevity," Arthur wrote to John Hope in July 1950. "But it was like old times as long as it lasted!"[70] After another visit to Evanston in 1956, Arthur wrote that "you could not have enjoyed being here any more than we enjoyed having you." Margaret's comment about John Hope after this visit was that he was a "perfect guest," who "seems to enjoy whether we have a party or a few friends in."[71]

Arthur and Margaret were feeling increasingly estranged by the white South's continued allegiance to white supremacy. In the fall of 1946, Arthur organized a conference at Princeton's School for Public and International Affairs that ran for much of the semester, focusing on the subject of race in southern politics, and under its auspices Arthur brought leading black political figures and prominent officials from the NAACP. He also continued to have active contacts with scholars of race, including African American scholars. In October 1946, he delivered a paper in Philadelphia on the Negro and the New Freedom before the Association for the Study of Negro Life. Margaret attended and noted the "assemblage of Negro intelligentsia and their questions and comments on the papers." She thought Arthur's paper was "masterly," and she noted that, in his introduction, John Hope Franklin described her husband as "a prodigious worker, prolific writer and one of the few young men in the profession enjoying a rapid and popular rise."[72] John Hope was delighted that Margaret attended, and he noted that her presence "topped the day off beautifully."[73]

Arthur remained an instructor for three years, but he soon became a rising star. The appearance of *The Road to the White House*, which Princeton University Press brought out in 1947, led to his promotion to assistant professor in 1948. "We are absolutely certain that Mr. Link will continue to produce important work in the field of recent American history," Strayer wrote in support of reappointing him as instructor in 1947. "He is more sure of what he wants to do in the next ten years than any other man of his age we have ever known."[74] To Arthur, Strayer provided a "very encouraging" assessment of his progress. He told him in early 1947 that he intended to seek a promotion for him in the near future. Certainly others were expecting that Arthur would advance at Princeton or move elsewhere. In May 1947, noting the favorable reception for his book,

John Hope Franklin asked what "tangible results" were coming from the Princeton department: "Have the offers come in so that you can use them to advance your position there?"[75] Strayer reached the same conclusion as John Hope: he told Arthur that the easiest and fastest way to advance was to obtain an offer. "I wish he could get an offer to use for blackmail purposes!" Margaret observed.[76]

After the appearance of *The Road to the White House*, Arthur considered possible moves. In late 1946, the Woman's College of the University of North Carolina—what later became UNCG, where I spent twenty-three years teaching—considered hiring him as head of the history department, but, at the ripe age of twenty-six, he was considered too young.[77] Two years later, in early 1948, a more serious possibility arose at the University of Maryland, after Arthur met with its history department chair Wesley Gewehr at the American Historical Association meetings in Cleveland. When Gewehr learned that Arthur might be movable from Princeton, Maryland courted Arthur and eventually offered him an assistant professorship at an annual salary of $3,800.

Arthur was attracted by the offer because he and Margaret had friends in the area and because of the proximity to Arthur's research materials in Washington. Another consideration, Arthur wrote to Margaret, was that a move to Maryland "might be a relief to get out of this company of demi-gods and breathe common air again."[78] Margaret was a full partner in these negotiations, and, as usual, her judgment was considerably less impulsive than Arthur's. There was, she said, "more to reach for at Princeton, even tho it's slower going." Despite "personal, social interests [that] would draw us to Maryland," these were not "the only thing to be considered." They were happy in Princeton and "would be happy anywhere together." Leaving Princeton, after all, meant departing the "hallowed circle."[79]

Strayer never took the threat from Maryland seriously, and he advised Arthur that he "could do a lot better than Maryland." When asked for his assessment, Howard Beale disagreed. He warned Arthur not to "accept pleasant assurances from Princeton . . . that they like me and want me to stay." He had seen too many instances in which younger scholars were kept on for a few years and then dropped.[80] In the end, Strayer came through quickly with a counteroffer: Princeton agreed to match, nearly, the Maryland salary—providing Arthur with $3,750—and to promise to push his appointment as assistant professor for the 1948–49 year, with a three-year contract rather than what Margaret called "this hand-to-mouth one-year instructor business." With that appointment came greater status in the department, what Arthur called "a more satisfactory position in the department": he would be able to teach graduate students, though he would remain unable to teach his own course. "I don't know how it will all end," Margaret wrote her parents in January 1948, "but I rather believe we'll be in Princeton next year." Very shortly, Arthur accepted the Princeton counteroffer. "The Maryland offer at least gave me a chance to find out where I stand here," he told Beale; he "wasn't bluffing," he added, and "if they had decided not to promote me I would have gone to Maryland." In any event, the external offer gave Arthur what he needed—leverage with Princeton—something that Strayer had advised him to obtain about a year earlier. "Now if we could just attain an associate professorship," Margaret observed, "we would have some tenure. But we'll have to wait awhile longer for that."[81]

Another point of negotiation with Princeton was the matter of housing. With Stanley's arrival, the Links had outgrown the Patton Avenue apartment, and Arthur and Margaret wanted their own house. "We need a house badly at this point," Margaret told her parents in early 1948.[82] There was some university housing available, and Arthur sought one of the row houses that the university owned on Edwards Place, just west of campus. As it happens, this house was right behind a house that my family would occupy between 1960 and 1975, at 26 Mercer Street; this was the house that I grew up in, and Edwards Place was part of our extended neighborhood. Since the university provided no improvement in housing, Arthur and Margaret decided to build their own home. In the spring of 1948, with some financial help from the Douglases, they purchased a lot at 66 Cedar Lane, only a few blocks east of the Patton Avenue apartment. During the summer of 1948, they contracted with a builder to put up a new, Cape Cod–style, two-story house, and they moved into it in September 1948.

As it turns out, Margaret and Arthur would occupy the Cedar Lane house for less than a year. Despite his promotion to assistant professor, Arthur had hit a brick wall at Princeton. His rapid ascent and the semi-celebrity that had come to him in the historical profession profoundly alienated Eric Goldman, by then a senior American historian at Princeton. Under the long chairmanship of Joe Strayer, who headed the department for twenty years after 1941, Princeton recruited and attempted to retain a vibrant department that was notably strong in European history, though perhaps weaker in U.S. history. The mainstay of the American side had long been early American historian Thomas Jefferson Wertenbaker, but his retirement in 1947 left a void that was filled by the appointment of Wesley Frank Craven three years later. That meant that, in the late 1940s, Arthur's future at Princeton pretty much depended on Goldman.

Like Arthur, Goldman was something of a wunderkind. Growing up in poverty in Baltimore, Goldman received a full scholarship to Johns Hopkins, and he stayed on there for graduate work. Receiving a Ph.D. from Johns Hopkins at the age of twenty-two, he had written for *Time* magazine between 1940 and 1944, and he wrote easily for a wide audience. From 1938 to 1941, he taught at Hopkins as an instructor until university president Isaac Bowman ordered that he be fired because he wanted no Jews on the faculty. Strayer, ever on the lookout for bright young scholars, recruited him to Princeton as an instructor in 1942. Notably, Strayer had a record of hiring Jewish faculty, three of whom served in a department of around twenty by the 1950s—an exception to the general trend in the immediate postwar period. Still, Goldman was also one of only a few Jewish faculty members at Princeton, an institution that had made restricting the admission of Jewish students through its "quota" system a matter of policy since the 1920s. After publishing two books, Goldman rose to the rank of assistant professor in 1943 and associate professor in 1947. Later, in 1952, he wrote *Rendezvous with Destiny*, a study of reform in modern America that won the prestigious Bancroft Prize; in 1956, a sequel, *The Crucial Decade and After, 1945–55*, appeared. In 1964, he joined the White House as a special adviser to Lyndon B. Johnson.[83]

Goldman, in the mid-1940s, was not especially happy at Princeton. Unlike most faculty, he did not live in Princeton, preferring instead to stay in New York and come to campus a few days a week to teach. (In later years, however, he lived around the corner from us on Alexander Street.) In part, this might have been so because he had always aspired to write a sort of history with wider appeal than professional historians normally achieve, and New York seemed a better locale for this. Between 1959 and 1967, he served as moderator of *Open Mind*, a news program on NBC that twice won Emmys. Later, in the mid-1970s, he worked as a special commentator for the *CBS Morning News* on national political affairs. At Princeton, Goldman taught a popular course on twentieth-century American history and commanded a devoted undergraduate following, but he never had much of a presence among graduate students. Moreover, despite his election to prestigious groups such as the Society of American Historians, Goldman never commanded wide respect among professional historians, many of whom considered him more of a popularizer than an original historian.

At first, relations between Arthur and Goldman were good. Beale knew Goldman, and soon after Arthur's appointment he urged Arthur to look Goldman up. After a dinner meeting, Arthur pronounced Goldman "certainly a swell fellow" whom both he and Margaret liked "very much."[84] A year later, in August 1946, Margaret noted that Goldman seemed unhappy. "I am really surprised that Eric is coming back to Princeton," she wrote Arthur. Evidently, he was looking for other jobs, but he "obviously couldn't find anything better (or maybe it was too far from N.Y.)." Married only one year, he divorced in 1945, and Margaret hoped he would be happier if he could have a happier personal life. Goldman had two unhappy marriages: the first, with Betty Ann Heilbrun, lasted a year (1944–45); the second, with Anne Metzger, lasted two years (1950–52). But the love of his life was concert pianist Joanna Ruth Jackson, whom he married in 1952. Joanna was eventually diagnosed as a schizophrenic, and he took care of her until her death in 1983.[85] By 1947, Arthur was suggesting that some distance had developed in his relationship with Goldman. "I have seen about as much of you as I have seen of Eric during the past six months," he wrote Beale. He further wondered whether Goldman had become a "little erratic in his judgments." At some point during Arthur's ascent at Princeton, relations with Goldman grew decidedly chilly, and he regarded Arthur as a threat to his position at the university.[86]

EVANSTON 5

The year after he received the Maryland offer, the history department at Northwestern courted Arthur. The department there had experienced a great deal of turnover. Ray Allen Billington, the distinguished historian of the West, arrived in 1944, followed by the diplomatic historian Richard W. "Dick" Leopold, who came to Northwestern in 1948. The departure of department chair Tracey E. Strevey, who became dean at the University of Southern California, created a gap. The department attempted to recruit David Potter, then at Yale, but he declined the offer. The Northwestern dean Simeon F. Leland and president Franklyn Snyder rejected the department's proposed hiring of Bell I. Wiley, a Civil War historian, then at Louisiana State University and later at Emory, because they believed he didn't meet their standards. There was little enthusiasm in the department about Arthur; he was at the bottom of the list of possible additions. Although he was regarded as a phenomenon, Northwestern faculty, according to Leopold, believed that "he lacked the prestige and experience initially sought by both the department and the university."[1]

Leopold became instrumental in bringing Arthur to Northwestern. In many ways enigmatic, Leopold was reared in New York City. He came from a background of wealthy Orthodox Jewish parents who were intent that their children should reject their Jewish identity and assimilate into the northeastern WASP elite. Leopold succeeded: many people were not even aware of his Jewish heritage in later years.[2] He attended Exeter, a leading boarding school, then entered Princeton as an undergraduate (graduating in 1929) and Harvard as a graduate student (where he received a doctorate in 1938). Serving as a naval officer stationed in Washington during the war, Leopold was appointed assistant professor at Harvard, but the department did not tenure him. At the December 1948 meetings of the AHA—only a few months into his appointment at Northwestern—he first met Arthur at the Mayflower Hotel in Washington. Leopold knew about Arthur's *Road to the White House*, and he had heard from Thomas J. Pressly, a former Harvard student who was an instructor at Princeton, about Arthur's prodigious work habits. Sometime before the AHA, the Northwestern administration decided on Arthur, in part because of his four years' experience at Princeton.

Arthur was invited for a campus interview to Northwestern on February 17, 1949. Dean Leland immediately indicated that he supported his appointment, saying that "we very much want you at Northwestern" and indicating that they would go beyond his present rank and salary at Princeton. Arthur returned to Princeton with an offer of an associate professorship and a salary of $5,500, plus the assurance of a wide berth in the range of courses and the potential for directing graduate students. Northwestern also promised him a research leave at half pay for the 1950–51 academic year. Leopold remained dubious, writing historian Arthur M. Schlesinger Jr. that "Princeton would not let him go, that it would feel compelled to jump him over the heads of his less distinguished seniors."[3]

Arthur immediately took Northwestern's offer to Strayer, who knew about his visit to Evanston. Princeton president Harold W. Dodds personally lobbied Arthur to remain at Princeton even before the offer came in.[4] Arthur later said that Strayer was "extremely anxious to keep me, as were, I think, most of the other members of the department." But even Strayer's magic could not overcome the dynamics of departmental politics. Princeton's counteroffer followed the usual procedure: they promised $500 less than Northwestern's offer, presumably on the assumption that remaining at Princeton was worth the difference. Despite the support of the administration, Strayer failed to get departmental support to make Arthur an associate professor. In essence, Goldman, perhaps along with a few others in the department, was able to block the promotion because of what Margaret described as a "standing grudge" against Arthur.

"For some reason which no one seems to be able to fathom," Arthur wrote Fletcher Green, "Eric has an enormous grudge against me," and, according to other members of the department, he was "almost psychotic about it." Goldman made the case that Arthur possessed an insufficient and deficient teaching record, a specious claim since the department didn't permit any teaching beyond precepting and senior thesis supervision.

Strayer then tried to persuade the Institute for Advanced Study in Princeton to offer Arthur an appointment. Founded in 1930 as an independent research organization on the western fringes of the Princeton campus, the institute had hosted German Jewish refugee scientists such as Albert Einstein. It was supported by the largesse of Louis Bamberger and his sister Caroline Bamberger Fuld, and their fortune from the Macy's department store. On the faculty at the institute, political scientist Edward Mead Earle tried, at Strayer's urging, to find a place for Arthur. But the best that Earle could offer was a two-year appointment with an uncertain future. Arthur saw no point in turning down Northwestern, "not only a bird in the hand, but a really grand opportunity," and on March 10, 1949, he decided to leave Princeton. Arthur and Margaret were both disappointed about Princeton's rejection. Margaret told her parents that both of them were "much upset" and "pretty bitter" because Princeton's response suggested a "lack of departmental approval" that would "block his ever getting an associate professorship." Margaret was especially disgusted by the ornate and complicated departmental politics. "It seems that academic advancement is worked on the same principle as admission into fraternities—one man can blackball you," she complained to her parents. Princeton would someday be "awfully sorry they lost Arthur—because he's going to be a great scholar (everybody says that)."[5]

Northwestern, for its part, was delighted to snag Arthur. Ray Allen Billington wrote Arthur in March, expressing his confidence that Arthur would never regret his decision to leave Princeton. "You will find the department the most congenial in the profession," he declared; Billington had never seen "such cooperation and understanding and friendship." "You will find Northwestern a lively place intellectually, with some first-rate graduate students and a faculty that offers a type of stimulation, for either mind or body." And Evanston, Billington said, was "pleasant and attractive," and he was "happier here than I could be in any other spot save Boston—which is my true love."[6]

Leopold was equally confident that Arthur's hiring was a triumph for the Northwestern department. To Pressly, Leopold wrote that he was "surprised as I could be when Old Nassau let us steal Link away," despite his "youth and teaching inexperience and whatever defects there may be."[7] "Everyone here is very gratified that you are coming," Leopold wrote in late March. He had received "some complimentary letters from people outside of Evanston on the excellence of our appointment," he added. Leopold had faced a difficult decision when he left Harvard just a year earlier; "I went through the same agony a year ago." But during his visit, Leopold had assured Arthur that the Northwestern move made sense. "I repeat what I said to you when you were here," he declared. "You will not regret your decision to come."[8]

Dick Leopold's prediction proved correct: the move to Northwestern, and the Links' departure for Evanston, marked the beginning of a happy period in Margaret and Arthur's life. In the eleven years spent in Evanston, their time would be consumed with raising a family, with three children born during the 1950s. Arthur found a welcome academic home in Northwestern; Margaret embraced the welcoming life of suburban Chicago. Their separation from the South was punctuated by the deaths of Margaret's parents, though she and Arthur maintained strong ties with their region. Yet their departure for Evanston in 1949 did not, at the same time, mean the end of their relationship with Princeton, and in 1960 a new set of circumstances would bring them back to New Jersey.

In many ways, Northwestern was a better fit for Arthur. In Evanston during the 1950s, Arthur's closest friends were fellow American historians Richard Leopold and Ray Allen Billington (who lived around the block on Central Street in Evanston), and—perhaps his and Margaret's best friends—Scandinavian historian Franklin Scott and his wife, Helen, who lived across the street at 2657 Orrington Avenue. Moving into a large, three-story house a few blocks from Lake Michigan in Evanston at 2726 Orrington Avenue, the Link family had plenty of room to grow. Evanston proved to be an idyllic midwestern community for the Links, with strong public schools, a collegial and welcoming department, and a neighborhood filled with intelligent, educated women very much like Margaret. To the south lived Al and Peg Bolton, whose three children were close to the Link children; Peg and Margaret became good friends. The Orrington Elementary School, which my brothers and sister and I attended, was a block south, and the children walked to school and came home for lunch.[9]

My sister, Peggy, who lived in Evanston until the age of nine, recalled their life in the community as a sort of "Norman Rockwell existence" in a place with a "warm, family feel." The children rode bikes around a neighborhood full of kids, and the schools enjoyed strong support. Christmases were especially warm and lively, with neighborhood gatherings and carol singing. Arthur and Margaret participated in an active social life. They belonged to a monthly dinner club, and they socialized frequently. Margaret was especially drawn to midwestern culture; Peggy remembered that she was "crazy about Evanston." Later in life, Margaret often commented how midwestern culture in many ways resembled southern culture in its openness, hospitality, and civility—all values she cherished, but felt were absent in Princeton's colder climate.[10]

Although the move to Northwestern resulted in more salary, Arthur continued to earn extra income by teaching summers and evening classes in downtown Evanston.[11] Money needs also meant taking in lodgers. From the time that they arrived, the Links rented a room in their house, usually to graduate students. In September 1951, their lodger was George Simmons, originally from Barbados and Trinidad. He had come to the United States in 1946 and had immediately experienced race prejudice in Baltimore, when a train conductor ordered him out of an all-white train compartment. Simmons attended the Seventh-Day Adventist Oakwood College, a historically black college in Huntsville, Alabama, and then transferred to the predominantly white Emmanuel Missionary College (now Andrews University) in Berrien Springs, Michigan. Simmons's experience at Emmanuel was eye-opening, and he arrived at Northwestern for graduate school acutely sensitive to white race prejudice. Early in the fall of 1951, Simmons telephoned the Links to see if a room was available. When Margaret answered the phone and spoke with a deep southern drawl, encouraging him to come over, he nearly skipped the appointment. But Simmons took the room, becoming a part of the Link household. Living at Orrington Avenue, he recalled years later, was "one of the pleasantest experiences I had in the United States." Margaret and Arthur, Simmons recalled, "recognized that there were black people who were intelligent and honest," who "longed for better race relationships." Whenever company came, Margaret and Arthur invited George to join them. On one occasion, John Hope Franklin came to visit, and George met him. The "question of racial prejudice," he recalled, "never surfaced."

My brother Stan, who was then four years old, remembered rising one

Links: My Family in American History

July morning in Davidson. Finding his grandfather collapsed in the hallway, Stan rushed to rouse his mother. "Mom, Grandfather is asleep in the hallway," he told her. Margaret dashed into the hallway, where she discovered her father on the floor, dead from a massive heart attack he had suffered in the middle of the night. Margaret's mother, Anniebelle, had never recovered from earlier heart attacks, and she suffered steady mental deterioration resulting from a hardening of the arteries. Only a few weeks before James Douglas's death, she had suffered a "complete collapse" and had been moved to a nursing home. The twin blows of losing her father and observing her mother's irreversible decline were too much for Margaret, who was then pregnant with my sister Peggy, her third child. She was, according to Arthur, "as devoted" to her father "as any daughter I have ever seen and his passing was a great blow." Not long after James's death, Margaret went into premature labor and nearly lost the baby—the fact that Peggy survived was, according to my father, always regarded as miraculous. My mother remained in North Carolina to settle her parents' affairs, and Peggy was born in Charlotte Presbyterian Hospital on August 30, 1951.[12]

Although by September 1951, Arthur described Margaret as "completely her old self again," the Links took on Simmons to do odd jobs, housework, and heavy labor, "things that would break Margaret down if she had to do them." Simmons took his meals with the family, interacted with them closely, and became close to the Links.[13] Simmons described Margaret as "a grand lady." "I didn't like her; I loved her," he said. She had a "soft, southern" way, and she was "sympathetic" and "empathized with people generally." Arthur was a "real scholar" who taught him, by example, "how a scholar lives, . . . what a scholar does." An ordained Seventh-Day Adventist pastor, Simmons had numerous religious conversations with Arthur. They also shared ideas about music, while Arthur introduced George to one of his great loves—eating waffles. "We both loved waffles," and to this day Simmons—who bought a waffle iron in the 1950s—continues to love them. Arthur taught him "the love of waffles" and the "love of learning." In 1953, when Simmons was married in an Evanston black neighborhood, Arthur and Margaret not only attended the ceremony but also stayed for dinner afterward. The other black guests were astounded that the Links took part in the dinner reception. Simmons recalled how the elderly black ladies who had never sat at a table with white people thought that this was "an amazing thing."[14]

The Links were in for a different cultural experience after Simmons left, and Gerald "Gerry" Grob joined the household in the fall of 1952. Grob completed his Ph.D. work under Arthur, subsequently becoming a long-standing faculty member at Rutgers University. The son of Polish Jewish immigrants who grew up in the southeastern Bronx, Grob had never lived anywhere but in the New York City area. He attended City College as an undergraduate and received his master's at Columbia, working under Richard Hofstadter. But he felt that Columbia was too large, a "money-making operation," and when Hofstadter urged him to look at Northwestern, he jumped at the opportunity. Grob worked at the New York Public Library for six years, and he met a Northwestern graduate student, Jack Blicksilver, in the reading room. Blicksilver suggested that Grob write to Arthur if he needed a room. With Simmons's departure, the room was available, and Grob moved in during September 1952.

Like Simmons, Grob became incorporated into the Link family. Before long, Arthur and Margaret invited him to participate in the weekend rituals—car trips with the children, visits to Chicago, and even Sunday dinner. Grob, who grew up in a community that was overwhelmingly Jewish, had attended Hebrew School in the afternoons after public school for five days a week for a decade. He came from a household that was observant and kept, or nearly kept, a kosher kitchen. Once Gerry was invited for Sunday dinner, and he came into the dining room and saw a "big pink thing." What is that? he asked. "What," said Arthur, "you've never seen a ham?" Noticing that there was also milk and butter on the table, he excused himself and went into the bathroom and threw up. After exposure to shellfish while he was out with Northwestern graduate students, Grob learned more of the ways of people outside the Jewish enclave of New York. At the same time, Margaret and Arthur were fascinated with Grob's cultural background. He introduced the family to strudel—his aunt sent one regularly from New York—and to the delicacy of halvah, which became a family favorite. Arthur also actively engaged Gerry in regular discussions about Judaism, in which he was intensely interested.[15]

Professionally, Arthur loved the Northwestern department, and he was promoted to full professor at the end of 1954. Northwestern provided ample time for leave: the entire family spent the 1950–51 year in the Washington area and the 1954–55 year at the Institute for Advanced Study in Princeton. Arthur taught the first of many graduate students at Northwestern, and he was fully engaged in teaching a popular course on twentieth-century American history. Arthur genuinely liked his colleagues at Northwestern. Along with three other Americanists—Billington, Leopold, and colonialist Clarence Ver Steeg—they ran a small but intimate department where the faculty often ate lunch with the small number of graduate students in the program. Billington was a legendary teacher. Not only was he a splendid undergraduate lecturer, his year-long graduate seminar was considered de rigueur for new graduate students.

As was true at Princeton, Arthur soon became known for his work habits and prodigious productivity. When Grob arrived in 1952, he was amazed to find Arthur working on two books simultaneously—the New American Nation volume, eventually published as *Woodrow Wilson and the Progressive Era*, and a new, synthetic textbook about twentieth-century America, *American Epoch*. Arthur worked in a third-floor study at the Orrington Avenue house, from which he could look out and call down to misbehaving children below. But the study was also quiet. Arthur told fellow historian Merle Curti that it was "almost hermetically sealed off from the noise and confusion that the children sometimes create below."[16] Arthur worked intensely—according to Grob, he was "absolutely compulsive" in his habits—every day from breakfast until dinner. Rarely did he work at nights, and very often he took weekends off: this was his pattern for the rest of his life. Grob remembered that Arthur once told him over morning coffee that he needed to write a review, which he hadn't started, that was due by the end of the day. At four o'clock that afternoon, Arthur asked Gerry if he wanted to walk with him to the post office to mail the completed review. After Grob asked to see a copy, he noticed that Arthur had produced an eighteen-page review in a single day's work. Grob was "awestruck" at the way Arthur worked.[17]

Arthur also directed Ph.D.s at Northwestern—he had directed one at Princeton, John R. Lambert, who received the degree in 1948 and taught for many years at N.C. State University—and during the eleven years that he was in Evanston he supervised eight dissertations. One of them was by Bill Harbaugh, his second Ph.D., who came to Northwestern in 1950, not long after Arthur had arrived in Evanston. Harbaugh, an artillery officer who during World War II saw action in North Africa, Italy, France, and Germany, was actually six months older than Arthur. Harbaugh, a person of great wisdom, wit, and style, would later be my dissertation supervisor at the University of Virginia. More important, he became a major twentieth-century American historian with what remains one of the best biographies of Theodore Roosevelt and a prize-winning study of the lawyer and politician John W. Davis.

Arthur's first doctoral student at Northwestern was George McGovern. Like Harbaugh, McGovern was a war veteran, having flown a B-24 bomber over the Pacific in thirty-five missions. When the war ended, McGovern completed his undergraduate degree at Dakota Wesleyan College, and then sought a theological degree at Garrett Seminary on the Northwestern campus. In 1947, he decided to enter graduate school at Northwestern, and when Arthur arrived two years later, he took McGovern on as his first Northwestern doctoral student. At one point during McGovern's graduate school days, Arthur described him as having "extremely high intelligence, keen analytical abilities, and fine balance." He was also a "splendid person—warm, friendly, sympathetic to students and an excellent teacher."[18] "I have seen perhaps one or two students who were as good as McGovern," Arthur told an interviewer. "But in twenty-six years of graduate teaching I have never seen any better."[19] In graduate school, the McGoverns had three children, with a young daughter born in 1949. My mother remembered visiting George and his wife, Eleanor, in their apartment in Evanston, where the infant children slept in dresser drawers that doubled as cribs. McGovern returned to his alma mater, Dakota Wesleyan College, in 1950, and finished his degree in three years; his dissertation concerned the Colorado Coal Strike of 1913–14. He taught for six years, until he was elected to the U.S. House of Representatives in 1956 and the U.S. Senate in 1962. In 1972, he ran as the Democratic nominee for president.[20]

Arthur maintained close contact with McGovern over subsequent years, in conversations and through correspondence. "Our friendship," Arthur wrote in 1989, was "one of the great blessings of my life." McGovern described his friendship with Arthur as "one of the genuine treasures of my life," and "long gaps between meetings do not seem to dim our friendship."[21] During the 1972 campaign, Arthur told an interviewer that McGovern was "too nice a guy" who would not "crack heads sometimes when he needs to." About the Nixon campaign's characterization of McGovern as a radical threat, Arthur described him as an "extraordinarily cautious and prudent man."[22]

Six months after McGovern's disastrous landslide loss to Richard Nixon in the presidential election of 1972, on June 9, 1973, George and Eleanor visited my parents and had lunch and spent the afternoon with them at their Mercer Street house in Princeton. I was home and sat in on the event, which I found fascinating. McGovern was still devastated by the enormity of the defeat, which was made bitter by the emerging revelations about the extent of Nixon's illegal activities. When McGovern was considering another, quixotic run for the White House in 1984, Arthur counseled him and even drafted the announcement of his candidacy.[23] (McGovern decided to run in the Democratic primaries of 1984, though his candidacy never gained traction.) In August 1983, we visited McGovern and Eleanor in Gatlinburg, in east Tennessee, and spent the afternoon with them. My wife, Susannah, and I, along with our two-month-old daughter, Percy, made the two-hour drive from Montreat for lunch and the afternoon. I remembered how McGovern held Percy with complete ease—suggesting the ample experience he had had as a father. When my mother was dying about ten years after that, McGovern made a special effort by traveling to visit with my parents in their North Carolina home.

Arthur, as a scholar of the presidency, enjoyed rare access to political leaders. During the summer of 1956, he shared an apartment in Chevy Chase with McGovern, and his next-door neighbor—who often came to visit—was Minnesota senator Hubert Humphrey. "After work, Humphrey would come cover and we'd have a beer," Arthur recalled, and "sit on the porch and discuss the state of the world."[24] During the 1950s, Arthur developed a relationship with Adlai Stevenson, who served as governor of Illinois (1948–52) and twice ran against and lost to Dwight D. Eisenhower for the presidency. In August 1955, Stevenson and Arthur began a correspondence when Stevenson asked for ideas about Wilson; Stevenson was preparing a speech on the occasion of the centennial of Wilson's birth.[25] Arthur responded enthusiastically—perhaps too enthusiastically. He urged that Stevenson take up the question of civil liberties, but this was a topic, in the age of McCarthyism, that Stevenson considered too politically sensitive. Still, in a letter in January 1956, Arthur made a strong civil libertarian case. The "present menace" to civil liberties lay mainly in the way in which the subversion of liberties had become "institutionalized and accepted as the normal machinery of government." The greater danger, Arthur wrote, was a "subtle and sophisticated McCarthyism—the tremendous, constant, steady pressure on all sides for not merely conformity but positive acceptance of prevailing ideas."[26]

My birth was something of an accident. Arthur had contracted a case of the mumps in 1951, and the common belief was that adult cases of the mumps usually resulted in sterility. My parents were convinced that Peggy would be their last child. As early as 1952, they had planned a year at the Institute for Advanced Study for 1954–55, not expecting to have an infant as part of the move to Princeton.[27] They were mistaken. "A fourth Link is on the way and due about the middle of August," Arthur wrote Ray Billington in June 1954. "We did this simply to demonstrate that I am as virile as ever and to end certain slanders about the mumps affair!"[28] My arrival was not especially convenient or easy: I was born in Evanston Hospital on August 18, 1954, but because my mother was Rh negative, and I am Rh positive, her antibodies caused a reaction. I was born a small baby at six pounds, thirteen ounces: my mother liked to say that I was a "puny" baby. The family moved to Princeton about a month after my birth. By November, Arthur could report that "little Billy" was "growing so fast that he will be little not much longer."[29]

My earliest memory was a trip that my family took to a cabin on a glacial lake in Grand Marais, Minnesota, in August 1957, when I was nearly three years old. Arthur described the "absolutely spectacular country—a wilderness of virgin forests with crystal-clear lakes and rugged terrain." I remember how my father took my brothers fishing. I wasn't old enough to fish, so Arthur put a string on the end of a stick, and I pretended. In a letter to John Hope—himself a great fisherman—Arthur described how the lake was a "fisherman's paradise." He caught his limit of bass every time he went out in the boat, usually within two hours. "Most of them were small," he reported, "but I did hook four two-three pounders, and they gave a wonderful fight. I thought about you and how you would enjoy it."[30]

For Margaret, the experience of raising a family in the 1950s was all-consuming, as the arrival of three children between 1950 and 1954 confined her to a domestic existence. Although she was a loving mother, I'm not sure that she ever completely enjoyed the role, especially the time that child rearing absorbed. Later, when my children came on the scene, she made it clear to me that she loved her grandchildren but had less interest in hands-on babysitting: she had done that with four children, and was grateful to have the free time. And managing Arthur was a full-time job, but it was a job that she eagerly took—and knew that she was taking when she married him.

During Arthur's leave at the institute in 1954–55, Joe Strayer made an attempt to woo him back. The Stanford historian Frank Freidel

Links: My Family in American History

had turned Princeton down for Harvard, and Strayer pursued Arthur. In early February 1955, Strayer made a formal offer of a full professorship at $10,000 salary. When it appeared that Arthur was tempted to leave Northwestern, Leopold insisted that he make a trip back to Evanston, where the department and the administration actively courted him. Northwestern, which had preemptively raised his salary to $8,000 in late 1954, met Princeton's offer by increasing him to $13,000. By mid-February, after many conversations with Margaret, he decided to stay at Northwestern. His increased salary, coming as a result of the Northwestern-Princeton bidding war, meant that there would be no more boarders at Orrington Avenue. Remaining in Evanston suited Margaret, who harbored some ill feelings toward Princeton about the way Arthur had been treated in 1949. "How glad I am that Arthur made the trip to Evanston and talked with you," Margaret wrote Dick.[31]

Arthur and Margaret's decision reflected the contrast between their chilly reception at Princeton and the warm embrace of Northwestern. Six years earlier, writing to Princeton president Harold Dodds in April 1949 when he formally submitted his resignation, Arthur declared that he had reached his decision "only after long consideration and with a feeling of regret that circumstances seemed to compel it." Princeton had been his and Margaret's home for the past four years, and they had "sunk our roots pretty deep here." He was deeply grateful to Princeton, he said. "No university could have given a young man greater encouragement and inspiration in scholarship than Princeton has given me. Nothing that I asked for in this respect has ever been refused." Even though he and Margaret left for Evanston, "we shall always carry Princeton with us in spirit and continue to wish for her prosperity and intellectual advancement."[32]

The truth was that, although Arthur felt bruised by his earlier experience in Princeton as an assistant professor, he regarded a return to the university as placing him at the very top of the profession. Professional recognition and achievement were part of his psyche, and he would never be satisfied with an institution like Northwestern—even though it was then becoming a major university. Arthur's attachment to Princeton remained unchanged when he turned Strayer's offer down in February 1955. The decision to remain in Evanston was agonizing, and Arthur noted that there were "many reasons why we should come and why we should stay." What probably tipped the matter in Northwestern's direction was Margaret's happiness and Arthur's personal ties to Northwestern faculty.

Writing to Strayer a little after he had made his decision, he described the "difficult time Margaret and I have been going through." "I think you understand what the call from Princeton meant to me personally, and why I nearly accepted." Arthur saw new opportunities at Princeton in terms of building up scholarship and graduate study in American history.

Princeton's offer in 1955 posed difficult choices, as professionally Arthur felt pulled to Princeton, but personally he and his family were strongly tied to Northwestern. Arthur's sense of identification with Princeton continued to pull at him. The chance to return "evoked strong and affectionate memories of the place in which I got my start and found my intellectual way." Despite the blow in 1949, he was "personally moved by the thought that the Department should want me back and by the thought that you have probably had calling me back in mind since I left in 1949." He had been "extremely happy" at Northwestern, where, as he wrote his colleague Franklin Scott, he was drawn by the "thought of being associated in the work of building a program." Arthur and Margaret had, in addition, become deeply involved in the Evanston community. Leaving Northwestern meant more to that institution than would his arrival in Princeton, and he would leave a "strong team" of American historians behind. Though the decision was "evenly balanced" in all considerations— suggesting a hint of regret on Arthur's part—"we think . . . we would not be justified in leaving."[33]

The recruiting war between Northwestern and Princeton, Arthur later observed to a friend, "nearly tore him to pieces." So distraught was Arthur that he suffered a physical collapse and required hospitalization.[34] But other forces continued to pull at Arthur. The year 1956 was the centennial of Woodrow Wilson's birth, and in April of that year, the Mississippi Valley Historical Association (the predecessor of the Organization of American Historians) asked Arthur and Dick Leopold to write a report about Woodrow Wilson's historical legacy. They recommended a full-scale editorial project of Wilson's papers, consisting of about thirty volumes.[35] Spurred on by the centennial commission, the Woodrow Wilson Foundation endorsed the idea in May 1957, promised to find ample financing to support the project, and appointed a special committee to search for an editor-director of a papers project. The two dominant figures on the committee were the foundation chair Raymond B. Fosdick, who had a long career in public service, including twelve years as head of the Rockefeller Foundation, and August C. "Augie" Heckscher, a New Yorker who had worked as chief editorial writer for the *New York Herald Tribune* and later served as New York City parks commissioner under Mayor John Lindsay.[36] Fosdick became a Wilsonian as a young man. While a Princeton undergraduate, he took Wilson's course on jurisprudence, and he recalled how his sentences "seemed to catch fire and crackled with sparks of eloquence."[37] Fosdick served as president of the Wilson Foundation's special committee, with Heckscher as vice chair. The committee consisted of luminaries such as North Carolina journalist Jonathan Daniels, diplomat and legal scholar Philip C. Jessup, and historian Arthur M. Schlesinger Jr. With Schlesinger urging a search for an editor possessing a "discriminating intelligence," Fosdick canvassed the field during the fall of 1957. In late October, Fosdick sent out letters to thirteen prominent historians seeking nominations.[38]

Although Arthur had already published two volumes of his biography of Wilson, there was some disquiet about him as a possible candidate. Dexter Perkins, a historian at Cornell, warned the committee about Arthur's "hypercritical and sometimes supercilious attitude toward Wilson,"[39] and this seemed sufficient to discourage interest. In late November, Fosdick noted that some believed that Arthur "had demonstrated judgments which were unsound in so young a man," and others on the committee agreed. Only Heckscher persisted, announcing that the committee could not "pass over him."[40] The committee seemed inclined toward Yale historian John Morton Blum, the author of a recent brief biography of Wilson and an editor of an edition of Theodore Roosevelt's letters. Arthur recommended "young-yet-not-so-young" historians; he thought Blum fit the bill.[41] Although Fosdick initially agreed, describing Blum as "our best bet," he had second thoughts. He worried that Blum would insist on having the project at Yale; Fosdick was insistent that it be housed at Princeton and published by the Princeton University Press.[42] Moreover, after reading Blum's book, he concluded that Blum was too critical of Wilson. By the end of the year, the committee remained uncertain. Arthur seemed the inevitable choice, however, though few seemed to think that he was interested. By late January 1958, former Princeton president Harold Dodds told Fosdick that Arthur had "grown a lot" and that he might be induced to return to Princeton. Augie and Jessup, in private conversations, agreed that he was "objective, fair, scholarly" and "devoted" to Wilson's memory. Schlesinger and others urged that the job be offered to Arthur. Fosdick called him on January 28, 1958, inviting him to visit the committee in New York. Arthur agreed to come in February.[43]

Fosdick's committee, meeting with Arthur on February 20, 1958, offered him the editorship of the Wilson Papers. But the most important point of negotiation remained the project's location. Arthur "expressed some disinclination" to leave Northwestern, where, he said, he was "more urgently needed." The committee agreed to defer matters for a year since Arthur was slated to visit Oxford University as the Harold Vyvyan Harmsworth Professor. Arthur accepted the position as editor, but over time he became increasingly convinced that editing the Wilson Papers was a sort of divine calling. He believed in a Calvinist calling; his was to edit the Wilson Papers. "I believe God created me to do this," he told an interviewer many years later. "Not many people in this day and age would think there was such a thing as a divine call, but I do." He also believed that the work would supersede the value of further publications. "This work is certainly worthy of the best that is in us all," he wrote to Fosdick, and "the more I think about it the more I believe we can make some contribution that will last and serve future generations of historians and scholars." For the rest of his life, he remained convinced that the Wilson Papers project would become his monument to American history.[44]

The decision to edit the Wilson Papers was wrapped up in the question of Arthur's academic home: the Wilson Foundation search committee early on declared the "natural location" for the project was in Princeton. Both Princeton University president Robert F. Goheen and Princeton University Press director Herb Bailey urged locating the papers there as well, and Goheen promised ample space in Princeton's Firestone Library. The Princeton history department was eager to recruit Arthur.[45] Soon after he was offered the editorship, Fosdick telegraphed Gray Boyce, chair of the Northwestern history department, and described Arthur as "preeminently qualified" in a way that "no other scholar in the country" could match. But, in addition, from "every point of view" Princeton offered advantages that "no other place affords."[46]

Arthur was, however, strongly tied to Evanston. "I got the impression," Fosdick wrote Augie in February 1958, that "his wife is not enthusiastic about the proposed move."[47] Arthur admitted to Fosdick that he was conflicted. "I hope that it will be possible for me to carry on this work in Evanston, as Wilson himself would say," he wrote to Fosdick in March

1958. He described his "great obligation" to Northwestern and the "deep personal roots that we have sunk in our church and community." At this point, however, Arthur saw the decision as "bigger than any individual"; he assured Fosdick that "individual preferences will have to give way if that is necessary."[48]

Northwestern, determined "to do everything possible to have Arthur Link remain at Northwestern,"[49] made an offer to house the project in Evanston, but the decision was deferred while Arthur assumed the Harmsworth Professorship at Oxford University during the 1958–59 year. The Harmsworth was a prestigious appointment that had been offered, before Arthur, to Ray Billington (who went to Oxford in 1954–55) and to Dick Leopold (who declined the opportunity). The year in England became a highlight of our family's history. It involved my earliest memories: I was almost four when we left, five when we returned. On the trip over we rode the Canadian Pacific liner *Empress of Britain* from Montreal, leaving at the end of June 1958.

Typically, there was a crisis involving my brother Jimmy. As the ship traveled up the St. Lawrence River to the Atlantic, Jimmy was nowhere to be found. Then seven years old, Jimmy had been a difficult child. As a toddler, he was demanding, and Stan remembered how my parents had trouble keeping him in his crib. Jimmy was a struggle, and he received attention by misbehaving. He had a kind of hyperactive energy that often drove him into disaster and crisis. Gerry Grob, who lived with the family when Jimmy was a toddler and young child, remembered him having "kinds of fits" and tantrums that attracted most of the family's attention. At a very young age, Jimmy climbed on top of a dresser, and brought it crashing down. Later, as a young boy, he crashed through a sliding-glass window, spewing broken glass everywhere.[50]

Only sixteen months old when my sister Peggy was born, Jimmy suffered from a bad case of sibling rivalry: my mother told me later that when she came home from the hospital with my sister, she noticed a dark look coming over Jimmy's face. Later, he would become Peggy's tormenter—and, to a lesser extent, mine. Peggy remembered him as a "mean-spirited brother" who, when she was four or five, took her favorite doll and, out of spite, destroyed it. Although a difficult child, Jimmy unquestionably lit up a room with his sparkle. Always bright, inventive, even brilliant, he had a slightly devilish laugh, an infectious sense of humor, and an easy, natural charm. In the family dynamic, Jimmy kept things churning as a way of focusing attention on himself. In high school, however, his life turned dark, as he descended into a series of problems that led to a mental breakdown in the fall of 1968.

In June 1958, the *Empress of Britain* had been commissioned only two years. It was a 25,500-ton ship that traveled at a maximum speed of 20 knots. One of the first North Atlantic liners to possess air-conditioning, the *Empress of Britain* made regular trips between Montreal and Liverpool. On the departure of the ship, Margaret and Arthur, unable to find Jimmy, were in a panic, and they discussed possible arrangements to have him transported across the Atlantic. But, as was typical of Jimmy, the crisis subsided: my parents discovered that, in the excitement of embarkation, he had gone to the top of the ship to view the departure—without, however, telling anyone where he was going.

The rest of the Atlantic crossing occurred without incident, with the *Empress of Britain* arriving in Liverpool on July 1, 1958. The ship, Arthur wrote, was new, with "large cabins and spacious public rooms," while the food was "nothing extraordinary, but it was good enough and there was of course more of it than one could begin to eat." The children, Arthur wrote Dick Leopold, "continued to behave themselves, except for rather rare occasions," and one of the nicest parts of the trip was the way in which "the children fell in and had a wonderful time on their own, thus leaving Margaret and me with more time to ourselves than we had ever thought possible." Jimmy became "well known throughout the ship before the trip was over—and favorably so." The ship ran into some rough weather on the fifth day of the crossing, but most of the family weathered it well. The main challenge was dinner, which involved a later mealtime than the children were used to. Margaret and Arthur solved things by feeding the children—"except Stanley, who does not consider himself a child"—at the afternoon tea so that the "three older Links could enjoy themselves at dinner." Meanwhile, Peggy, Jimmy, and Billy occupied themselves in the lounge or ship playroom.[51]

One advantage of taking the *Empress of Britain* across the Atlantic was that my parents could transport their roomy, but also very conspicuous, American station wagon to England. In 1950s England, our large American car became a curiosity, and as we traveled across England and Europe during that year we attracted stares everywhere we went. Arriving in Liverpool, which was still suffering the terrible effects of the German blitz during World War II, we drove southeast to our first destination,

Cambridge, where we spent July, August, and part of September 1958. Arthur had made arrangements to rent a medium-sized, four-bedroom house on Grange Road. The house also included a study, and Arthur commented that his view while working was "all so pleasant and seductive that I wonder whether I will get any work done."[52]

That summer, and the following year, was distinguished by the presence of a young German au pair, Ortrun Lenz, who spent the year with us, minding the children and doing household chores in exchange for room, board, and a small allowance. Ortrun came to Cambridge to study English at a local technical college, and she lived at a local hostel. Graziana Rossi, an Italian friend of hers, had worked for us briefly as an au pair in Cambridge, but she had to return to Italy. When she left, Graziana recommended Ortrun, and, after an interview by Arthur and Margaret, Ortrun described the relationship as "love at first sight." Arthur liked Ortrun's German discipline and orderliness, and he eventually persuaded her to accompany the family to Oxford. By August, Arthur was describing her as caring for things "magnificently."[53]

Ortrun was a woman with an interesting past. Her mother had been a member of the Nazi Party who lived in Munich and, like other Nazis, had been encouraged to produce healthy Aryan children. Ortrun was the product of these efforts; her mother bore her out of wedlock. Because of Allied bombing late in the war, German children were sent out to schools in supposedly safer areas; Ortrun was placed in one such facility in Poland. Toward the end of the war, the school's headmistress ignored warnings about the approaching Red Army, and the camp was overrun by Russian troops. Trapped in Poland, the German teachers and students were subject to abuse and privation; the teachers, Ortrun remembered, practiced prostitution in order to survive. The teachers organized an attempt to gather the children and secretly return to Germany, but they were caught by Russian troops at the border. The troops lined the group up against the wall, prepared to execute them, when one of the children burst into tears. The Russian soldiers took pity on them and let them go. Eventually, Ortrun returned to Germany and, in the turmoil, located her mother.[54]

Ortrun became a part of our family: she organized outings for the children and became responsible for much of the day-to-day child care. She later recalled that, at four years old, I was very attached to my mother and suffered from separation anxiety when she would leave, crying bitterly when my parents left on trips. All four children "tested me," Ortrun remembered. Jimmy was a "troubled child" who occupied much of the family's attention and who had an "evil streak" that would appear out of nowhere. Stanley and Peggy felt a little neglected, according to her recollection, because of the time my parents spent on Jimmy. In her relationship with my parents, Ortrun maintained business dealings with Arthur, whom she regarded as "very remote" and emotionally disconnected. She was baffled by his stinginess with small things and generosity with large things—which was, in truth, one of Arthur's basic qualities—and she noted his "charming arrogance." Arthur "knew who he was; he did not hold back bragging about himself." Somehow, Ortrun recalled, "you had to chuckle" about him. At times they disagreed, and Ortrun, strong-minded, stood up to Arthur, and he eventually backed down. She remembered Margaret as a "real southern lady with a lot of backbone," and she noted that in Margaret's soft style of personal relations, she was also very "powerful." Margaret knew how to manage Arthur, who had an "emotional dependence, as well as intellectual" on his wife. They had a "solid" marriage, Ortrun believed. Not only were they close emotionally, she noted that there was a "sexual energy" between the two of them, and they had a "good intimate life." She later told my brother that, in Oxford, the walls were thin enough for her to hear my parents at night: Arthur, she told him, was a "lusty lover." Margaret adopted Ortrun as a kind of daughter, often counseling her about various personal issues. Her stay with the Links, for Ortrun, became an emotional anchor. The Links were "my family, my first family."[55]

Having Ortrun in the family provided a new life for my parents. Until their year in England, my parents were consumed—Arthur by his work, my mother by the demands of four children. There were few opportunities in particular for Margaret, who had left an interesting life as a professional woman and adopted the domestic lifestyle of the 1950s. She enjoyed that role, yet it was also clear that she needed some space from her children. The arrival of Ortrun provided that space, especially for Margaret, and the year in England opened up a new world for her.

Arthur, too, enjoyed more time with Margaret alone. After we left England, Ortrun and Arthur maintained a correspondence—she noted that Arthur, rather than Margaret, was the person who wrote. His main motivation was to get her to come to the United States and continue her au pair work. Ortrun was working as an interpreter in Germany and was reluctant to abandon her education. When she wrote Arthur and told him that she was free of obligations, he responded with a letter saying how glad they were that she was joining them. "That's your dad," Ortrun later told me. She came to Princeton in 1961–62, but Ortrun agreed to work only one year, and, in 1962, she obtained a job in Princeton. In 1963, when she married a graduate student studying French at Princeton, we all attended the wedding in Millville, Massachusetts.

Ortrun became especially close to Stanley, who as a young preteen had always considered himself nearer in affiliation to the adults than to the other children. Stan remembered that Ortrun was thoroughly German in her attitudes. She taught us a little German, and we sang German marching songs—such as "Wenn die Soldaten durch die Stadt marschieren." According to Stanley, Ortrun told him that Nazism wasn't a bad thing, that Hitler did some good things for the German people. Early in her tenure, when Peggy spoke rudely to her, Ortrun slapped her across the face. My mother gently but firmly told Ortrun—outside of the presence of the children—that this wouldn't be tolerated. But she was a fair-minded disciplinarian who didn't hesitate to use other forms of corporal punishment—one of her favorites was to hit our knuckles with her knitting needles. Ortrun often clashed with Jimmy, and attempted to protect Peggy against his teasing and bullying; later in life, he said that he had hated her. Ortrun met her match in Jimmy, but he also encountered a strong force in her. As early as August 1958, Arthur described Jimmy as "subdued, although he is having the time of his life, as are all the little Links."[56]

The Cambridge summer was followed by a move during the academic year to Oxford. Beginning in October 1958, the family lived at a rented house at 30 Blandford Ave., in the northern part of Oxford, off the road that went to Woodstock and eventually became the A44 highway. The house, by English standards, was modern, constructed in 1957 with central heating, which was unusual for England in the 1950s.[57] Arthur commented to Ray Billington that this was a "house that will make you old Oxonians drool with envy" and was "elegant even by the best American standards." In addition to the heat, there was an automatic washing machine, a large refrigerator, and a large garden maintained by a gardener.[58] The children enjoyed a range of activities. Jimmy and Stanley became active horseback riders, and both began a long interest in equestrianism. When Dick Leopold heard about Jimmy's new interest, he wanted to know more details. "What is this about Jimmy riding? Horseback or ti-gers? There cannot be wild west shows in Cambridge."[59]

All four Link children attended English schools in Oxford. About a quarter mile from our house, my sister and I attended the Greycotes School on North Banbury Road, where boys and girls wore gray uniforms and gray socks. Jimmy went to Crescent School, an elementary school in Oxford. Stanley attended Magdalen College School, a boys' preparatory school that was founded in 1480 and was attached to Oxford's Magdalen College. Every day he rode a double-decker bus to school on his own for thruppence, half—half fare because he was a student. At four years old, I quickly acquired English ways; in December 1958, Arthur noted that "lit-tle Billy is acquiring very much of an English accent—he more than any of the others."[60]

As was true of all holders of the Harmsworth Professorship, Arthur was based at Queens College, founded in 1341. Arthur had few academic responsibilities, aside from delivering public lectures twice a week for the first seven weeks during the fall of 1958, followed by seven weeks in the spring. Arthur had plenty of time to work in foreign archives, including the British Foreign Office records, and he made contacts with German scholars when he gave a lecture on Wilson and American intervention in World War I at Cologne in December 1958. Most of Arthur's year was spent working with his usual ferocity; he wrote in December that "I have gotten a great deal more work done here than I ever could have accom-plished at home." During the year in England, Arthur wrote the third vol-ume of his Wilson biography, *Wilson: The Struggle for Neutrality*, which took Wilson's life up to 1915, was published in 1960, and won the presti-gious Bancroft Prize in American history. By late November 1958, Arthur had completed a handwritten pencil draft. At the same time, he indulged in the ancient traditions of Queens College. He frequently ate lunch and dinners at High Table, and faculty and administrators regularly enter-tained Margaret and him. Arthur achieved some fame by singing the "Boar's Head" carol in the annual Christmas processional at Queens. At Oxford, the start of the Christmas season was marked by a large feast that involved a faculty member singing this carol, which recounted the sacrifice of the boar and the presentation of its head. Arthur became the first American to perform this duty; my mother overheard a random comment that "some American scientist" would be the singer.[61]

The year abroad concluded with a summer in Bavaria. There, we resided in a pension that was operated by Frau Lieberman, the former mistress of Ludwig Thoma (1867–1921), a minor regional Bavarian author. Located near Tegernsee and south of Munich in the Bavarian Alps, the pension offered a beautiful locale. In the summer of 1959, while in Bavaria, Arthur and Margaret took numerous side trips with Stanley and Jimmy, and left Peggy and me behind in the care of Ortrun in the Ludwig-Thoma-Haus. Ortrun organized numerous excursions while my parents were gone: hiking and berry picking, and she taught all of us how to knit. All four of us wore *lederhosen*, the leather shorts that serve as the Bavarian national uniform. After one hike, we stopped for a drink out of a well. When my turn came, I tumbled into the well, but Ortrun caught me on my way down.

Arthur described the year in Oxford, in a letter to John Hope, as "proceeding in a very wonderful and diverse way for us." Oxford, he declared, "must be the most exciting and stimulating place in the world in which to live." People there had overwhelmed him with hospitality; he had met "scores of interesting people." But he had worked hard during the year, in his capacity as Harmsworth Professor and in writing the third volume of the Wilson biography. "At this point," he wrote, "I feel pretty well worn out intellectually."[62]

While the Links were in England, Dick Leopold worried about the prospect of losing Arthur, though little was mentioned in their ample correspondence during 1958–59. When Arthur and Margaret prepared to leave for England in June 1958, he wrote hopefully: "As you move about in distant lands and in novel surroundings, do not forget old friends at home. We shall be waiting for you fourteen months from now; I personally have not yet abandoned the hope that your return then will mark the resumption, not the incipient end, of the close relationship and collaboration that has made my first decade in Evanston so delightful and so profitable."[63]

For the entire year in England, Arthur had maintained a long-distance correspondence with Fosdick and other Wilson Foundation officials to set up the Papers of Woodrow Wilson project. Fosdick and Arthur agreed that the Harmsworth appointment provided a year's respite in which they could make concrete plans. "All of us had a feeling," Fosdick wrote in February 1958, "that your appointment as Harmsworth professor at

Oxford was, from our point of view, a happy one, because it afforded ample opportunity to shape the project in a way that would minimize any inconvenience."[64] The 1958–59 year provided Fosdick time to raise funds. He and others such as Heckscher sought to amass a war chest of about $1 million to finance the papers project. By May 1959, Fosdick had raised nearly $400,000, including $150,000 from the Rockefeller Foundation and $175,000 from the Ford Foundation.[65] In March 1958, Arthur recruited John Wells Davidson, a Tennessean who had edited Wilson's speeches from the 1912 presidential campaign, and Davidson set up an office in Study Room 128 in the Library of Congress Annex in Washington. Arthur described Davidson as "very competent," yet also as "slow and unimaginative," though he realized that Davidson anchored the project. Davidson moved to Washington and began the process of surveying the Wilson Papers.[66] In September 1959, the offices moved to 132 Third St. SE in Washington, and David W. Hirst, who had received a Ph.D. under Arthur at Northwestern, joined the staff as assistant editor. Davidson and Hirst, who hired a slew of temporary workers, pored through the Wilson Papers at the Library of Congress, along with seventy other collections there, and they conducted a national campaign to locate documents. By 1963, Davidson and Hirst had photocopied nineteen filing cabinets of documents, totaling 250,000 documents and 500,000 pages.[67]

Soon after Arthur returned to Northwestern, the pressure mounted for a decision: would he agree that the Wilson Papers should be located at Princeton, or would he remain in Evanston? Despite strong arguments advanced by Leopold, in alliance with Margaret, to remain at Evanston, Arthur became convinced, with near religious certitude, that it was his calling to edit the Wilson Papers, and that this could only be done properly in Princeton. There were other factors drawing Arthur back to Princeton. He had never fully accepted his departure, despite his acquired affection for Northwestern, and the prestige of the Princeton platform—and a larger department (composed of twenty-six faculty, rather than eleven at Northwestern) was appealing. Arthur's claim that Providence had driven him back to Princeton was more likely an expression of his inner desire to return to the scene of his defeat in 1949. He had to "prove to himself," Peggy said later, that he was acceptable at Princeton; and the "sore spot" regarding his departure in 1949 had stuck in his craw for eleven years. No matter how wonderful Northwestern was for him personally and professionally, it "was not an Ivy League school," with the accompanying recognition and status.[68]

In September 1959, not long after the return to Evanston, the decision was made to move to Princeton, and Arthur informed the Northwestern administration and his closest friends in the department. In part, Arthur delayed the decision because Margaret was unenthusiastic. But over the previous eighteen months, he was also awaiting better terms from Princeton. He wanted assurances that he would hold full faculty status, would teach on a regular basis, and could supervise graduate students. Arthur was also very concerned about housing in Princeton. "We simply cannot afford to bankrupt ourselves," he wrote, "by buying a house at Princeton prices."[69] This was "one of the hardest decisions that we have ever had to make," Arthur told Merle Curti in March 1960. "We could hardly bear to think of leaving our friends here," and the prospect of leaving the department was "almost intolerable." But the decision, he believed, was "inevitable."[70] He realized how important Northwestern had been as an academic home. "If I have come to some maturity as a scholar and teacher," he wrote the dean of the faculty, "then much of the credit for this miracle must go to Northwestern University. I shall always feel that I am an integral part of this institution, and I will leave a part of myself here when we go to Princeton."[71]

Arthur's professional impulse ran contrary to my mother's love for Evanston, the children's desire to remain in what had become their home, and the close friends and professional connections that they all enjoyed. The Links' departure from Northwestern was especially painful for Dick Leopold. Dick exuded imperiousness to graduate students and junior colleagues: the joke was that new graduate students joined the "I Hate Dick Leopold Club" when they entered the program. Grob recalled that Leopold convened class exactly on time, with military precision, and both his campus office and his downtown apartment (where he often held class) were meticulously organized and maintained. Grob came to understand that Leopold was deeply involved with students, and that they benefited from his methodical and thorough critiques.[72]

By the late 1950s, Arthur and Margaret had become Dick's closest friends. He and Arthur had partnered professionally in teaching the United States survey course, in working as allies in the Northwestern Department, and in coediting a major critical reader, *Problems in American*

History (which appeared in 1952). In 1956, when Arthur published the second biographical volume, *Wilson: The New Freedom*, he dedicated the book to Dick. They sat together at football games and were close confidants. Margaret was one of his dearest friends. Dick lived alone in an apartment in downtown Evanston, with no family life aside from that of his friends. He was a member of our family; all the children called him "Dick," and he enjoyed the status as a sort of uncle. Though he was completely professional, Leopold admitted that "it took the very greatest will power to discuss your problem objectively and without the intrusion of personal feelings and appeals." But he realized that Arthur should do "what is best for your family and your career," and "loyalty and affection for friends and other institutions must be a secondary consideration. . . . So there will be no appeal to you on the grounds of friendship and emotion."[73]

Once Arthur made the decision to return to Princeton in 1959, Leopold was more fully honest about his feelings in a letter written to Yale historian John Morton Blum. This was a "cruel blow to the university, to the department, and to me personally." The process of losing Arthur to Princeton was initiated by Leopold as part of the search for an editor for the Wilson Papers project; this "came about in an ironical way that few outsiders can appreciate." He was unable to "persuade Arthur that God was not calling him to the task." In the end, what Arthur perceived as the best interests of the Wilson Papers won out, along with skillful wooing this time by Strayer and Princeton president Robert Goheen. "We lost to the facts of geography and distance," Leopold concluded. Arthur preferred to remain at Northwestern, "but he believes, and he is probably right, that the job can be done more efficiently along the Atlantic seaboard."[74]

NORTH TO SOUTH

6

My family's move from Evanston to Princeton followed a long, circuitous path during the summer of 1960. Stanley and Jimmy spent these months at camp in the North Carolina mountains, while Peggy and I accompanied our parents on the cross-country trip that took us, in the old red station wagon, to Palo Alto, California, where Arthur had a summer appointment to teach at Stanford University. Joining us for the trip was historian Charlie Sellers, who saved money along the way by sleeping in the car while we stayed in cheap motels. Arthur had known Charlie for about a decade. A native of Charlotte, Sellers received his doctorate at UNC and, like Arthur, worked under Fletcher Green. Sellers's work was mostly about Jacksonian America; he wrote a multivolume biography of President James K. Polk. He joined the faculty at Princeton after Arthur left, and, in 1958, after Arthur endorsed his candidacy for a job at Berkeley, the Princeton history department refused to make a counteroffer. Charlie's fate at the hands of the Princeton department rang true for Arthur. He was "appalled" by Princeton's willingness to let Charlie go, he wrote to Sellers, "without the hardest kind of fight." Princeton's history department exhibited a "smugness and egotism of its collective entity."[1]

Although Charlie was only three years younger, Arthur and Charlie enjoyed a mentor/mentee relationship—Arthur described him as a "dear friend" in one letter, and their friendship rested on a common North Carolina heritage. Their correspondence indicated a rich friendship—rich enough for Charlie to advise Arthur in February 1958 to "let up a little" in his fanatical work habits. "Woodrow will wait," he advised, and "anyhow, he isn't worth killing yourself over."[2] When Sellers came to Berkeley, he joined the Congress of Racial Equality, and participated in Bay Area civil rights sit-ins. In July 1961, he was arrested in Jackson, Mississippi, when he joined the Freedom Rides. Subsequently, Charlie's radicalization over civil rights spilled over into participation in the 1964 Free Speech Movement at Berkeley.

Arthur was no such radical, and, unlike Margaret, he possessed confidence in the ability of the system to correct itself. Nonetheless, he held strong beliefs about civil liberties, religious toleration, and civil rights that were rooted in his experiences at UNC. In the 1960s, Arthur served as a vice president of the National Council of Churches, at precisely the time that it was attacked by conservatives for its liberal civil rights positions. In December 1964, Arthur wrote to the president of Abbott Laboratories on the pretext that Margaret was a shareholder. He had read in Arnold Foster and B. R. Epstein's *Danger on the Right* that Abbott contributed to the Church League of America, a right-wing organization that hunted "subversives" in American life. The Church League, Arthur wrote, was "one of the most reprehensible" organizations in the United States, and it "constantly slanders and misrepresents" the activities of the National Council. He demanded that Abbott change its investment policies.[3]

The camp where my brothers spent the summer of 1960 was located south of Hendersonville, North Carolina. Arthur had found it by asking friends, "What is the best summer camp in the United States?" The answer, apparently, was Camp Mondamin, in Tuxedo, North Carolina. It lasted nearly two months, a long separation for a family never apart for that long. My parents sorely missed their two eldest sons. The separation, Arthur wrote the boys in July, "has not been easy." "I am sure that we will all be glad to return to autumn and the beginning of a new life for us all together in Princeton," he added. The one good thing about their separation, he believed, was that it made "us realize how much we mean to one another."[4] The separation was especially hard on Jimmy. Frank Bell, who ran the camp and was known as "Chief," wrote in July that Jimmy's adjustment was "not a rapid and ready one." Jimmy did not "respond readily to new people, and places," and his social adaptability was "not yet highly developed." Still, Chief thought Jimmy's mind was "quite keen, and that it is, therefore, important not only that he be exposed to a community of this sort, but that he learn to adapt himself to it." Margaret's brother, John, and sister-in-law Marjorie visited Jimmy and Stanley and reported problems, even suggesting that Jimmy should leave camp. But Chief assured my parents that Marjorie had a "slightly exaggerated impression of his unhappiness." Jimmy was a "fine boy with a high intellectual potential, but converting him to an ardent extrovert is a business we have not yet achieved, nor are we at all sure we shall." Chief recounted how he took Jimmy on a ride on local mountain roads in his World War II–era Jeep—Chief was a notoriously fast driver—and he reportedly had a "grand time."[5] By late July, Chief reported that Jimmy had "settled in nicely."[6]

Stanley and Jimmy's experiences in camp exposed them both to southern culture. When Jimmy told my mother how much he enjoyed the camp food, she interpreted this as a result of the fact that it was southern food. "Probably the reason that you like it so well," she said, "is that you are used to my cooking the Southern way." Arthur, she added, "likes food best cooked the Southern way."[7] Stanley reported a different cultural encounter. In conversation with other boys at camp, he made a passing reference to his racially integrated school in Evanston. "Everyone immediately looked up and stared at me with disbelief," he wrote my parents. "I heard one boy say, 'Fool Yankys.'"[8] Arthur also had cultural experience with his southernness in California. Attending a Palo Alto dinner party in July, he described how Californians viewed the South. "You should have heard some of the things they said about the South! You would have thought they were talking about South Africa!" Arthur did not hold back, and he "made some people pretty mad by talking back, as I am inclined to do when irritated."[9]

In California, Peggy and I had the first opportunity to spend time alone together, the start of a close relationship that I have had with her ever since. My parents rented a house a few miles east of the Stanford campus, a single-level ranch house at 1088 Metro Circle. I was five years old, and my memories include the warm California sun (I complained in a letter to my brothers that "it's so hot that I get boiling"),[10] the Creamsicles that we ate at a day camp on campus, and the sound of planes preparing to land at nearby Moffett Field as I fell asleep. We returned across the country along the southern route, taking U.S. Highway 66 most of the way. Our destination was western North Carolina, where we would eventually pick up my brothers. We stayed with Chief at his guest lodge, arriving about August 19, 1960, after a six-day cross-country trip. My birthday, which had occurred a day earlier, on August 18, was celebrated on the road.

We then headed north to Princeton, to an older house that the university rented to my family at a subsidized price. During the year-long negotiations with Princeton, Arthur had insisted that he needed cheaper housing before he could afford to take the job. The university found an older residence that it could rent, at 26 Mercer Street, a few blocks west of campus. My parents remained in that house for fifteen years, and it was the house where I spent most of my childhood. Donated to the university by a trustee, the house was a combination of three houses: a two-story rear section that was an eighteenth-century farmhouse, a middle section built in the early nineteenth century; and a three-story front section constructed after the Civil War with a large bay window and a front porch. Toward Nassau Street, on the other side of 26 Mercer, was a house occupied by the families of Princeton medievalist Durant Robertson and, later, the English historian Lawrence Stone. Two doors away was Sheldon House, a large, early-nineteenth-century Greek Revival house, with pillars in front. Originally located in Northampton, Massachusetts, Sheldon House was transported by barge and wagon to Princeton after the Civil War. The Rev. George Sheldon, a Congregational minister, had inherited the house, but the terms of inheritance required him to live there. Sheldon wanted to be a Princeton resident, however, so he solved his problem by arranging for the house to be floated down the Connecticut River, across Long Island Sound, and through the Delaware and Raritan Canal to Princeton. Donated to the university in 1929, Sheldon House had fallen on hard times by the 1960s, and it was broken into apartments for unmarried faculty.

The backyard of the Mercer Street house led into the parking lot for the U-Store, the campus store that sold textbooks, books, clothing, records, and virtually everything else. Across the parking lot was University Place, which led directly into the university, which was no more than 200 yards behind the Mercer Street house. Down Mercer Street was a series of houses, including one occupied by Albert Einstein's daughter, and the Princeton Theological Seminary campus. My neighborhood friends and I used the seminary's lush grounds for pickup baseball and football games. One block away was Stockton Street, where Morven, the home of the Revolutionary leader and Declaration of Independence signer Richard Stockton, served as the executive mansion for the governor of New Jersey.

My brother Stan unhappily started Princeton High School in the fall of 1960. His adjustment proved the most difficult. Stan had left Princeton in 1949, when he was not yet three years old; Evanston was his home. One day in the fall of 1959, he recalled, Arthur had taken him to a Northwestern football game. How would Stan like to move to Princeton? Arthur had asked him as they walked out of the stadium toward home. In eighth grade, about ready to begin high school, Stan thought his father was joking. He answered unequivocally: he definitely did not want to move. Well, his father responded, that was what they were going to do. "My life as I know it is now over," Stanley melodramatically informed his mother. My mother was acutely aware of Stanley's unhappiness. In the summer of 1960, she wrote to him about Linda Waggoner, the daughter of a friend who had moved a year earlier from Evanston to Princeton. A year older than Stanley, Linda, according to Margaret, predicted that he would "really like the high school." Like him, she did not want to leave Evanston, "but now she wouldn't want to go back."[11]

The rest of us enjoyed Princeton, even if we found moving in as new inhabitants challenging. In an odd way, the community was more urban than Evanston. Working-class and African American neighborhoods were a part of the Princeton Borough, where we lived. Evanston, in contrast, was entirely suburban, and, for all of its tranquility, was sanitized of anything beyond middle-class white people; I don't recall seeing many black people as a young child. Moving to Princeton when I had just turned six, I attended local public schools from first grade through high school. Princeton schools were fully integrated, with about a fifth of the students African American. I remember my early days at Nassau Street School, an easy walk from Mercer Street, where my first friends were African Americans and where making friends seemed hard. Later, Jimmy, Peggy, and I attended Witherspoon Junior High School, which was constructed in 1922 and served as the segregated black high school until 1947. Thereafter, it served as a junior high school for Princeton Borough students until 1966, my seventh-grade year, when it was closed, subsequently becoming a nursing home and, more recently, condominiums. The old Witherspoon

School had a decidedly African American character: its principal, Mr. Waxwood, dated to the days of segregation. In order to get to school, we rode bikes through the historically black neighborhood in Princeton. When school ended, we went by a small and somewhat dank shop owned by an elderly black man, Mr. Ball, that offered an amazing array of candy.

The move back to Princeton fell hard on Margaret. Jane DeHart Mathews arrived at Princeton in 1962 when her husband, historian Don Mathews, joined the department as an untenured faculty member. Arthur, Don later recalled, "more or less adopted me" and mentored him professionally and academically.[12] Jane was finishing her dissertation at Duke University, and felt out of place in Princeton. Jane remembered Princeton as formal, cold, and unwelcoming, especially to women, as the traditions of a men's college persisted. At the inns and clubs of Princeton, women were excluded from some functions and even certain rooms. Jane remembered dinners at faculty homes in which, after the meal, men went to one room, women to another, for conversation. One of her first events at Princeton when she and Don arrived in the fall of 1962 was to attend a meeting of faculty wives held in the living room of the wife of Dean of the Faculty J. Douglas Brown. Introductions occurred as each woman was asked to identify her husband's name and rank, and to indicate the groups—bread making, reading, or other volunteer activities—in which they intended to participate. Incensed, Jane called Margaret and asked to meet with her privately. Margaret counseled Jane, and she acknowledged the gender hierarchy at Princeton. Jane and Margaret became fast friends. Over time, Margaret revealed her own attitudes about Princeton. Living in the South, she said, had not "really prepared her for Princeton." Margaret recalled that she found Chapel Hill "much freer in relation to gender."[13]

Later, when women began to become more a part of Princeton, Margaret made an effort to ease their ability to cope with the all-male culture. She took care not only to mentor young female faculty but also female graduate students as they arrived at Princeton during the onset of coeducation during the 1970s. Margaret "took on such a wide range of women to be supportive of," remembered one graduate student. If she had problems or worries, this graduate student felt free to call up Margaret, whom she called by her first name. She had a "really positive influence" in helping female graduate students learn how to deal with Princeton.[14]

Over time, my parents came to embrace Princeton. Being there energized them both. "We have long since settled in here," Arthur wrote in May 1961, "and are beginning to think that Princeton is about the most exciting place, except for Oxford, that we have ever known."[15] Unlike the Northwestern department, the Princeton history department was bigger, more self-consciously high-powered, and full of prima donnas—but not a place where Arthur and Margaret had their best and closest friends. As a faculty member, Arthur was, according to his colleague James McPherson, "in the Department but, for the most part, not of it." In Princeton, the department's medievalists and Europeanists had long dominated affairs. They looked down on the American historians, whom they considered second-best. Moreover, Arthur's type of history—presidential, political history—was regarded as old-fashioned in the face of the new wave of social history during the 1960s and 1970s. Still, Arthur remained involved in departmental affairs, and fellow faculty members remembered him as a good colleague. McPherson recalled that, although he "could be dogmatic at times, . . . he never tried to punish or undermine me if I disagreed with him, as I occasionally did, and we remained friendly." Yet McPherson reported that some of his colleagues "found [Arthur] more remote and less accessible than I did."[16]

Certainly, elements remained of the Old Princeton that Arthur had encountered in the 1940s. When Arthur returned from Northwestern, the history department remained entirely white and male; the first female member hired was Nancy Weiss, who arrived in 1969, the year that Princeton admitted female undergraduates. The department of the 1960s, remembered James McPherson, was "quite elitist," with an Old Guard led by Joe Strayer still in charge. The Old Guard was also "resistant or at least lukewarm about the winds of change moving universities toward diversity in race and gender among both students and faculty." As had been the case in the 1940s, junior faculty were "treated as indeed quite junior—not in a vicious but in a sort of patronizing way." But changes were coming to the department. Jerome Blum followed Strayer as chair in 1961. But especially important was the chairmanship of Lawrence Stone, who instituted more democratic procedures in departmental governance. Weiss remembered things as significantly more "inclusive" and "participatory" by the time she arrived.[17]

Arthur often took an interest in new faculty. Weiss remembered how, during the spring of 1970, Arthur worked closely with her in the teaching of the twentieth-century American history course. Arthur permitted her to deliver six lectures in anticipation of turning the course over to her—if she measured up to his expectations. Having Arthur observe her teaching in order to decide whether to give her the course was, she said, "a little intimidating." He liked her lectures, though he advised her to be a little more theatrical. Unlike his own experience in the 1940s, he believed that junior faculty should have their own courses. Moreover, he made an effort to mentor Weiss as a young faculty member, and he and my mother took a special interest in her. She remembered them both as among the "warmest, more hospitable" people in the department who went out of their way to make young faculty feel welcome. Nancy was often invited out to the Mercer Street house. McPherson remembered that, while socializing at Princeton was "segregated by rank and age," Arthur was one of the few senior faculty with whom he socialized frequently.[18]

After 1960, Arthur entered a new phase in his career. The third volume of the Wilson biography appeared in 1960, and two more volumes were published in 1964 and 1965. Arthur won the prestigious Bancroft Prize— awarded for the best book in U.S. history—twice for the second and third volumes. But after 1965 he stopped further work on the biography—volume 5 ended with American entry into World War I in April 1917—and devoted the rest of his career to the publication of the *Papers of Woodrow Wilson* (*PWW*). The project was among the best-funded such enterprises in the newly emerging world of modern documentary editing. An ample endowment from the Wilson Foundation and Raymond Fosdick's successful fund-raising made the project financially secure and—unique among documentary editing projects—independent of public funding. In addition, Arthur was able to hire two senior editors, John Wells Davidson and David W. Hirst, and several more assistant editors. Princeton provided space in Firestone Library. In addition, in January 1963 the Wilson Foundation decided to devote its full resources to the *PWW*. The foundation and its assets moved to Princeton University, with Pendleton Herring serving as president.[19]

John E. Little was a colonial historian, with a new Ph.D. from Princeton, in need of a job. In 1962, he began what he thought would be a temporary job with the Wilson Papers. Little remained for the next thirty years. He attributed its successful completion to several factors. The Wilson Foundation largesse meant that we "never lacked for anything that we really needed." That most of the corpus of the Wilson Papers was typed made transcription less time consuming. Most important of all was the editorial staff, especially Davidson, Hirst, and Little, and, above all, Arthur. Little described him as "the living embodiment of the Protestant Work Ethic." To know Arthur "at all was to realize from the outset that the Wilson project would indeed be completed within his working lifetime." "It simply had to be, and that was all there was to it." Arriving early and staying late, Arthur engaged in every part of the editorial process—selecting documents, writing notes, transcription, and reading proofs. Arthur was proficient in French and translated many of the documents from the Paris Peace Conference.[20]

Editing the Wilson Papers became an all-consuming enterprise, upon which Arthur focused all of his energies. Unlike most academics, he kept regular, nine-to-five hours at the library, and worked with feverish intensity. He drove his staff relentlessly. The drive and intensity bore fruit. The first volume of the *PWW* appeared in 1966, with several volumes appearing annually thereafter. By 1993, the last volume of sixty-nine volumes was published. Unique among documentary collections of this size, the Wilson project was finished after about thirty-two years of work. It represented a major accomplishment. As one historian concluded, the *PWW* "were almost universally recognized as the standard by which all such projects should be measured." As another assessment put it, "the Wilson series is one of the great scholarly achievements of this generation."[21]

As a presidential scholar, Arthur enjoyed unusual access to U.S. presidents. He enjoyed the celebrity thoroughly. On June 17, 1963, he was invited to a White House luncheon of presidential scholars, hosted by President John F. Kennedy. His family was thrilled. We had watched in some excitement in October 1960, during the presidential campaign, when Kennedy drove down Nassau Street in his campaign motorcade. During Arthur's luncheon at the White House, the entire family drove to stay with our grandparents in Shepherdstown and eagerly awaited Arthur's return. We were not disappointed. He returned to Shepherdstown describing how he sat next to Kennedy and talked about presidential history and the need to preserve presidential records. Mentioning that his children were bursting with excitement about the White House visit, Kennedy asked Arthur his children's names. The president took his placecard, and scribbled out: "For Peggy, Stanley, Billy, and Jimmy, Best wishes, John F. Kennedy."

Arthur never cared for Richard Nixon. During the 1950s, he despised Nixon's political tactics and his strident anticommunism. During the 1960 campaign against Kennedy, Arthur announced that we would move to England if Nixon won the election. After the Watergate crisis occurred, his premonitions about Nixon rang true. When the story of the Watergate cover-up broke and two of Nixon's top aides, Bob Haldeman and John Ehrlichman, resigned on April 30, 1973, Arthur was asked to provide a commentary on an NBC national broadcast, which I watched while in college in North Carolina. Arthur reviewed the history of Watergate and concluded that the degree of constitutional corruption was unprecedented. "History," he told the audience, "will not judge the president leniently." Arthur later supported impeachment, writing to his friend George McGovern that Nixon's had become "the most shameful administration in American history." This was so, he thought, because Nixon "simply has no ethical system." "Poor fellow, he seems unable to tell right from wrong."[22]

Arthur liked Jimmy Carter, though he had his doubts about his presidency. When comparisons were made between Woodrow Wilson and Jimmy Carter because both were driven by religious ideology, Arthur liked to say that if Wilson was a theology professor, Carter was a graduate student. In a piece that was published in the *Washington Post*, Arthur compared Wilson and Carter. Both were intelligent progressive Democrats, but after that the comparison fell off. Carter was a "managerial" problem-solver who lacked Wilson's erudition. Carter had little charisma and was "unable to communicate great ideas and to formulate great programs in language that will capture the hearts and inspire the minds of the people, as Wilson could." Wilson was a skilled rhetorician; Carter was a dull public speaker.[23]

Carter apparently was not offended. After his defeat by Ronald Reagan in the presidential election of November 1980, Carter sought out Arthur and other presidential scholars, visiting Princeton on March 17 and 18, 1981. He consulted with Arthur about his presidential papers and how he should organize his biographical materials. Carter wrote in his diary that Arthur advised him "not to read any more biographies or histories concerning Presidents," but to keep his "native, perhaps naive, inclinations intact." Carter was also on the lookout for a research assistant. Arthur recommended Steven Hochman, the longtime assistant of Jefferson biographer Dumas Malone. Hochman joined Carter, and has remained on his staff ever since.[24]

Arthur's final brush with presidential celebrity was an encounter with Ronald Reagan that occurred on Valentine's Day 1983. Senator Mark Hatfield of Oregon had organized a dinner at his Georgetown townhouse to encourage Reagan to consider planning for his historical legacy. Hatfield provided a birthday cake to celebrate the 124th anniversary of Oregon's statehood. Arthur attended with Theodore Roosevelt biographer Edmund Morris, Franklin Roosevelt biographer Frank Freidel, Hoover biographer George Nash, and Librarian of Congress Daniel Boorstin. My mother attended, as did Morris's wife, Sylvia; Freidel's wife, Madeleine; and Boorstin's wife, Ruth.[25] A significant outcome of the meeting was that Morris became Reagan's official biographer and was granted unrestricted access to his papers and to the White House. In November 1985, Morris signed a contract with Random House that provided him with a $3 million advance.[26]

Originally scheduled for publication in 1991, Morris's biography, *Dutch*, did not appear until 1999. The Georgetown dinner with Reagan featured prominently in the beginning of Morris's book. Arthur's "detestation of the Gipper was legendary in academe," said Morris, and "some of us had taken bets that Arthur would not show up." He described how Arthur met Reagan, who shook "his disapproving Democratic hand." Arthur "straightened and tried to smile—a mirthless iguana gape." Morris's point in using the semi-satirical anecdote was to illustrate how Reagan could irresistibly turn on the charm. Reagan's charm, Morris maintained, had converted Arthur, his most skeptical dinner companion, because he was "determined at all costs to captivate every person in the room."[27]

In reality, Arthur thought little of Reagan. He once reassured a friend during the summer of 1980 that there was no way that Reagan could win the presidential election that November. "This country will never elect a right-wing president," he announced with certainty. His memory of the Reagan dinner, and my mother's memory of the event, differed significantly from Morris's account. Writing an account for the record about ten days after the event, Arthur described how Reagan seemed to have little conception of the importance of his role in history. When Arthur told him how Wilson's private secretary used to save the contents of the president's wastebasket for posterity—documents, Arthur said, which were "monumentally important"—Reagan "looked startled at the idea that his wastebasket might be scavenged!" Arthur concluded that he was impressed by Reagan's "warmth, friendliness, and poise," along with a "lack of any ostentation."[28]

Still, Morris's account, while exaggerated, contained an element of truth: Arthur's love of celebrity prevailed, and he would not have missed a presidential dinner, no matter who the president. Afterward, I questioned why he would attend such an event. He replied that it was out of respect for the office. But I'm sure it was also out of excitement over participating in something important. In numerous conversations with me he expressed views about Reagan that remained basically unchanged. Indeed, he and Margaret left the meeting convinced that, mentally, Reagan wasn't entirely all there.[29]

At Princeton, Arthur attracted some of the best undergraduates. In 1964–65, he supervised Bill Bradley, then a spectacular basketball player and icon on the Princeton campus, who wrote a senior thesis—required of all Princeton students—about Harry Truman's 1940 senatorial campaign. Bradley became the subject of a profile by John McPhee, originally published by the *New Yorker* and then as a book entitled *A Sense of Where You Are*. Bradley used to receive loads of fan mail, as many as four dozen letters a week. He was a hero to millions of kids, and as a ten-year-old I remember the utter unbelievability of seeing him teaching Sunday school at Princeton's First Presbyterian Church or in having him over for Sunday dinner, which my parents did on several occasions. Arthur thought a great deal of him. Though Bradley was not at the top of his class, Arthur wrote in his letter of recommendation for the Rhodes Scholarship, he was "somewhat better than his record would indicate." Bradley's record would have been better "if he had not spent quite so much time in sports. . . . He is not brilliant in the way that a few students are, but he has plenty of intelligence and is extremely well disciplined and a steady and reliable worker." Describing him as a "young man of very deep religious convictions," he described his "only defect" as "excessive modesty."[30]

After Bradley won a Rhodes Scholarship before he graduated from Princeton in 1965, Arthur remained in regular contact. "I was lucky to have had you as my adviser," he wrote to Arthur soon after he arrived in

Oxford in October 1965, because of the "friendship that was kindled" and the "technical skill which you imparted" in writing in what Arthur described as his preference for the "simplest, clearest, most vigorous prose." He also appreciated Arthur as a "Christian sage in an age of indecision and moral rationalization."[31] As Bradley finished up his Rhodes, he contemplated his future. Writing to Arthur in October 1966, he considered law school. Bradley also faced the draft: this was the height of the Vietnam War, and Bradley's graduate school deferment was about to expire. One alternative that Bradley mentioned was the possibility of teaching two years at West Point while fulfilling his obligations.[32] Arthur advised him to "go ahead and get one's military service out of the way," and he saw West Point as a good opportunity. "I would certainly do everything that I could to nail down this arrangement."[33] Teaching at West Point didn't materialize, however, and Bradley continued to worry about his future.[34]

During the spring of 1967, the National Basketball Association's New York Knicks, who had drafted Bradley in 1965 and still possessed his rights, pursued him. Bradley was able to arrange a six-month stint in the Air Force, which, in essence, provided a way for him to avoid Vietnam service. Bradley came to my parents in Princeton sometime in April 1967 to discuss this move, and I remember Bradley and Arthur sitting together in the Mercer Street kitchen. Arthur had discouraged law school. If Bradley wanted a political career, the law provided no easy pathway. If he loved basketball, he should sign with the Knicks. In late April, Bradley signed a contract that would pay him over $100,000 annually, making him one of the best-paid players in the NBA. Bradley, who joined the Knicks in January 1968 after active duty in the Air Force, earned the nickname "Dollar Bill." From then on, I became a lifelong Knicks fan.[35]

Perhaps Arthur's most distinguished undergraduate was Steven Oxman, who was student body president, and, like Bradley, a Rhodes Scholar. Oxman, who later became an assistant secretary of state under Bill Clinton (he knew Clinton and became one of his inner circle, a so-called "Friend of Bill," while at Oxford), first met Arthur while he was an undergraduate major at the Woodrow Wilson School of Public Affairs at Princeton. He wanted to write a senior thesis under Arthur, but he had never met him before and never had a course with him. So he got up his nerve in the spring of 1966 and went to meet Arthur in his office in Firestone Library. Arthur was known as an "intimidating figure," "so substantive, so focused on thinking," someone "too high" for a "lowly undergraduate." Arthur welcomed him in immediately, "incredibly friendly," exuding warmth and a sense of humor, with his pipe in hand. Oxman thought to himself: "I sure wish I'd knocked on his door earlier." Looking up at the ceiling while thinking—a favorite habit—Arthur suggested a topic, a study of British reaction to Wilson's peace efforts prior to 1917. Arthur realized that British Foreign Office records were now opening up. Oxman, whose girlfriend was in England that summer, leapt at the opportunity to do research in London. Oxman ended up producing a high-quality one-hundred-page thesis, despite his procrastination (he turned in his only draft at the deadline). That "little conversation" led to Oxman's preoccupation with Wilson, and while a Rhodes Scholar, at Arthur's urging, he would write a doctoral dissertation on the same subject. Oxman remained one of Arthur's most loyal former students, though he never called him anything but "Dr. Link."[36]

During the 1960s, Arthur supervised three Princeton doctoral students; in the 1970s, five students; and during the 1980s, ten students. A number of them produced work on the Wilson era. Thomas Knock wrote a book about Wilson and the League of Nations; Danish scholar Nils Thorsen published what became one of the best intellectual histories of Wilson; and John Mulder wrote a classic work on Wilson's religious ideology. Not everyone worked on Wilson topics. Steven Ross, for example, produced a dissertation, and then a book, about meatpacking in nineteenth-century Cincinnati. He went on to become a distinguished historian of filmmaking and American culture at the University of Southern California. Catherine Clinton, who worked under Jim McPherson, considered Arthur a major influence. Arthur's emphasis on empiricism taught her that "you could go so deep into your subject that you thought they were there." His insistence on the careful use of evidence "demanded neutrality," though Clinton's impulses were different in writing women's history. Clinton considered Arthur a "paternalist" in his views toward women, and recalled that he believed women graduate students should "man up" and do the hard work of becoming historians.[37]

Clinton observed that Arthur was often quite "stern and dismissive" when he heard opposing views about Wilson.[38] Steve Ross, who wrote about labor history, remembered that students working on Wilson topics "found him a harsh taskmaster." Arthur was "so invested in Wilson, that it was difficult for his students to stray too far from the 'master.'" Ross was struck at first by the "ramrod upright position" in which Arthur held himself, and how he first seemed "quite an intimidating figure" in gradu-ate seminars.[39] Historian Andrew Bacevich, who took a seminar with Ar-thur and had him on his doctoral committee, also found Arthur intimi-dating. Arthur "modeled professionalism in everything he did," according to Bacevich, but "it was a model that seemed beyond the reach of mere mortals" because he "just knew so much, facts large and obscure, histori-ography recent and obsolete." And that graduate students were expected to meet that standard, Bacevich recalled, seemed impossible. Arthur's particular passion in teaching, as in everything else, was Woodrow Wil-son. Students had a sense that Arthur was "channeling Wilson himself—that Wilson's spirit was present in the seminar room." Although Bacev-ich observed that Arthur had an "excessively benign" view of Wilson, he greatly admired him as a scholar who "lived, breathed, and slept work," and whose "work ethic and powers of concentration were astonishing."[40]

Other grad students remembered Arthur the same way. Justus Doe-necke, who worked with Arthur in the 1960s, described him as "ex-tremely imposing" and as a person who was "very fair but did not suffer fools lightly," especially with regard to Wilson. He was known as "impos-ing but fair," and there was "great respect among the graduate students for Arthur Link." Students working with him were considered "lucky" because he always treated students "fairly."[41] Another of Arthur's gradu-ate students, foreign relations historian Ralph Levering, recalled taking two seminars with Arthur in 1966 and 1967. A UNC graduate and native North Carolinian, Levering came to Princeton with some rough edges. He recalled Arthur as generally kind and understanding. Still, Levering remembered a research seminar when another graduate student pro-posed an interpretation of Wilson and World War I that ran contrary to Arthur's view. When the student presented his research proposal, Arthur launched a tirade that left a pall over the room. Students realized that working in the Wilson era was dangerous unless one toed the line. Le-vering remembered that this was in stark contrast to every other aspect of Arthur's disposition, which was generous, kind, and accessible toward graduate students.[42]

While absorbed in child rearing, Margaret became active in Princeton affairs during the 1960s. She became active again in the lo-cal YWCA, and, in 1962, as chair of its Public-Affairs Committee, led an examination of open housing in Princeton. Since the mid-1950s, various church and voluntary organizations in Princeton had studied housing segregation in an interdenominational gathering, the Princeton Housing Group. Like most communities in the North, the town was strictly segregated, and the practice of real estate agents was to avoid showing black buyers housing in white neighborhoods. For many years, according to one account, Princeton "kept its Negro citizens confined within a ghetto-like area regardless of their educational or economic achievements." After the national YWCA endorsed integrated housing, the local Y made it a priority. Only two years after returning to Princeton, Margaret took on a high-visibility role.[43]

In October 1962, Margaret's YWCA Public-Affairs Committee began a town-wide campaign for open housing. Under a plan proposed by Margaret's committee, the Y served as a clearinghouse for complaints about housing discrimination, while it encouraged voluntary integration by real estate agents and sellers and urged churches and synagogues to encourage members to sign open-occupancy agreements. The committee obtained endorsements for open housing from Princeton University president Robert F. Goheen, Institute for Advanced Study director J. Robert Oppenheimer, and Princeton Theological Seminary president James McCord. The Y's open-housing campaign involved writing letters to real estate agents, door-to-door campaigning, and a public-relations effort through local newspapers. The open-housing campaign coincided with the onset of the civil rights struggle as a national drama in 1962–65. The Y's Public-Affairs Committee was integrated, but it also cooperated with the Princeton Association for Human Rights (PAHR), which was organized by Princeton African Americans to press for racial equality on issues of jobs, housing, and education. Margaret's involvement culminated with her participation in a televised panel discussion on CBS in New York in October 1964. The discussion, which was entitled "Power, Persons, and the Gospel," focused on efforts by church and synagogue groups against discrimination.

The open-housing campaign became Margaret's first foray into civil rights in Princeton. The town, and New Jersey generally, had a long history of subtle and open racial discrimination, and the public response to the efforts ranged from muted to open opposition. Although open housing became an accepted standard in Princeton by the mid-1960s, the experience was eye-opening for Margaret. There was, perhaps predictably, a great deal of foot dragging. She often told me that she believed that Princetonians were hypocritical in their assumption of superiority over white southerners about racial bigotry. Martin Luther King's March on Washington in August 1963 had an impact on her. A few months after, in the fall of 1963, she told a YWCA group about her experiences in working toward racial justice. Building Christian fellowship, she believed, meant "an active, growing relationship." Christians interested in social justice should "never assume that we have nothing to learn in the art of communicating with people, in the art of fellowship." Christians should "learn to listen, and not just to speak," and should never take for granted "that we are above prejudice against different races, creeds, cultures, and economic backgrounds." "We need to closely examine our own hearts and listen to what we think, not just listen to what we say."[44]

Margaret and Arthur were periodically separated by Arthur's travel to the archives, though that occurred much less frequently. Their only long separation occurred during the last three weeks of July 1964, when Arthur worked in Princeton while Margaret took the children to Montreat. Their weeks apart spawned a spate of daily letter writing that recalled the intense correspondence during the 1940s. Arthur frequently complained about his loneliness. A day after he rode the overnight train from Montreat to Princeton, he went to get a glass of sherry and brought two glasses out to the kitchen. That, he declared, "shows you how unreal it is not to have you here." The Princeton house was "dead and lonely . . . without the various noises of my dear ones."[45] His dinners were dreary, Arthur complained, featuring Swanson's TV dinners and frozen Chungking Chinese food. In another letter, Arthur reassured Margaret about his health—always a concern for her. "Just worry about my loneliness, which only an end of our separation can cure."[46] Arthur also took care to write to me (I was then ten years old) in order to assure me his "main trouble" was that "I miss you and Mother and the other children." Still, he chided me about my bad handwriting, suggesting that it would be a "wonderful thing" if Margaret or Peggy would give me "some lessons in handwriting. Yours is getting hard to read!"[47]

Margaret's letters were filled with descriptions of the activities of the Montreat summer—how my sister and I spent our days; visits and reunions with the Douglases in Charlotte; and housekeeping matters for the new cottage. On a Sunday afternoon, she described the "quiet calm of the Montreat Sabbath—shades of my childhood!"[48] These activities filled the time for Margaret, she wrote, "but [don't] keep me from missing you sorely." Jimmy, as usual, stirred the pot and, during a visit to Charlotte in mid-July, quarreled with Aunt Marjorie. Arthur assured Margaret, who was taking Jimmy's side, that it was "very hard to know how much or little Jimmy exaggerates such things, as he is very sensitive." "Remember that you have heard only one side of it, and that Jimmy unfortunately has a peculiar capacity to rub all sorts of people the wrong way."[49]

As always, much of the correspondence focused on books, public affairs, and politics. Margaret read Erich Maria Remarque's last novel, *The Night in Lisbon* (1962), and judged it one of "his weaker efforts." She far preferred John Updike's *The Centaur* (1963), which, she said, revealed him as a "tremendously fine craftsman and *literate* writer." His writing was "sheer poetry with an all-enveloping sexual theme."[50]

Arthur reported skeptically about the comments of Princeton constitutional scholar Alpheus Mason, who expressed "grave doubts" about the public-accommodations clause of the Civil Rights Act. "Before he knew it," Arthur noted, Mason was pronouncing "Negro" as "Nigra!"[51] Margaret kept Arthur updated about the Republican National Convention, which met in San Francisco July 13–16, 1964, and nominated conservative Barry M. Goldwater. Margaret complained that "I can't take too much and too many Republicans," and she wished "you were here for me to mutter to and [to] hear you mutter (among other things!)." Arthur sent back his own assessment, describing Goldwater's acceptance speech as "about the worst I have ever heard." Arthur predicted that Goldwater would run his campaign on "strident nationalism and disguised racism" and that the campaign would pit "humane liberalism" against "reaction and even evil."[52] When African Americans rioted in Harlem in July 1964, Arthur commented that this was "just what Goldwater needs at this point—it would really help his cause."[53] He feared that Goldwater was "apparently eager to profit from the backlash."[54]

Isolated in Montreat during the tumultuous summer of 1964, Margaret was eager to discuss current events. She sent Arthur a clipping about a black church in Elm City, North Carolina, about sixty miles east of Raleigh, where white and black Presbyterians fought off efforts to burn the church down.[55] Arthur, meanwhile, dispatched clippings from the *New York Times*, including news stories and columns from James Reston, along with a package of magazines that had arrived at the Princeton house. *Time* magazine, he noted, had reported the Goldwater campaign fairly, though it would be a "real test of their integrity whether they go all out for Goldwater." It was simply "too much to expect them to support a Democrat."[56]

For most of his childhood, my parents worried about Jimmy's intense sibling rivalry with Peggy, though they tried to protect her from his bullying. As the two younger children, Peggy and I faced a looming presence. Moody and unpredictable, Jimmy tyrannized his younger siblings. Growing into a dashing and handsome teenager with great personal charm, Jimmy found that the best teachers gravitated to him, spotting a rare talent. But, as he entered adolescence, Jimmy exhibited certain personality characteristics—a contrariness, a tendency to withdraw socially, and often manic behavior—that grew worse. Waking him up in the morning became a daily struggle for my parents, and getting him to high school provided regular excitement. These were all characteristics typical of teenagers, but my parents' anxieties were realized after Jimmy started his freshman year as a student at the University of North Carolina. In December 1968, late in his first semester there, Jimmy suffered a psychological breakdown and was hospitalized for a few months at Memorial Hospital in Chapel Hill.

Jimmy often expressed himself with great sensitivity and eloquence. His letters, written in a beautiful script, described his affection for his parents. "Please, please, know deep within my heart, that I love both of you very much," he wrote in August 1972. Although he admitted that he had been a "peevish child," he remembered "so much of what you gave me as a child." "I associate with you your teaching me the importance of the law; of living right and doing good," he told his father. He praised Arthur's "wisdom and teaching" and his ability to "show God's law in action." Margaret, he said, exuded "warmth and care" that was "deep within your heart and nature," along with a "warmth and strength of your full heart." Rarely modest, Jimmy told his parents how they had bequeathed him with a "brilliant and sensitive mind." Jimmy wrote poetry, some of it quite good. He promised his parents that he would be a "great and good poet," something that was "destiny and God's will." "No matter what hour this letter and these words greet you," Jimmy wrote, "let the message be true and stay lasting." "Rise; rise; and see the light beyond the dark at the end of the day."[57]

The late 1960s were a rather primitive period for the care of the mentally ill. Psychiatrists relied on therapy, sometimes even badly outdated Freudian therapy, to treat patients. In more severe cases, they used medication. The newly developed antipsychotic drug chlorpromazine (or thorazine) became one of the most popular in the phenothiazine category of drugs developed during the 1950s to treat the mentally ill population. The advent of phenothiazines made possible the deinstitutionalization movement—the closing of large state-run mental hospitals that had been used to warehouse the gravely mentally ill.

Jimmy, however, never responded well to thorazine. He complained about its side effects, which included restlessness and nervousness, and he took the medication reluctantly and erratically. After hospitalization in Chapel Hill, Jimmy moved to the Institute of Living, a long-term care facility in Hartford, Connecticut, where he spent about eighteen months in a mostly futile effort to cure him. The Institute of Living was constructed in 1823 as one of the earliest mental health centers in the United States. I remember visiting Jimmy on weekends, making the three-hour drive with my parents from Princeton, through New York City. Located on 35-acre grounds designed by Frederick Law Olmsted, the building stood in a beautiful location in central Hartford.

Jimmy reenrolled at UNC during the fall semester of 1971, yet he couldn't manage the demands of school. By the summer of 1972, he had moved back to Princeton, and his mental health dominated much of my parents' lives for the next two decades. His illness resulted in frequent stints back in the hospital, and, after 1972, he was hospitalized in Trenton State Hospital. Jimmy was kept usually only a few weeks at a time, enough to get him medicated. There were some instances in which Jimmy disappeared; he once went to Southern California on his own for a few months and led a homeless existence. Jimmy's situation fell especially hard on Margaret, who worried constantly about his welfare. Most of her emotional energy during her last twenty years in Princeton was devoted to Jimmy's psychological welfare and to Arthur's health problems.

Jimmy, who preferred in adulthood to be called "James," took a decided turn for the better with the advent of second-generation antipsychotic medication. Unlike the earlier phenothiazines, these drugs, known as atypical antipsychotics, managed his illness by blocking receptors in the brain's dopamine pathways. James underwent a regime of atypical antipsychotics in the late 1980s, and his response was nearly immediate. For the past twenty years, his life and mental health have improved significantly.

Among Arthur's most important and long-lasting friendships was his relationship with John Hope Franklin. "I hang my head in shame," Arthur wrote to John Hope in October 1959, "when I think how long it has been since I have written to you." Whenever he was in the New York area, Arthur sought time with John Hope (who was then teaching at Brooklyn College), Aurelia, and their son, Whit. When he visited in April 1957, he scolded John Hope: "For goodness sake, please do not drive all the way [to LaGuardia Airport] to meet me." But Arthur so appreciated staying with the Franklins "that I am willing even to put you to the trouble involved."[58] When Arthur worked on revising David Saville Muzzey's very traditional high school American history textbook, he turned to John Hope for advice. Muzzey's account of Reconstruction was retrograde; black people remained nearly completely absent. Muzzey's text had made African Americans "overlooked, ignored, or forgotten altogether," John Hope agreed. He sympathized with the plight of rewriting a book written from a point of view that "was entirely different" from theirs. Arthur wanted a text, he said, that "at the least, will not be insulting and offensive to Negroes, to say nothing of being inaccurate."[59]

Arthur and John Hope's friendship survived the years. When John Hope received an honorary degree from Princeton in 1972, the Franklins stayed at 26 Mercer. After a visit at the Franklin home in Durham, North Carolina, in the 1980s, Arthur declared that they were "such dear friends, and we love you very much."[60] Arthur wrote in 1978 that their bond was "based upon our love for each other as human beings, and nothing else. I can honestly say that I have never thought of you as anything but John Hope, and I know you can say the same about me."[61] Both men attended historical meetings faithfully; Arthur stopped when he retired in 1992, though John Hope continued attending as late as 2007, when he was ninety-two.

After my parents had passed away, James renewed his friendship with John Hope Franklin. James had always had a special relationship with John Hope. As a young boy, John Hope recalled, James developed a "strong feeling for me." At five or six years old, he identified John Hope as his best friend, and insisted when he visited that John Hope pay special attention to him. As John Hope entered his nineties, James began the practice of calling him every Sunday night to check in. When John Hope gave him copies of his books when James visited North Carolina in 2006, he inscribed them: "To my best friend."[62]

Arthur was supremely happy at Princeton, which was a place that, especially over time, revered him and his status as the preeminent Wilson biographer. But my parents' social contacts were largely oriented toward the community and especially the Nassau Presbyterian Church, located on the front side of the campus on Nassau Street. Both my parents were actively involved as elders and leaders, and their closest friends and contacts worshipped there.

Over time, Arthur had less and less directly to do with the history department. The 1970s witnessed divisions over hiring and political tensions. After giving up his lecture course, Arthur rarely taught undergraduates, and he focused on graduate students and the Wilson Papers. In the 1970s, he taught a seminar in which graduate students presented dissertation research, as well as a course on historical editing.[63] In 1980, after he turned down an offer to become the head of the Manuscripts Division at the Library of Congress, he gave up most of his teaching. Dan Rodgers, who came to the Princeton history department in 1980, remembered "a certain amount of tension" between Arthur and other senior figures in the department, though Rodgers was "too junior to know how much of that was real and if it was real where it might have come from." Arthur, by the 1980s, "was no longer playing an active part in appointments or faculty rebuilding, and everyone accepted the division of labor that kept him focused on the papers."[64] Others noticed that Arthur had less and less to do with departmental affairs. During his last decade at Princeton, according to colleague John Murrin, Arthur "had withdrawn almost completely into the Wilson Papers."[65] Another colleague, medievalist Bill Jordan, noted that, once Arthur gave up teaching, it became clear that he was no longer "as committed to being in the department as he was to working on the editing," and he "less and less attended faculty meetings."[66]

In the 1980s, Arthur became involved in a bitter conflict with Stanford political scientist Alexander George and his wife, Juliette. The Georges' *Woodrow Wilson and Colonel House: A Personality Study* (1956) argued that

Wilson's career should be understood as a product of his dysfunctional Freudian relationship with a dominant father and excessively dependent mother. As evidence, the Georges cited Wilson's difficulty in learning how to read; he could not read until age eleven. Woodrow Wilson, the Georges contended, possessed "a ruinously self-defeating refusal to compromise with his opponents on certain key issues that became emotionally charged for him." Wilson's inability to compromise—for example, during the political fight to ratify the Treaty of Versailles—thus reflected his childhood relationship with his father.[67]

Over the years, Arthur came to prefer a neurological rather than a psychological explanation of Wilson's behavior. Beginning with volume 9 of the *PWW*, when the editors identified Wilson as having had a stroke in May 1896, definitive references to strokes in 1906 and 1907 occurred frequently.[68] Increasingly, he interpreted Wilson's erratic behavior at crucial points in his life as the product of a neurological illness that culminated in a massive, debilitating stroke during the fall of 1919. Arthur's interest in Wilson's health paralleled his obsessions with his own health. Arthur enjoyed the company of physicians, and Wilson's medical history—and presidential medical history—became an abiding interest.

While the *PWW* editor, Arthur sponsored research by a retired neuropsychiatrist at Mount Sinai Hospital, Edwin A. Weinstein. Ed became a fixture in the *PWW*'s offices. In 1979, Ed sent his manuscript to me while I was a graduate student at the University of Virginia. I earned extra money by tracking down missing quotations and correcting his citations; Ed's propensity for mistakes kept me busy. In 1978, Arthur and Ed, along with clinical psychologist James Anderson, coauthored an article appearing in *Political Science Quarterly* (*PSQ*). The article sharply attacked *Woodrow Wilson and Colonel House* for its lack of research and misuse of evidence. Most importantly, the article criticized the Georges' failure to recognize the importance of how neurological disorders and cerebral vascular disease influenced Wilson's behavior during his most important crises.[69]

The long controversy that followed was a direct result of the *PSQ* article; Arthur and his collaborators had started a fight. Soon after the article was published, Arthur heard from the Georges. In threatening, legalistic correspondence, they requested a listing of all the evidence available about Wilson's medical history. Arthur responded cordially and helpfully, offering to provide copies of any materials in the *PWW* office. The

Georges wanted the complete documentary record, and they expected that Arthur should provide it. In addition, their letters suggested that Arthur might be withholding evidence, a suggestion he tried to dispel.[70] The Georges indicated that they would seek their own "competent medical expert" to evaluate the contentions in the *Political Science Quarterly* essay.[71] Arthur hosted Juliette when she came to visit Firestone Library in November 1980, providing her with full access to their files, free use of the photocopier, and office space. Later, Arthur's staff made numerous photocopies for the ever-needy Georges.[72]

The Georges' rejoinder appeared in pieces in the *Political Science Quarterly* (1982) and the *Journal of American History* (1984). The Georges included, in an appendix to the *PSQ* article, a medical evaluation by Michael F. Marmor, a Stanford University ophthalmologist, that disputed Weinstein's claims about Wilson's neurology. The Georges and Marmor contended that Wilson did not suffer from strokes prior to 1919. In the *New England Journal of Medicine* (1982) and *Science* (1983), Marmor questioned whether Wilson's 1906 illness, where he experienced severe pain in his right arm and a hemorrhage in the eye, constituted a stroke. Arthur was especially criticized for presenting the pre-1919 strokes as "fact" in thirty unequivocal references in his annotation of the *Papers of Woodrow Wilson*. While describing the *PWW* as a product of Arthur's "prodigious scholarship," the Georges questioned his willingness to publish, in editorial notes, "hypothesis" as "fact." Arthur's incorporation of a highly speculative hypothesis, they said, had "prejudiced the objectivity" of the documentary series.[73] The purported strokes, the Georges and their allies contended, were "highly questionable and certainly controversial on medical grounds." As a result, they argued, the "objectivity of the *Papers of Woodrow Wilson*" had become compromised because of this "serious editorial flaw."[74]

For a time, it appeared that Arthur and the Georges might find a middle ground. The Georges proposed a session at an academic conference in which the two views would be presented; Arthur suggested creating an independent commission of medical experts to evaluate Wilson's health. But the Georges really wanted a full retraction, a white flag of surrender. While writing that they were "truly eager to understand your views," they pressed Arthur further. Facing a back operation in 1982, he complained that he lacked the "strength to consider the matter further at this point."

Nonetheless, he said, "I am open to all scientific evidence—at least I hope that I am."[75]

Arthur's initial reaction was to ignore the Georges' attack: let people make up their own mind based on the evidence, he said. But the impending appearance of the Georges' 1984 critique in the *Journal of American History* required an answer. The journal editors asked Arthur to respond, and he composed a rejoinder in Montreat in August 1983. The charge that *PWW* had failed to maintain historical objectivity was wrong, Arthur asserted, because the original documentation was there, "'unvarnished,' plain for all to read." Editorial annotation fell into the category of secondary historical writing—and thus involved informed inference that all historians make.[76] The *PWW* editors were interested only in obtaining the truth about Wilson. Healthy scholarly dialogue should continue, but "let us carry on our dialogues without accusing one another of irresponsible scholarship and of deliberately distorting the historical record, primary and secondary."[77]

Marmor, the Georges' medical expert, was unrelenting. For several years after the publication of his *New England Journal* attack, Marmor wrote a series of letters to Arthur seeking to engage him in a "direct and frank dialog that will help us both to move closer to a valid understanding of Wilson, the man."[78] Arthur refused to engage him, though he wrote privately that he was sorely tempted.[79] Arthur became frustrated with Marmor, who was confrontational in his correspondence. In a letter that remained unsent, Arthur complained about Marmor's "rude" and "condescending" barrage of letters. "I have been amazed at your assumption that I am a schoolboy who needs lecturing on proper historical methods," and at Marmor's "inability to see the difference between documents and annotation." Arthur was offended at Marmor's attack on his "scholarly integrity and independence."[80]

The controversy over Wilson's medical history exposed a blind spot in Arthur's lifelong association with Wilson. Arthur had unquestionably become fascinated with his subject. Some of his critics often murmured that he had become worshipful, excessively so. And his sense of hyperbole—so much a part of Arthur's personality—made it easy for him to be misunderstood. "I've read a lot of history in my life," he once told an interviewer, "and I think that aside from St. Paul, Jesus, and the great religious prophets, Woodrow Wilson was the most admirable character

I've ever encountered in history." Wilson remained endlessly interesting to him. "Most of the Hitler and Stalin scholars I know," he declared, "are depressed people."[81]

The Georges correctly pointed out that no definitive evidence could ever explain Wilson's neurological history. No medical records about Wilson's health prior to 1919 survive. Arthur rested his assertions on informed speculation by Ed Weinstein, but Ed's conclusions remained highly speculative and were based on a reading of fragmentary evidence. Reviews of the *PWW* series generally acknowledge that the Georges had a point about whether it could be proven that strokes occurred prior to 1919.[82] The tendency to explain all of Wilson's major mistakes as Princeton University president and as president of the United States as a consequence of his neurological affliction tended to diminish the impact of personality and human error.[83] The medical model became a catch-all for Wilson's weaknesses, but, like most human beings, he made mistakes and had weaknesses.

Still, the Georges' assertions about the *PWW*'s integrity was ludicrous. Tom Knock later described these assertions as "nonsense."[84] Dan Carter made an important point: Arthur possessed such "great faith in factuality as a path to truth," but he "never once confused his own strongly held views with absolute truth."[85] "If there were transgressions," Wilson biographer John Cooper later said, they were "minor, compared to the achievement." Editors, as historians, are free to make inferences and advance explanation; that is their role. As long as all the documents are presented, readers would surely make up their own minds. The Georges' assault, as John Cooper later observed, reflected a reputation for "striking like adders."[86]

The controversy over Wilson's health eventually became a point of contention with Wilson Foundation president Penn Herring. At first, Herring was supportive. Annotation, he wrote Arthur in December 1982, was not "a final word but rather a useful guide to further amplification and enlarged understanding." But Herring was unenthusiastic about maintaining a controversy with Alexander George, a leading figure in political science—Herring's own academic field—and in this same letter he urged Arthur to indicate editorially that "varying viewpoints exist." Even more ominously, Herring asserted that the foundation "cannot take sides" and should stand for "free discussion."[87]

Arthur seemed to miss Herring's skittishness. Four years later, when

Arthur composed an extended note about Wilson's health in volume 58 of the *PWW*, Herring expressed concern to other foundation board members.[88] Arthur made no effort to placate Herring.[89] Indeed, in one of his final volumes, volume 58, Arthur asserted that Wilson was "long the victim of a dangerous cerebrovascular disease," and that this disease had "an important impact" on his public career and decision making. There was now "a general agreement on the etiology, nature, and consequences of Wilson's longtime hypertension and cerebrovascular disease."[90]

Cooper believes that a number of people associated with Arthur let him down. He was "really quite hurt" by the lack of support at the foundation. Cooper contends that Herring, for his part, never forgave Arthur for the controversy, and that it formed the basis of a breach between the two men. Cooper recalled that when he and colleague Charles Neu organized a festschrift conference in Arthur's honor at Princeton in 1989, the Wilson Foundation did not contribute a penny. Nor did Herring contribute to an event honoring his retirement three years later.[91]

There is little question that the Georges' controversy personally hurt Arthur, and he felt a lack of support not just at Princeton but also among his colleagues in the profession. Though he maintained a cordial tone in all correspondence with his adversaries, privately he was frustrated. In 1986, when another physician, Bert Park, published a book on presidential health that vindicated Arthur's position on Wilson's strokes, he gleefully wrote how Marmor's diagnosis was "wrong"; Park's book would make Marmor "look like an ignoramus."[92] Although not usually a bitter person, Arthur came to see scholars' positions on the controversy with the Georges as either supportive or adversarial. When University of South Carolina historian Kendrick Clements delivered a paper at the Association of Documentary Editing meeting in Williamsburg in 1991, Arthur privately complained that Clements was a "hypocrite" because he gave credence to the Georges' position. In addition, after Vanderbilt historian Dewey Grantham, an old friend of Arthur and fellow UNC graduate, published a review of the *PWW* that acknowledged the validity of the Georges' critique, Arthur responded, "I have my doubts about Dewey Grantham." Clements and Grantham, he wrote a friend, had both said that *PWW* was "a great achievement, but - but - but. And some of their comments are low blows, particularly on the health issue." He admitted, however, that "I may be paranoid about them."[93]

Despite these conflicts, Arthur remained deeply attached to Princeton, dedicated to the institution and appreciative of his long tenure there. That is to say, Arthur's later years in the profession in no sense turned him against the university. In part this reflected his own sense of himself. He believed that Princeton was his destiny, and that, as a scholar of Woodrow Wilson, there was no other place more fitting for him to teach. He realized certain tradeoffs teaching there, but he was more than willing to make the tradeoffs. Whatever his frustrations with the Wilson Foundation, those didn't generally translate to a negative attitude toward the university. Arthur would always remain a Princetonian, though he retained a strong identity that was attached to his southern roots. His relationship with Princeton thus exemplified the conflictive nature of his own life experience as a southerner.

In April 1992, my parents returned to North Carolina, becoming, once again, southerners. They moved to Bermuda Village, a retirement community west of Winston-Salem, where my brother Stan lives, and a forty-five-minute drive west of Greensboro, where I lived. In January 1992, just prior to the move, Arthur described Bermuda Village as "really posh."[94] "This is a truly beautiful place with marvelous facilities and amenities," he wrote in June 1992. He was now enjoying the "absence of a coercive regime and the freedom to spend more time with Margaret."[95]

My parents did not have long to enjoy their North Carolina retirement. In the mid-1990s, in their seventies and after a half century of marriage, they suffered a series of grievous blows. Only three years after retirement, in July 1995, Arthur was diagnosed with lung cancer and had a large part of one of his lungs removed. He had started smoking in his teens; by his twenties, he was a hopeless addict. Arthur drank heavily during his period of chronic pain; scotch provided self-medication. Drinking and alcoholism contributed to his general debilitation, along with tobacco. Smoking was one of Arthur's main pleasures in life, and all the attempts to quit were only halfhearted. The toll that the smoking took on his health was obvious. He often described himself as having "a little emphysema," but he had obvious difficulties breathing as he grew older. In August 1992, while spending a damp and cold month in Montreat, he developed bronchitis and suffered from a paralyzed vocal cord that resulted in him "very nearly strangling."[96] That August, he spent two weeks in a Winston-Salem hospital and required a tracheoscopy and a permanent trach apparatus to permit him to breathe. These were the results of smoking, as were frequent bronchial infections during the last decade of his life. After the lung cancer surgery, the doctors were evasive but not especially optimistic. His physical and mental decline occurred slowly over the next three years, and he never recovered.[97]

A more devastating setback was the sudden illness afflicting Margaret, the result of an intestinal blockage and recommended emergency surgery. My mother's health had always been precarious. In the fall of 1959, when I was five years old in Evanston, Illinois, she experienced, out of the blue, a burst ovarian cyst one night, and Arthur rushed her to the Evanston Hospital for an emergency hysterectomy. Beginning in 1965, she was diagnosed as suffering from angina, a condition she medicated with nitroglycerin. But when she experienced another bout of chest pains in 1983, an arteriogram revealed no heart disease whatsoever. Arthur ascribed this to a "miracle," but, in retrospect, her "recovery" reflected a serious misdiagnosis by Princeton doctors.

In 1986, Margaret was diagnosed with breast cancer, and doctors at Princeton Hospital performed a radical mastectomy. After the surgery, my sister happened to be in the hospital room with her when she noticed that the back of her gown was soaked in blood: my mother had hemorrhaged in an incident that was probably life-threatening. In this case, doctors had medicated her with blood-thinning medication, but they had not calibrated the dosage during the postsurgical recovery. This made her especially susceptible to hemorrhaging. Suffering from the loss of a considerable amount of blood, she took six months to recover. Peggy remembered visiting Margaret after her surgery and being struck by the fact that "she had no strength." The surgeon was shocked by the postsurgical turn of events: he had done hundreds of identical surgeries and never had anything like this occur.[98]

In the late 1980s and 1990s, Margaret was treated for a clotting problem in which she produced too many or sometimes too few platelets. Any kind of surgery posed unusual risks for her; there was no such thing as "routine surgery." For some inexplicable reason, in October 1995 her Winston-Salem physician did not put her on blood thinners after the intestinal surgery. Without blood-thinning medication, her body, after her surgery, rushed to produce platelets, but so much so that the clotting process led to further complications. About three days after her surgery, Margaret developed a clot in her intestine that led to thrombosis and a nearly lethal explosion of the intestine in her abdominal cavity. After emergency surgery in which she nearly died, my mother survived, but only with a series of subsequent complications that eventually killed her. Not too long after Mother's Day 1996, she died in a Winston-Salem hospital.

Arthur had had a long history of health problems, and frequent crises. In August 1955, he had suffered an allergic reaction to penicillin that he took for a chest infection. Margaret noted afterward that Arthur "doesn't go in for run-of-the-mill maladies."[99] The reaction was nearly lethal, and my Uncle John drove up to the North Carolina mountains and drove him back to Charlotte, where he spent a week in the hospital. In the fall of 1965, he experienced what started out as a gall bladder problem that then developed into pancreatitis. Arthur developed continuing stomach problems that sometimes, in the late evenings, developed into terrifying episodes in which he seemed to lose his ability to breathe. In the mid-1970s, he had a knee operation when he slipped off a ladder cleaning the gutters of his Princeton house.

Through all of these experiences, he never lost faith in hospitals and doctors. He always believed in the power of surgery and surgeons, and he confidently and optimistically predicted success. The joke in the family was that there wasn't anyone more ready to jump onto the operating table. He was delighted when my eldest brother, Stanley, decided to go to medical school and become a physician.

From middle age until the end of his life, my father's life was defined by a terrible struggle with back problems. In May 1964, Arthur had a major back operation after nearly three years of pain. In one of the earliest spinal fusions of that era, he went to the Neurological Institute in New York City and spent two weeks recovering on his stomach.[100] Although pain-free for the next eight years, beginning in 1972 he experienced the return of severe back problems that resulted in back operations in 1973, 1974, 1975, and 1983. He tried various nonsurgical options, such as the use of the synthetic corticosteroid drug prednisone. In May 1990, a neurosurgeon at Pennsylvania Medical College inserted a dorsal column implant that was operated by a battery installed in his abdomen. But the battery wore out within three years, and the pain returned. Another stimulator was installed in November 1993; it brought no pain relief. After 1995, the doctors were resigned to a program of narcotic pain medication, but that brought on its own set of problems.[101]

Arthur's chronic back pain meant that he required more and more care—something that eventually became draining on my mother. But her caregiver instincts were paramount. Her good friend Katie Aldridge later complained that she spent too much time "waiting on him." Katie wondered how Margaret dealt with the all-consuming experience of being with Arthur, how the dominating character of his personality didn't frustrate her. She was "an enabler," Katie said, though "we're all enablers." Occasionally, Margaret escaped and got "out on her own"—and did so eagerly. With Katie and other Princeton friends, she went on lunches, while she sometimes drove up to Flemington, New Jersey, to visit the ceramic factories.[102] My sister Peggy remembered one weekend that they spent in New York City while Arthur attended a conference at the Carter Center in Atlanta. But after Arthur returned, he blacked out and ended up on the kitchen floor. My mother rushed home to attend to him, ending their weekend in New York.

Arthur's constant chronic pain was increasingly relieved only by pain medication and scotch. Although this regime contributed to his debilitation, my mother's illness, and then her death on May 26, 1996, devastated him. Married for almost fifty-one years, they had fashioned a relationship of mutual dependency. Arthur's health problems were connected to that relationship: for many years, his health became a way of securing my mother's love and attracting her undivided attention. He was always eager to consult with doctors and had an unlimited faith in their abilities, even when that faith was misplaced. And my mother had a need to help as a caregiver, and she was unstinting in her willingness to give love by looking after his health. By 1995, when she was seventy-seven years old and he seventy-five, his chronic medical problems had finally taken a toll on them both.

My father lived on for nearly two years past Margaret's death, but most people realized that there was only part of him there without her in his life. My brother Stan took him on cruises to Europe, which he loved, even while his health was very poor. He planned more cruises as his way of charting an uncertain future. Stan also took him to the Metropolitan Opera in New York City to hear his beloved music, and he would hobble down the aisle to his matinee seats. In November 1997, when he received a terminal cancer diagnosis, he was probably not completely unhappy at the news. Arthur remained confident that he would go to a better place, that his body could not go on much further, and that he would receive heavy pain medication that would finally dull his constant pain. In late March, I visited him on a Saturday with my youngest daughter, Josie, then eight years old. As we left, Arthur widened his eyes, grasping Josie's hand as if to say good-bye one last time. A few days later, on March 26, 1998, he died in the middle of the night.

Three days later, I delivered a eulogy at his funeral. Two years before, I had been asked to speak about my mother at her funeral, and I had been simply unable to do it. Had I been able, I would have described Margaret as a person of intelligence, compassion, and human interest. Possessing wide capacity for being interested in everything and everyone—and an almost innate empathy for people—she was an acute people-watcher, a sympathetic and ironic observer of human beings. She lit up a room, but in her own way, and there was little in that room that escaped her gaze. She was a dyed-in-the-wool political progressive of the old school. But probably Margaret's most important characteristic was her sense of helping people in need. All four of her children looked to her for support, but she had a wider circle of people who depended on her. Probably the most important of these was her husband, and their relationship was founded on his neediness and her desire to help those in need.

I surprised myself by being able to speak at my father's funeral, held in a small Presbyterian church in Lewisville, North Carolina, that my parents had been attending. "Arthur Link should be remembered as a people person," I said.

> He truly liked people around him. He didn't enjoy solitude. He engaged individuals on their own terms, listening to what they knew and usually establishing some sort of connection. He enjoyed speaking to Nobel Prize winners, but he also appreciated gas station attendants and fruit stand owners. Although the level of his accomplishment often intimidated people who didn't know him, those who did know him marveled at his willingness to listen and learn, and to teach and tell. Despite his tremendous reservoir of knowledge, he could talk easily with anyone, and wherever he went this gregarious aura followed. He accepted humanity with a great sense of humor, and this sense of humor constantly informed his thinking and his conversation. . . .

Another of his basic qualities was optimistic and purposeful action. He believed in doing. He was a thinking person, but he also had an intuitive sense of how to do things, how to translate ideas into results, and to be around him was often to be swept up in his tide of optimism and activity. That optimism was rooted in his religious faith: Arthur Link was a person who lived and believed the Reformed faith. His God was not remote. His faith was not quiet and reserved. He did not easily acquiesce in things that he could change, and he believed he could change many things. Whenever he had the chance, he told people around him that he was a Christian, but he abhorred religious faith that was sanctimonious or self-serving, or that choked off thinking and doing. Question all you can, he said. God is creator, redeemer. The one God is a God of truth—wherever that truth may lead. This faith of doing rejected simple answers, and it informed his entire life.

NOTES

Abbreviations used in the notes

AMD	Anniebelle Munroe Douglas
ASL	Arthur S. Link
ASLP	Arthur S. Link Papers, Seeley G. Mudd Library, Princeton University
DCA	Davidson College Archives
DFP	Douglas Family Papers (in author's possession)
ECU	Joyner Library, East Carolina University Library
ELC	Elinor Link Cagan
JHF	John Hope Franklin
JHFP	John Hope Franklin Papers, Duke University Library
JMcDD	James McDowell Douglas
JMD	John Munroe Douglas
JPM	John Peter Munroe
JRF	Julius Rosenwald Fund Archives, Fisk University, Nashville
LFP	Link Family Papers (in author's possession)
MD	Margaret Douglas
MDL	Margaret Douglas Link
PUL	Seeley Mudd Library, Princeton University
PWW	*The Papers of Woodrow Wilson*
SHC	Southern Historical Collection, UNC–Chapel Hill Library
SOHP	Southern Oral History Program, Southern Historical Collection
WAL	William A. Link
WHS	Wisconsin Historical Society, Madison
WWF	Woodrow Wilson Foundation Archives, Princeton University

Prologue

1. Richard W. Leopold to Thomas D. Clark, January 11, 1960, ASLP, Box 65.
2. Dick Gilbert interview, March 31, 2009; Peggy Link-Weil interview, April 1, 2009. Unless otherwise stated, interviews were conducted by the author.
3. Link-Weil interview, April 1, 2009.
4. ASL to Gerry Grob, June 12, 1992, ASLP, Box 102.
5. Arthur S. Link, "Woodrow Wilson and His Presbyterian Influence," in *The Higher Realism of Woodrow Wilson and Other Essays* (Nashville: Vanderbilt University Press, 1971), 7.
6. www.aamh.org/about.asp.
7. Blan Aldridge interview, January 21, 2009.
8. ASL to MDL, July 26, 1964, LFP.
9. Gilbert interview, March 31, 2009.
10. Ibid.
11. Gilbert interview, April 1, 2009; Link-Weil interview, April 1, 2009.
12. Gilbert interview, March 31, 2009; Link-Weil interview, April 1, 2009.
13. Catherine Clinton interview, November 6, 2010.
14. ASL to MDL, June 25, 1946, LFP.

Chapter 1. Chapel Hill

1. George B. Tindall, "The Formative Years," in John Milton Cooper Jr. and Charles E. Neu, eds., *The Wilson Era: Essays in Honor of Arthur S. Link* (Arlington Heights, Ill.: Harlan Davidson, 1991), 13.
2. Ibid., 19; MD to ASL, April 24, 1944, LFP.
3. MD to her parents, August 19, 1942, LFP.
4. ASL to MD, March 5, 1943, LFP.
5. Bennett H. Wall interview, August 13, 1982, SOHP.
6. Wall interviews, August 11, 1981, August 13, 1982, SOHP; Fletcher M. Green, recommendation for ASL, 1942, JRF.
7. Jane Zimmerman to Fletcher Green, January 29, 1945, Fletcher M. Green Papers, SHC.
8. Isaac Copeland interview, August 12, 1981, SOHP.
9. Tindall, "The Formative Years," 17.
10. ASL to Joseph F. Steelman, July 28, 1944, Joseph F. and Lala Carr Steelman Papers, ECU, Box 1.
11. Howard K. Beale to Paul Mooney, June 5, 1936, Howard K. Beale Papers, WHS.
12. Beale to Albert Ray Newsome, March 7, 1944; Beale to Frank Porter Graham, September 12, 1945, Beale Papers.
13. Tindall, "The Formative Years," 19.
14. ASL to Steelman, July 28, 1944, Steelman Papers.
15. Ibid.
16. Beale to admissions committee, University of Chicago, February 18, 1941,

Beale Papers; ASL to Steelman, July 28, 1944, Steelman Papers; Tindall, "The Formative Years," 18.

17. Beale to Newsome, March 7, 1944, ASLP; Beale to ASL, December 29, 1942, Beale Papers; Wall interview, August 11, 1981; ASL to Steelman, February 22, 1946, Steelman Papers.

18. ASL to Steelman, June 26, 1944, Steelman Papers.

19. John Hope Franklin, *Mirror to America: The Autobiography of John Hope Franklin* (New York: Farrar, Straus, and Giroux, 2005), 132–33.

20. Beale to ASL, June 2, 1945, Beale Papers.

21. ASL to Beale, August 15, 1945, Beale Papers.

22. ASL to Steelman, March 20, 1947, Steelman Papers; Wall interview, August 9, 1983.

23. ASL to Green, July 10, 1942, Green Papers.

24. ASL to Green, August 17, September 21, October 15, 1942, Green Papers; ASL to Miss Eldridge, September 1, 1942; ASL to William Haygood, October 24, November 27, 1942, JRF; ASL to Steelman, January 19, 1944, January 27, 1948, Steelman Papers.

25. Helen Link to ASL, ca. February 1944, LFP.

26. Rheumatic fever "very treacherous," she wrote about John William (Helen Link to ASL, ca. January 1, 1945, LFP).

27. Helen Link to ASL, ca. February 1, 1944, LFP.

28. William Edward Eisenberg, *The Lutheran Church in Virginia, 1717–1962* (Roanoke: Trustees of the Virginia Synod, 1967), 509.

29. Helen Link to ASL, ca. April 1943, LFP.

30. ELC to ASL, April 1, 1943, LFP.

31. ELC interview, May 5, 1996.

32. ASL interview, February 1, 1997; Wall interview, August 13, 1982.

33. My subsequent account of the Douglases is based largely on the extensive family research conducted by my cousin Robert L. Douglas Jr. I am indebted to him for sharing this with me (see Robert L. Douglas Jr., "Douglas Family: A History," in author's possession).

34. MD to JMcDD, February 14, 1943, LFP.

35. Faculty resolution on the death of JMcDD, July 1951, DCA.

36. JMD interview, December 2, 2001. For an account of life in Davidson, see James B. Puckett, *Olin, Oskeegum & Gizmo: Growing Up in a Small Southern College Town, 1950–1970* (Davidson: Blackwell Ink, 2003).

37. JMD interview, September 15, 2001.

38. AMD to JMcDD, January 5, 1924, DFP, indicates that James attended a Sunday rally in Charlotte. On Presbyterian fundamentalism, see Willard B. Gatewood, *Preachers, Pedagogues & Politicians: The Evolution Controversy in North Carolina 1920–1927* (Chapel Hill: University of North Carolina Press, 1966).

39. JMcDD to AMD, December 25, 1919, LFP.

40. JPM to JMcDD, February 22, 1909; John M. Douglas interview, September 15, 2001.

41. AMD to MD, ca. May 1938, LFP; records of JPM's estate, DFP.

42. "Anna Belle Munroe Douglas, J. M. Douglas, and J. P. Munroe, January 1928," notes on real estate transaction, DFP; JMD interview, September 15, 2001.

43. "I hope sometime to build a house on this plan," Anniebelle noted on clipping from the *Woman's Home Companion* in 1924.

44. JMD interview, September 15, 2001.

45. Ibid.

46. ELC interview.

47. "Around Town," *Davidsonian*, May 16, 1934.

48. Walter Edward McNair, *Lest We Forget: An Account of Agnes Scott College* (Atlanta: Agnes Scott College, 1983), 78–81; *Agnes Scott College Bulletin, 1936–1937*, 16; *Agonistic*, October 7, 1936.

49. MDL to AMD, July 18, 1935, LFP.

50. See the registrar's records, Agnes Scott College.

51. "Town Tattle," *Davidsonian*, September 23, 1936.

52. The Agnes Scott student yearbook, *The Silhouette*, 1938, documents Margaret's activities. See, on antiwar activities, "College Has Anti-War Program," *Agonistic*, April 27, 1938.

53. *The Silhouette*, 1938; "Sociology Students Go to Copper Hill," *Agonistic*, October 27, 1937.

54. Louis Mazzari, *Southern Modernist: Arthur Raper from the New Deal to the Cold War* (Baton Rouge: Louisiana State University Press, 2006).

55. MD, report card, June 1938, LFP.

56. Appointment Committee records, March 1938, Agnes Scott College Archives.

57. JMcDD to MD, undated, LFP.

58. John Fairley to MD, May 27, 1938, LFP.

59. JMcDD to MD, ca. May 1938; AMD to MD, ca. May 1938, LFP.

60. MD to her parents, July 6, 1939, LFP.

61. ASL to MD, March 13, 1945, LFP.

62. ASL transcript, UNC archives. Regarding ASL's grades, Tindall erroneously states, "after the freshman year . . . the undergraduate record was all A's, except for a B in the required hygiene course." In fact, ASL received a C in Hygiene in his freshman year (Tindall, "The Formative Years," 13).

63. Tindall, "The Formative Years," 15; Truman Hobbs to WAL, December 16, 2008.

64. Junius Scales and Richard Nickson, *Cause at Heart: A Former Communist Remembers* (Athens: University of Georgia Press, 1987).

65. ASL to MD, August 3, 1944, LFP.

66. Olive Stone interview, August 13, 1975, SOHP.

67. Kay Richards Broschart, "Research in the Service of Society: Women at the Institute for Research in Social Science," *American Sociologist* 33 (Fall 2002): 92–106. See also Guy Benton Johnson and Guion Griffis Johnson, *Research in Service to Society: The First Fifty Years of the Institute for Research in Social Science at the University of North Carolina* (Chapel Hill: University of North Carolina Press, 1980).

68. MD to her father, August 19, 1942, LFP.

69. MD to her parents, August 19, 1942, LFP.

70. John William Link Jr. to ASL, January 13, 1942, LFP.

71. John William Link Jr. to ASL, February 18, 1942, LFP.

72. Wesley Bagby to ASL, May 5, 1945, ASLP, Box 2. Arthur would later admit that the "monumental events since we were roommates have brought us much closer together" (ASL to Bagby, April 15, 1993, ASLP, Box 102).

73. Bagby to ASL, June 10, 1943, ASLP, Box 2; ASL to Steelman, January 19, 1944, Steelman Papers.

74. ASL to Green, August 17, 1942, Green Papers; Lewis Williams to ASL, April 12, 1942, ASLP.

75. ASL to Haygood, October 24, 1942, January 20, 1943, JRF.

76. Helen Link to ASL, ca. April 1943; John W. Link to ASL, March 14, 1943, LFP.

77. Helen Link to ASL, ca. April 1943, LFP. Arthur's father also urged him to get an examination (John W. Link to ASL, April 19, 1943, LFP).

78. ASL to Beale, July 22, 1943, Beale Papers; ASL to Haygood, May 4, 1943, JRF.

79. Helen Link to ASL, ca. May 1, 1943, LFP.

Chapter 2. Charlotte

1. MD to ASL, April 1, 1943; MD to her parents, March 17, 1943; MD to Hunter Blakely, March 10, 1943; MD to ASL, March 14, 1943, LFP.

2. Student's Handbook, 1944–1945 (Charlotte: Student Government Association of Queens College, 1945), 3. On the history of Queens, see Mildred Morse McEwen, Queens College: Yesterday and Today (Charlotte: Queens College, 1980).

3. MD to ASL, July 30, 1943, LFP.

4. MD to ASL, March 23, 1945, LFP.

5. MD to ASL, November 16, 1943, January 28, 1944, LFP.

6. MD to ASL, January 19, 1945, LFP.

7. MD to ASL, January 28, February 12, 20, March 20, 1944, January 5, February 6, 1945, LFP.

8. MD to ASL, January 25, 1945, LFP.

9. MD to ASL, March 5, 1944, LFP.

10. MD to ASL, September 7, 1943, LFP.

11. MD to ASL, March 25, 1945, LFP. "Hurrah for your defense of love-making youth!" Arthur responded. "Boy, you all must have a lot of Miss Prisses at Queens to suspend a girl for courting in public" (ASL to MD, March 31, 1945, LFP).

12. MD to ASL, September 29, 1943, LFP.

13. MD to ASL, December 1, 1944, LFP.

14. MD to ASL, September 23, 1944, LFP.

15. "Now As You Seniors Graduate, Nothing's Certain but Uncertainty," Queens Blues, May 24, 1944.

16. Wall interview, August 9, 1983; James Patton to ASL, February 23, 1943, ASL.

17. ASL to Haygood, February 23, 1943; ASL to Mrs. William Haygood, November 3, 1943, JRF.

18. ASL to Steelman, August 31, 1943, Steelman Papers; ASL to Beale, May 17, 1943, Beale Papers.

19. ASL to Beale, May 17, 1943, Beale Papers.

20. Franklin, *Mirror to America*, chaps. 6–8.

21. John Hope Franklin interview, July 27, 1990, SOHP.

22. Tindall, "The Formative Years," 24.

23. ASL to Beale, May 17, 1943, Beale Papers; ASL to JRF, November 3, 1943, JRF. See also John Hope Franklin to ASL, November 24, 1944, ASLP, Box 6.

24. John Hope Franklin interview, July 22, 2008.

25. ASL to MD, December 31, 1944, LFP.

26. Franklin interview, July 22, 2008; Franklin to ASL, November 12, 1944, ASLP, Box 6.

27. ASL to Green, October 28, 1943, Green Papers.

28. ASL to MD, November 8, 1943; Helen Link to ASL, ca. October 1943, LFP.

29. ASL to Beale, July 22, 1943, Beale Papers; ASL to Green, October 28, 1943, Green Papers; ASL to Steelman, January 19, 1943, Steelman Papers.

30. ASL to Green, February 21, 1944, Green Papers; Patton to ASL, March 2, 1944, ASLP, Box 17.

31. Juanita Kreps interview, January 17, 1986, SOHP; "Kreps Is Found Wounded," *Durham Morning Herald*, June 30, 1979.

32. Carrington Gretter to ASL, February 25, 1944, ASLP, Box 6.

33. MD to ASL, March 14, 1943, LFP.

34. ASL to MD, March 5, 1943, LFP.

35. ASL to MD, March 14, 1945, LFP.

36. William McCleery, *Conversations on the Character of Princeton* (Princeton: Princeton University Press, 1986), 75.

37. Gilbert interview, April 1, 2009.

38. ASL to MDL, July 17, 1946, LFP.

39. ASL to MD, January 21, 1945, LFP.

40. ASL to MD, February 18, 1945, LFP.

41. ASL to MD, May 1, 1944, January 12, 1945, LFP.

42. MD to ASL, July 31, 1944, LFP.

43. MD to ASL, April 29, 1944, LFP.

44. ASL to MD, May 1, 1944, LFP.

45. MD to ASL, March 14, 1943, LFP.

46. MD to ASL, July 30, 1943, January 28, 1944, January 19, 1945, LFP.

47. MD to ASL, September 7, 1943, LFP.

48. ASL to MD, May 20, 1943, LFP. See also ASL to MD, July 21, 1943; MD to ASL, June 26, July 7, 1943, LFP.

49. MD to ASL, July 20, 1943, LFP.

50. MD to ASL, July 1, 20, 1943; ASL to MD, July 21, 1943, LFP.

51. MD to ASL, October 18, 1943, LFP.

52. MD to ASL, January 4, 11, 18, March 5, 1944, LFP.

53. ASL to MD, April 7, 1944, LFP.

54. ASL to MD, April 26, 1944, LFP.

55. MD to ASL, May 21, August 16, 1944, LFP.

56. MD to ASL, April 12, 1944, LFP.

57. MD to ASL, April 18, June 12, 1944, LFP.

58. MD to ASL, July 19, 1944, LFP.

59. MD to ASL, July 10, 1944, LFP.

60. MD to ASL, July 10, 18, 24, 31, 1944, LFP.

61. MD to ASL, July 10, 1944, LFP.

62. MD to ASL, February 3, 1945, LFP.

63. MD to ASL, August 16, 1944, LFP.

64. ASL to MD, May 1, July 27, August 3, 1944; Helen Link to ASL, ca. February 1944, LFP; ASL to Beale, August 4, 1944, Beale Papers; ASL to Steelman, July 28, August 23, 1944, Steelman Papers.

65. ASL to Carrington Gretter, April 4, 1944, ASLP, Box 6.

66. MD to ASL, July 5, 1944, LFP.

67. ASL to Steelman, August 31, 1943, Steelman Papers.

68. James Robert Carroll, *The Real Woodrow Wilson: An Interview with Arthur S. Link, Editor of the Wilson Papers* (Bennington, Vt.: Images from the Past, 2001), 3; ASL to Steelman, January 19, 1944, Steelman Papers; ASL to Green, September 13, October 28, November 3, 19, 1943, Green Papers.

69. ASL to Green, December 1, 1943, Green Papers.

70. ASL to Mrs. Haygood, November 3, December 6, 10, 1943, January 17, 1944; Haygood to ASL, November 15, 29, December 16, 1943, April 19, 1944, JRF; MD to ASL, April 12, 1944, LFP; ASL to Newsome, April 21, 1944, UNC History Department records, copy in ASLP, Box 82.

71. ASL to MD, January 7, 1944, LFP.

72. ASL to Beale, August 12, 1944, Beale Papers; ASL to Mrs. Haygood, May 31, 1944, JRF.

73. ASL to Mrs. Haygood, January 10, 1945, JRF.

74. ASL to Steelman, October 4, 1944, Steelman Papers; ASL to MD, October 17, 1944; MD to ASL, October 20, 1944, LFP.

75. ASL to MD, September 27, 1944, LFP.

76. ASL to MD, October 30, 1944, January 21, 1945, LFP.

77. ASL to Steelman, November 8, 1944, Steelman Papers.

78. MD to ASL, October 31, 1944, LFP.

79. ASL to MD, November 8, 1944, LFP.

80. ASL to MD, November 18, 1944, LFP.

81. Carroll, *The Real Woodrow Wilson*, 4; MD to ASL, January 28, 1945, LFP.

82. MD to ASL, November 20, 1944, LFP.

83. ASL to Green, January 10, 1945, Green Papers; ASL to MD, April 20, 1944, January 8, 9, 1945, LFP.

84. ASL to MD, January 11, 1945, LFP.

85. MD to ASL, February 7, 1945, LFP.

86. MD to ASL, February 15, 1945, LFP.

87. MD to ASL, October 18, 1943, LFP.

88. MD to ASL, April 29, 1944, LFP.

89. MD to ASL, November 8, 1944, LFP.

90. MD to ASL, March 1, 1945, LFP.

91. MD to ASL, May 24, 1944, LFP.

92. MD to ASL, September 30, 1944, LFP.

93. MD to ASL, July 31, 1944, LFP.

94. ASL to MD, July 27, 1944, LFP.

95. MD to ASL, October 22, 1944, LFP.

96. MD to ASL, October 31, 1944, LFP.

97. MD to ASL, March 9, 1945, LFP.

98. MD to ASL, March 5, September 23, 1944, LFP.

99. MD to ASL, January 11, 1945, LFP.

100. MD to ASL, November 15, December 8, 1944, LFP.

101. MD to ASL, December 4, 1944, LFP.

102. MD to ASL, November 21, 1944; ASL to MD, November 24, 1944, LFP.

103. ASL to MD, December 7, 1944, LFP.

104. ASL to MD, August 4, 1944, LFP.

105. Beale to ASL, November 18, 1945; ASL to Beale, December 1, 1945, Beale Papers; MD to ASL, December 4, 1944, LFP. The furor surrounding Jones is described more fully in his papers (see Jones, "The Christian Church and Race," July 18, 1944, Charles M. Jones Papers, SHC).

106. "College Withdraws Job Offer to a Jew, Touching Off Furor," *New York Times*, May 1, 1977.

107. ASL to MD, January 16, 1945, LFP.

108. ASL to Steelman, January 27, 1948, Steelman Papers.

109. ASL to MD, May 22, 1944, LFP.

110. ASL to MD, November 12, 1944, LFP.

111. ASL to MD, March 12, 1945, LFP. Arthur may have been influenced by historian Francis Simkins's opinion of the book. Simkins declared that Fast was a "bad psychologist" whose account missed the "half tones" of the Reconstruction-era South (Simkins to ASL, November 5, 1944, ASLP, Box 32).

112. MD to ASL, March 4, 15, 16, 1945; ASL to MD, March 19, 1945, LFP.

113. MD to ASL, June 5, 1944, LFP.

114. ASL to MD, May 27, 1944, LFP.

115. October 19, 1944, LFP; ASL to Steelman, April 11, 1945, Steelman Papers.

116. ASL to MD, November 2, 1944, LFP.

117. ASL to MD, February 5, 23, April 14, 1945, LFP.

118. ASL to Steelman, April 11, 1945, Steelman Papers.

Chapter 3. New York

1. ASL to Steelman, April 15, 1945, Steelman Papers.

2. ASL to MD, July 27, 1944, LFP; ASL to Steelman, January 19, 1944, Steelman Papers.

3. ASL to MD, September 28, 1944, LFP.

4. ASL to MD, November 12, 1944, LFP.

5. ASL to MD, October 30, 1944, LFP.

6. MD to ASL, June 26, 1943, LFP.

7. MD to ASL, May 21, 24, 1944, LFP.

8. MD to ASL, July 24, 1944, LFP.

9. MD to ASL, July 31, 1944, LFP.

10. MD to ASL, September 26, 1944, LFP.

11. MD to ASL, October 10, 1944, LFP.

12. MD to ASL, October 12, 1944, LFP.

13. ASL to MD, October 30, 1944, LFP.

14. ASL to MD, November 8, 1944, LFP.

15. MD to ASL, September 30, 1944, LFP.

16. MD to ASL, October 30, November 8, 9, 1944, LFP.

17. ASL to MD, March 16, 1945, LFP.

18. ASL to Steelman, November 8, 1944, LFP.

19. ASL to MD, January 31, 1945, LFP.

20. ASL to MD, November 29, 1944, LFP.

21. ASL to MD, January 11, 14, 1945, LFP.

22. ASL to MD, January 24, 1945, LFP.

23. ASL to MD, February 1, 1945, LFP.

24. ASL to Steelman, November 8, 1944, Steelman Papers; ASL to MD, January 28, 1945, LFP.

25. ASL to MD, January 19, 1945, LFP.

26. ASL to MD, January 20, 1945, LFP.

27. ASL to MD, March 3, 1945, LFP.

28. ASL to MD, February 4, 1945, LFP. For another Sunday like this, see ASL to MD, January 29, 1945, LFP.

29. ASL to Steelman, December 5, 1944, Steelman Papers; ASL to MD, December 11, 1944, LFP; ASL to Newsome, December 11, 1944, UNC History Department records, copy in ASLP, Box 82.

30. ASL to MD, January 26, 1945, LFP.

31. ASL to MD, January 27, 1945, LFP.

32. ASL to MD, February 3, 1945, LFP.

33. ASL to MD, February 8, 13, 24, March 1, 7, 9, 17, 22, 28, 29, 1945, LFP; ASL to Steelman, December 5, 1944, Steelman Papers.

34. ASL to Beale, May 28, 1945, Beale Papers.

35. MD to ASL, September 27, 1944, LFP.

36. ASL to MD, November 29, 1944, LFP.

37. ASL to MD, November 12, 1944, LFP.

38. MD to ASL, December 1, 1944, LFP.

39. ASL to MD, December 11, 1944; MD to ASL, December 15, 1944, LFP.

40. In MD to ASL, January 28, 1945, Margaret described Christmas as like a "beautiful spring day."

41. MD to ASL, January 1, 1945, LFP.

42. MD to ASL, January 15, 1945, LFP.

43. MD to ASL, January 4, 1945, LFP.

44. ASL to Steelman, January 10, 1945, Steelman Papers.

45. ASL to Green, January 10, 1945, Green Papers.

46. ASL to MD, December 31, 1944, LFP.

47. ASL to MD, January 10, 1945, LFP.

48. John W. Link to ASL, January 28, 1945, LFP.

49. MD to ASL, January 15, 1945, LFP.

50. MD to ASL, January 26, 1945, LFP.

51. ASL to MD, February 3, 1945, LFP.

52. MD to ASL, January 8, 1945, LFP.

53. ASL to MD, January 25, 1945, LFP.

54. ASL to MD, January 29, 1945, LFP.

55. MD to ASL, February 13, 1945, LFP.

56. ASL to MD, March 1, 1945, LFP.

57. ASL to MD, March 9, 1945, LFP.

58. MD to ASL, February 8, 1945, LFP.

59. MD to ASL, January 8, 27, 1945, LFP.

60. ASL to MD, January 16, February 24, 1945; MD to ASL, February 13, March 1, 1945, LFP. "I will have the hairpins out of the way so they won't bother you, my sweet, when next I see you!" Margaret wrote (MD to ASL, January 18, 1945, LFP). "I heard that your new hair-do is very becoming, honey," Arthur later wrote. "I am anxious to see it and you" (ASL to MD, February 2, 1945, LFP).

61. ASL to Haygood, January 10, 1945, JRF.

62. ASL to MD, January 8, 1945, LFP.

63. ASL to MD, January 16, 1945, LFP.

64. Helen Link to ASL, ca. January 1945, LFP.

65. ASL to MD, January 22, February 2, 1945, LFP.

66. MD to ASL, January 23, 1945, LFP.

67. ASL to MD, January 25, 1945, LFP.

68. MD to ASL, January 29, 1945, LFP.

69. MD to ASL, February 2, 3, 1945, LFP.

70. John W. Link to ASL, January 5, 28, February 12, 1945, LFP.

71. ASL to MD, March 2, 1945, LFP; ASL to Steelman, April 11, 1945, Steelman Papers.

72. ASL to MD, March 16, 1945, LFP.

73. ASL to MD, March 17, 1945, LFP.

74. MD to ASL, February 6, 1945, LFP.

75. ASL to MD, February 9, 12, 1945, LFP.

76. MD to ASL, February 12, 1945, LFP.

77. MD to ASL, March 9, April 3, 1945, LFP.

78. MD to ASL, March 20, 1945, LFP.

79. ASL to MD, March 22, 1945, LFP.

80. MD to ASL, March 24, 1945, LFP.

81. ASL to Steelman, April 11, 1945, Steelman Papers.

82. ASL to MD, April 8, 1945; MD to ASL, April 9, 1945, LFP.

83. ASL to MD, January 14, February 12, 1945, LFP.

84. ASL to Katherine Brand, December 21, 1944, Katherine E. Brand Papers, Smith College Archives; ASL to Green, May 2, 1945, Green Papers; ASL to Beale, May 28, 1945, Beale Papers.

85. ASL to MD, January 12, 1945, LFP; ASL to Beale, December 14, 1944, Beale Papers; Emily Morrison to ASL, November 29, 1944, January 5, 26, 1945, ASLP, Box 14.

86. ASL to Steelman, April 15, 1945, Steelman Papers; ASL to Green, May 2, 1945, Green Papers.

87. Datus Smith Jr. to ASL, April 16, 20, May 7, 1945, ASLP, Box 21.

88. Smith to ASL, March 19, 1946, ASLP, Box 21.

89. Reader's report, in Smith to ASL, July 13, 1945, ASLP, Box 21.

90. ASL to MD, January 4, 15, 1945, LFP; Patton to ASL, February 14, 1945, ASLP, Box 17.

91. MD to ASL, January 30, 1945; ASL to MD, January 31, February 16, 1945, LFP.

92. ASL to Newsome, April 14, 1945, UNC History Department records, copy in ASLP, Box 82.

93. ASL to MD, January 26, 27, 30, 1945; ASL to MD, February 5, 7, 14, 16, 19, March 8, 20, 27, 1945, LFP.

94. MD to ASL, February 8, 1945, LFP.

95. ASL to MD, March 27, 1945, LFP.

96. ASL to MD, May 27, 1944, LFP.

97. ASL to MD, October 23, 1944, LFP.

98. ASL to Green, April 27, 1945, Green Papers.

99. Smith to ASL, April 20, 1945; Strayer to ASL, April 26, May 5, 1945, ASLP, Box 21; ASL to MD, April 27, 1945, LFP.

100. ASL to MD, May 4, 1945, LFP.

101. ASL to MD, May 11, 1945, LFP.

102. ASL to MD, May 15, 1945, LFP.

103. ASL to MD, May 13, 1945, LFP.

104. Strayer to ASL, May 15, 1945, ASLP, Box 21; ASL to MD, May 17, 22, 1945; MD to ASL, May 17, 1945, LFP; ASL to Steelman, May 17, 1945, Steelman Papers; Newsome to ASL, May 18, 1945, ASLP, Box 17.

Chapter 4. Princeton

1. MD to ASL, May 23, 1945, LFP.

2. MD to ASL, May 10, 12, 1945; ASL to MD, May 14, 1945, LFP.

3. ASL to Steelman, June 10, 1945, Steelman Papers; ASL to Beale, May 28, 1945, Beale Papers.

4. ASL to Steelman, June 10, 1945, Steelman Papers.

5. "Miss Margaret MacDowell Douglas Is Bride of Arthur Stanley Link," *Charlotte Observer*, June 3, 1945.

6. ASL to Steelman, June 10, 1945, Steelman Papers.

7. Ibid.

8. ASL to Beale, November 23, 1955, Beale Papers.

9. ASL to MD, May 17, 1945, LFP.

10. Patton to ASL, May 23, 1945, ASLP, Box 17.

11. Franklin interview, July 22, 2008; Franklin, *Mirror to America*, 132; Franklin to ASL, May 31, July 12, 1945, ASLP, Box 6.

12. ASL to MD, May 17, 1945, LFP; ASL to Green, June 28, 1945, Green Papers.

13. ASL to Steelman, July 23, 1945, Steelman Papers.

14. ASL to Steelman, September 18, 1945, Steelman Papers.

15. MDL to ASL, August 12, 1946, LFP.

16. MDL to ASL, October 16, 30, 1946, LFP.

17. MDL to her parents, October 31, 1946, LFP.

18. MDL to her parents, November 10, 14, 1946, LFP; ASL to Beale, December 4, 1946, Beale Papers.

19. MDL to her parents, November 10, 1946, LFP.

20. MDL to her parents, November 14, 1946, LFP.

21. Ibid.; John W. Link to MDL and ASL, April 13, 1947, LFP.

22. MDL to ASL, March 23, 1948, LFP.

23. MDL to her parents, November 14, 1946, LFP.

24. MDL to her parents, November 30, 1946, LFP.

25. MDL to ASL, July 30, 1948, LFP; Stan Link interview, November 24, 2008.

26. ASL to MDL, August 26, 1948, LFP.

27. ASL to MDL, August 1, 1948, LFP.

28. ASL to Steelman, July 7, 23, 1945, LFP.

29. ASL to Steelman, September 18, December 29, 1945, Steelman Papers; ASL to Beale, September 8, 16, October 19, December 26, 1945, Beale Papers.

30. ASL to Steelman, February 1, 1946, Steelman Papers.

31. ASL to Merle Curti, March 1, 1960, Merle Curti Papers, WHS.

32. ASL to John Hope Franklin, September 17, 1946, ASLP, Box 6.

33. ASL to MDL, July 30, 1946, LFP. John Milton Cooper Jr. calls *Woodrow Wilson and the Progressive Era* a "deft blending of narrative and analysis" (Cooper, "Arthur S. Link," in Robert Allen Rutland, *Clio's Favorites: Leading Historians of the United States, 1945–2000* [Columbia: University of Missouri Press, 2000], 113).

34. ASL to MDL, June 26, July 7, 10, 1946; MDL to ASL, July 8, 1946; Smith to ASL, July 17, 1946, LFP; ASL to Strayer, July 29, 1946; Strayer to ASL, July 31, 1946, ASLP, Box 21.

35. ASL to Beale, April 11, 1947, Beale Papers.

36. MDL to her parents, October 27, 1946, LFP.

37. MDL to her parents, December 9, 1945, LFP.

38. Helen Link to ASL, ca. July 1945, LFP.

39. Richard W. Leopold, "Arthur S. Link at Northwestern: The Maturing of a Scholar," in Cooper and Neu, *The Wilson Era*, 31–32.

40. Tindall, "The Formative Years," 27.

41. MDL to her parents, October 15, 1947, LFP.

42. Ibid.; MDL to ASL, July 18, 1946, LFP.

43. MDL to her parents, October 16, December 11, 1946; MDL to ASL, June 27, 1946, LFP.

44. ASL to MDL, July 1, 1947, LFP.

45. ASL to MDL, July 5, 1946, LFP.

46. ASL to MDL, July 18, 1946, LFP.

47. Clinton interview, November 6, 2010.

48. MDL to ASL, June 24, 1946, LFP.

49. MDL to ASL, July 17, 1946, LFP.

50. MDL to her parents, December 11, 1946, LFP.

51. MDL to her parents, January 8, 1947, LFP.

52. MDL to her parents, October 15, 1947, May 25, 31, 1948, LFP.

53. MDL to her parents, October 27, 31, 1946, January 8, 1947, LFP.

54. MDL to her parents, April 19, 1947; MDL to ASL, August 7, 1946; ASL to MDL, June 30, July 1, 1947, LFP.

55. Paul Robeson, *Here I Stand* (1958; Boston: Beacon, 1988), 10.

56. Jack Washington, *The Long Journey Home: A Bicentennial History of the Black Community of Princeton, New Jersey, 1776–1976* (Trenton, N.J.: Africa World Press, 2005).

57. Norman F. Cantor, *Inventing Norman Cantor: Confessions of a Medievalist* (Tempe: Arizona Center for Medieval and Renaissance Studies, 2002), 30.

58. ASL to Green, February 16, 1946, Green Papers. On Princeton, see James Axtell's *The Making of Princeton University: From Woodrow Wilson to the Present* (Princeton: Princeton University Press, 2006); and William Palmer, *From Gentleman's Club to Professional Body: The Evolution of the History Department in the United States, 1940-1980* (New York: Booksurge, 2008), chap. 4. On Strayer, see William Chester Jordan and Teofilo F. Ruiz, "Joseph Reese Strayer," in Patricia H. Marks, ed., *Luminaries: Princeton Faculty Remembered* (Princeton: Association of Princeton Graduate Alumni, 1996), 297–304. The quotation comes from Cooper, "Arthur S. Link," 120.

59. Cantor, *Inventing Norman Cantor*, 38.

60. MDL to her parents, May 1, October 27, 1946, LFP.

61. MDL to ASL, June 29, 1946, LFP.

62. MDL to ASL, July 9, 1946, LFP.

63. ASL to MDL, July 15, 1946; MDL to ASL, July 17, 1946, LFP.

64. ASL to Green, April 19, 1948, Green Papers.

65. ASL to MDL, July 19, 1946, LFP.

66. ASL to MDL, July 3, 1946, LFP.

67. MDL to her parents, October 22, 1946, LFP.

68. ASL to MDL, November 13, 1947, LFP.

69. ASL to MDL, July 31, 1948, LFP; ASL to JHF, July 5, 1950, JHFP; Franklin interview, July 22, 2008.

70. ASL to JHF, July 5, 1950, JHFP, Box 11.

71. ASL to JHF, November 16, 1956, JHFP, Box 25.

72. MDL to her parents, October 27, 1946, LFP; ASL to Franklin, October 28, 1946, ASLP, Box 6.

73. JHF to ASL, November 17, 1946, ASLP, Box 6; ASL to Beale, December 4, 1946, Beale Papers.

74. ASL, personnel file, Princeton University Archives.

75. JHF to ASL, May 23, 1947, ASLP, Box 6.

76. MDL to her parents, January 8, 1947, LFP.

77. Ibid.

78. ASL to MDL, January 2, 1948, LFP.

79. MDL to ASL, January 5, 1948, LFP.

80. ASL to Beale, January 14, 1948; Beale to ASL, January 22, 1948, Beale Papers.

81. ASL to Beale, February 9, 1948, Beale Papers; MDL to her parents, January 19, 22, 31, 1948, LFP; ASL to Green, April 19, 1948, Green Papers.

82. MDL to her parents, January 19, 1948, LFP.

83. Daniel J. Kevles, "Eric Frederick Goldman," *Luminaries*, 86–108.

84. ASL to Beale, August 15, 1945, Beale Papers.

85. MDL to ASL, August 15, 1946, LFP; Cantor, *Inventing Norman Cantor*, 38.

86. ASL to Beale, February 17, 1947, Beale Papers.

Chapter 5. Evanston

1. Leopold, "Link at Northwestern," 31; Steven J. Harper, *Straddling Worlds: The Jewish-American Journey of Professor Richard W. Leopold* (Evanston: Northwestern University Press, 2008), 115–17.

2. Gerald Grob interview, December 31, 2008.

3. Leopold, "Link at Northwestern," 32.

4. Harold Dodds to ASL, February 15, 1949, ASLP, Box 5.

5. MDL to her parents, ca. March 1, 1949; ASL to Green, March 24, 1949, LFP; Leopold, "Link at Northwestern," 32.

6. Ray Allen Billington to ASL, March 15, 1949, ASLP, Box 2.

7. Leopold, "Link at Northwestern," 32.

8. Leopold to ASL, March 26, 1949, ASLP, Box 12.

9. Stan Link interview, December 28, 2008.

10. Link-Weil interview, December 30, 2008.

11. ASL to Leopold, February 26, 1951, Northwestern University Archives, Box 65, mentioned the money woes.

12. ASL to Merle Curti, Curti Papers; Link-Weil interview, December 20, 2008.

13. ASL to Curti, October 24, 1951, Curti Papers.

14. George Simmons interview, December 18, 2008.

15. Grob interview.

16. ASL to Merle Curti, February 6, 1952, Curti Papers.

17. Grob interview.

18. ASL to William Aydelotte, November 3, 1952, ASLP, Box 65.

19. Kerry North, "Link Views McGovern as Friend, Pupil," *Daily Princetonian*, ca. October 1972, clipping in LFP.

20. George McGovern, *Grassroots: The Autobiography of George McGovern* (New York: Random House, 1977), 43, mentions that Arthur "imposed a work schedule on me that left no possibility for the kind of procrastination that has produced so many incomplete doctoral careers."

21. ASL to McGovern, July 28, 1989; McGovern to ASL, August 31, 1984, ASLP, Box 70; Tom Knock interview, December 4, 2010.

22. North, "Link Views McGovern as Friend, Pupil."

23. See ASL, draft announcement of a McGovern presidential candidacy, ca. August 1983, ASLP, Box 65. See also McGovern to ASL, August 11, 1983, ibid.

24. North, "Link Views McGovern as Friend, Pupil."

25. Adlai Stevenson to ASL, August 1, 1955, ASLP, Box 33.

26. ASL to Stevenson, January 25, 1956, ASLP, Box 33.

27. See ASL to Edward Mead Earle, October 8, 20, 1952; Earle to ASL, October 13, November 25, 1952, Edward Mead Earle Papers, PUL.

28. ASL to Billington, June 19, 1954, ASLP, Box 2.

29. ASL to Curti, November 20, 1954, Curti Papers.

30. ASL to JHF, September 1, 1957, JHFP, Box 25.

31. Strayer to ASL, February 7, 1955, ASLP, Box 21; Leopold, "Link at Northwestern," 36–37.

32. ASL to Harold Dodds, April 21, 1949, ASLP, Box 5.

33. ASL to Strayer, February 18, 1955; ASL to Franklin Scott, February 17, 1955, ASLP, Box 21. See Beale to ASL, April 26, 1955, in which he describes the decision to stay at Northwestern as a "happy choice and one that you will not regret" (Beale to ASL, April 26, 1955, Beale Papers).

34. Raymond B. Fosdick to August Heckscher, February 27, 1958, WWF, Box 26.

35. See ASL and Leopold to Edmund C. Gass, April 23, 1956, ASLP, Box 74 (copy from Richard W. Leopold Papers); David W. Hirst, who prepared a survey of Wilson materials for the foundation, made this estimate. Subsequently, Julian Boyd, editor of the Thomas Jefferson Papers at Princeton, estimated that a Wilson Papers project would result in more than one hundred volumes (*PWW* committee minutes, November 21, 1957, WWF, Box 28).

36. Heckscher, memorandum of meeting, April 15, 1957; report, May 3, 1957; Woodrow Wilson Foundation minutes, May 16, 1957, WWF, Box 7.

37. Fosdick to ASL, June 1, 1971, ASLP, Box 42.

38. Minutes of the committee on Woodrow Wilson Letters and Papers, October 24, 1957, WWF, Box 28.

39. Dexter Perkins to Fosdick, November 4, 1957, WWF, Box 28.

40. Minutes of the committee on Woodrow Wilson Letters and Papers, November 21, 1957, WWF, Box 28.

41. ASL to Fosdick, November 13, 1957, WWF, Box 28.

42. Fosdick to Heckscher, November 22, 1957, WWF, Box 28.

43. Fosdick, notes of conversations, January 23, 28, 1958, WWF, Box 28.

44. ASL to Fosdick, telegram, January 30, 1958; Fosdick to ASL, telegrams,

January 29 and 30, 1958; minutes of the committee on Woodrow Wilson Letters and Papers, February 20, 1958, WWF, Box 28; ASL to Fosdick, March 24, 1958, WWF, Box 26; *New York Times Book Review*, October 31, 1993.

45. Minutes of the committee on Woodrow Wilson Letters and Papers, November 21, 1957; Fosdick, notes of conversation with Robert F. Goheen, November 6, 1957, WWF, Box 28.

46. Fosdick to Boyce, February 21, 1958, WWF, Box 26.

47. Fosdick to Heckscher, February 27, 1958, WWF, Box 26.

48. ASL to Fosdick, March 4, 1958, WWF, Box 26.

49. Boyce to Fosdick, February 21, 1958, WWF, Box 26.

50. Grob interview; Link-Weil interview, December 30, 2008.

51. ASL to Leopold, July 9, 1958, ASLP, Box 12; ASL to Beale, July 4, 1958, Beale Papers.

52. ASL to Beale, July 4, 1958, Beale Papers.

53. ASL to Leopold, July 9, August 10, 1958, ASLP, Box 12.

54. Stan Link interview, December 28, 2008.

55. Ortrun Gauthier interview, January 9, 2009; Stan Link interview, December 28, 2008.

56. ASL to Leopold, August 10, 1958, ASLP, Box 12; Stan Link interview, December 28, 2008.

57. ASL to Billington, February 3, 1959, ASLP, Box 2.

58. ASL to Billington, October 1, 1958, ASLP, Box 2.

59. Leopold to ASL, August 1, 1958, ASLP, Box 12.

60. ASL to Franklin and Helen Scott, December 5, 1958, ASLP, Box 20.

61. Ibid.; Leopold, "Link at Northwestern," 43.

62. ASL to JHF, March 20, 1959, JHFP, Box 25.

63. Leopold to ASL, June 20, 1958, ASLP, Box 12.

64. Fosdick to ASL, February 28, 1958, WWF, Box 26.

65. Heckscher to ASL, May 4, 1959, WWF, Box 26.

66. ASL to Fosdick, March 12, April 2, 1958, WWF, Box 26.

67. *PWW*, 1: xiii–xiv.

68. Link-Weil interview, December 30, 2008.

69. ASL to Heckscher, May 8, 1959, WWF, Box 26.

70. ASL to Curti, March 1, 1960, Curti Papers.

71. Leopold, "Link at Northwestern," 39–46.

72. Grob interview.

73. *New York Times Book Review*, October 31, 1993.

74. Leopold, "Link at Northwestern," 46–47.

Chapter 6. North to South

1. ASL to Charles G. Sellers, February 5, 1958, ASLP, Box 32.

2. Ibid.; Sellers to ASL, February 1, 1958, ASLP, Box 32.

3. ASL to Abbott Laboratories, Inc., December 7, 1964. Arthur received a response admitting that Abbott had contributed but asserting that the company had no knowledge of the Church League's political activities (Franklin Gill to ASL, December 10, 1964, ASLP, Box 26).

4. ASL to Stanley and Jimmy, July 24, 1966, LFP.

5. Frank D. Bell to Marjorie Douglas, July 12, 1960, LFP.

6. Bell to ASL, July 25, 1960, LFP.

7. MDL to Jimmy and Stanley, July 12, 1960, LFP.

8. Stan Link to his family, June 28, 1960, LFP.

9. ASL to Stanley and Jimmy, July 24, 1960, LFP.

10. This was a letter that I dictated to my mother (see WAL to his brothers, July 12, 1960, LFP).

11. MDL to Stanley Link, August 3, 1960, LFP.

12. Donald Mathews to the author, April 6, 2009, in author's possession.

13. Jane DeHart interview, July 7, 2009. Catherine Clinton as a graduate student during the 1970s concluded that Margaret looked out for women grad students and was conscious of the barriers that they were overcoming in the all-male Princeton culture (Clinton interview).

14. Clinton interview.

15. ASL to Curti, May 10, 1961, Curti Papers.

16. James McPherson to the author, February 27, 2009, in author's possession.

17. McPherson to the author, February 27, 2009; Nancy Weiss Malkiel interview, February 24, 2009.

18. Malkiel interview.

19. Arthur S. Link et al., eds., *The Papers of Woodrow Wilson*, 69 vols. (Princeton: Princeton University Press, 1966–94), 1: xii–xiii.

20. John E. Little, "The Work of the Project: An Inside View," paper presented at the American Association of Documentary Editing conference, October 15, 1992, ASLP, Box 102.

21. Dan Carter, "Arthur Link and the Woodrow Wilson Papers," in Roberto Maccarini, ed., *L'unomo e il Presidente: Studi su Woodrow Wilson* (Milan: Selene Edizioni, 2001), 13–25. The second quotation is from Dewey W. Grantham, *Journal of American History* 81 (March 1995): 1789.

22. ASL to McGovern, February 27, 1984, ASLP, Box 47.

23. ASL, "A Wilson-Watcher Measures Carter," *Washington Post*, April 7, 1979. This piece came from an interview conducted by William McCleery for the *Princeton Alumni Weekly*.

24. Albin Krebs and Robert McG. Thomas Jr., "Carter Seeks Privacy during Princeton Visit," *Washington Post*, March 18, 1981. Douglas Brinkley notes that Carter "particularly" sought out Arthur (Brinkley, *The Unfinished Presidency: Jimmy Carter's Journey beyond the White House* [New York: Viking, 1998], 49). Carter makes brief mention of the meeting in his *White House Diary* ([New York: Farrar, Straus, and Giroux, 2010], 523). More detailed diary entries were provided to the author by Steven Hochman, on behalf of President Carter, May 9, 2011.

25. *Washington Post,* February 15, 1983; Hugh Sidey, "Taking Notes for History," *Time,* February 28, 1983.

26. Edwin McDowell, "Random House Buys Reagan Book," *New York Times,* November 27, 1985.

27. Edmund Morris, *Dutch: A Memoir of Ronald Reagan* (New York: Random House, 1999), xxv, xxviii.

28. ASL, account of the Reagan dinner, February 23, 1983, ASLP, Box 63.

29. The account of one participant, George H. Nash, seems to contain none of Morris's emphases (see Nash, "An Evening with the President of the United States," February 19, 1983, in author's possession).

30. ASL to Robert Lasch, November 6, 1964, ASLP, Box 26.

31. Bill Bradley to ASL, October 21, 1965; see also ASL to Bradley, November 20, 1965, ASLP, Box 26.

32. Bradley to ASL, October 18, 1966, ASLP, Box 26.

33. ASL to Bradley, November 8, 1966, ASLP, Box 26.

34. Bradley to ASL, December 5, 1966, ASLP, Box 26; Barton Gellman, "Following Rules, Finding Advantage: Bradley Chose Reserves after Advice," *Washington Post,* November 2, 1999.

35. Bradley to ASL, May 9, 1967, ASLP, Box 26; Leonard Koppett, "Knicks Sign Bradley to a $500,000 Contract," *New York Times,* April 28, 1967.

36. Steve Oxman interview, March 12, 2009.

37. Clinton interview.

38. Ibid.

39. Steve Ross to the author, December 20, 2010.

40. Andrew J. Bacevich to the author, December 5, 2010.

41. Justus Doenecke interview, December 4, 2010.

42. Ralph Levering interview, September 23, 2010. Clinton noted that Arthur could be "stern and dismissive" when dealing with matters related to Wilson (Clinton interview).

43. Frances W. Saunders, "Some of My Best Neighbors Are Negroes," reprint of *Presbyterian Life* article, in LFP.

44. MDL, comments to YWCA meeting, ca. October 1963, LFP.

45. ASL to MDL, July 8, 1964, LFP.

46. ASL to MDL, July 14, 1964, LFP.

47. ASL to WAL, July 16, 1964, LFP.

48. MDL to ASL, July 18, 1964, LFP.

49. ASL to MDL, July 20, 1964, LFP.

50. MDL to ASL, July 24, 1964, LFP.

51. ASL to MDL, July 25, 1964, LFP.

52. ASL to MDL, July 17, 1964, LFP.

53. ASL to MDL, July 19, 1964, LFP.

54. ASL to MDL, July 27, 1964, LFP.

55. MDL to ASL, July 15, 1964, LFP.

56. ASL to MDL, July 23, 1964, LFP.

57. James D. Link to his parents, August 28, 1972, LFP.

58. ASL to JHF, April 11, 1957, October 21, 1959, JHFP, Box 25.

59. ASL to JHF, February 3, 1962, JHFP, Box 25.

60. ASL to JHF, December 6, 1987, JHFP, Box 25.

61. ASL to JHF, February 6, 1978, JHFP, Box 25.

62. JHF interview.

63. William C. Jordan to WAL, March 12, 2009, in author's possession.

64. Dan Rodgers to WAL, February 23, 2009, in author's possession.

65. John Murrin to WAL, February 23, 2009, in author's possession.

66. Jordan to WAL, March 12, 2009.

67. Juliette L. George and Alexander L. George, "Woodrow Wilson and Colonel House: A Reply to Weinstein, Anderson, and Link," *Political Science Quarterly* 96, no. 4 (Winter 1981–82): 641–65.

68. *PWW*, 9: vi, 507; 10: 3; 11: 138; 16: vi, 593; 19: 193.

69. Edwin A. Weinstein, James William Anderson, and Arthur S. Link, "Woodrow Wilson's Political Personality: A Reappraisal," *Political Science Quarterly* 93, no. 4 (Winter 1978–79): 585–98. The Georges first responded in George and George, "Woodrow Wilson and Colonel House: A Reply," 641–66.

70. Alexander and Juliette George to ASL, January 31, March 16, April 30, 1979, March 10, 1980; ASL to the Georges, March 1, May 9, 11, 23, 1979, March 17, 1980; Weinstein to the Georges, ASLP, Box 62. A key document—the diary of Wilson's personal physician, Cary T. Grayson—remained under the Grayson family's control, and they insisted that Arthur use it only as a background source. The Georges were suspicious of Arthur's intentions. Arthur then obtained permission from the Graysons that gave the Georges access to the diary (ASL to the Georges, October 22, 1980, ASLP, Box 62).

71. The Georges to ASL, June 25, 1979, ASLP, Box 62.

72. Alexander L. George to ASL, November 28, 1980; ASL to the Georges, May 21, 1981, ASLP, Box 62.

73. George and George, "Woodrow Wilson and Colonel House: A Reply"; Michael F. Marmor, "Wilson, Strokes, and Zebras," *New England Journal of Medicine* 307 (August 26, 1982): 528–35; Marmor, "A Bad Case of History," *Science* 23 (January-February 1983): 36–38. Privately, the Georges wrote Arthur that they believed that he committed a "significant error of historical judgment" (the Georges to ASL, February 4, 1982, ASLP, Box 62).

74. Juliette L. George, Michael F. Marmor, and Alexander L. George, "Research Note/Issues in Wilson Scholarship: References to Early 'Strokes' in the *Papers of Woodrow Wilson*," *Journal of American History* 70, no. 4 (March 1984): 846.

75. The Georges to ASL, March 31, 1982; ASL to the Georges, April 8, 1982, ASLP, Box 62.

76. ASL et al., response, *Journal of American History* 70 (March 1984): 946.

77. Ibid., 955.

78. Marmor to ASL, January 29, 1983, ASLP, Box 65.

79. ASL to Marmor, September 23, 1982, in response to Marmor to ASL, August 27, 1982, ASLP, Box 65. For Marmor's combativeness, see Marmor to ASL, August 12, 1985, ibid.

80. ASL to Marmor, May 10, 1983, ASLP, Box 65.

81. Michael Kaufman, "Arthur Link, 77, Who Edited Woodrow Wilson Papers, Dies," *New York Times,* March 26, 1998.

82. One of the best assessments is Dan T. Carter, "Arthur Link and the Wilson Papers." Carter concluded that Arthur erred "in endorsing one point of view on such a contentious (and essentially unresolvable) issue," but Carter also maintained that the matter was a "tempest in a teapot."

83. Dewey W. Grantham, "*The Papers of Woodrow Wilson*: A Preliminary Appraisal," in Cooper and Neu, eds., *The Wilson Era,* 281–301; Kendrick A. Clements, "*The Papers of Woodrow Wilson* and the Interpretation of the Wilson Era," *History Teacher* 27, no. 4 (August 1994): 475–89. I remember making precisely this point to my father, something I immediately realized he didn't appreciate.

84. Knock interview.

85. Carter, "Arthur Link and the Wilson Papers."

86. John Cooper interview, September 22, 2010.

87. Pendleton Herring to ASL, December 17, 1982, ASLP, Box 9. Arthur responded by thanking Herring for his "wonderful letter" (ASL to Herring, December 27, 1982, ibid.).

88. Tom Wright to ASL, January 4, 1983, February 25, 1986, ASLP, Box 70.

89. ASL to Herring, May 18, 1987, ASLP, Box 63.

90. *PWW,* 58: 640. In the introduction to volume 64, the editors declared that "it can now be said definitively that Wilson had long suffered from carotid artery disease, malignant hypertension, and what is called the lacunar state." Their conclusion was based on new documents found (and published in *PWW*) in recently opened papers of Cary T. Grayson, Wilson's personal physician. Three examinations by Francis X. Dercum following Wilson's massive stroke in October 1919 indicated a "devastating trauma" with a long history of disease (ibid., 64: ix).

91. Cooper interview; Charles Neu to the author, October 26, 2010, recalled a "cool response" and no money from Herring.

92. ASL to Wright, February 26, 1986, ASLP, Box 70.

93. ASL to Neu, October 22, 1993, ASLP, Box 104.

94. ASL to Leopold, January 21, 1992, ASLP, Box 102.

95. ASL to Grob, June 12, 1992, ASLP, Box 102.

96. ASL to Heckscher, September 24, 1992, ASLP, Box 102.

97. William Satterwhite, memo, June 30, 1993, ASLP, Box 102.

98. Link-Weil interview, December 30, 2008.

99. MDL to Leopold, August 2, 1955; ASL to Leopold, August 17, 1955, Leopold Papers, copy in ASLP, Box 74.

100. He came home on May 30, 1964, reporting that "I really feel already like a new person" and that "my doctors assure me that my operation is a complete success" (ASL to well-wishers, June 5, 1964, LFP).

101. MDL, "Back History of ASL," undated in ASLP, Box 102.

102. Katie Aldridge interview, January 21, 2009.

William A. Link is the Richard J. Milbauer Professor of History at the University of Florida, where he has been since 2004. Among other works, he is the author of *The Paradox of Southern Progressivism, 1880–1930* (1992); *William Friday: Power and Purpose in American Higher Education* (1995); *Roots of Secession: Slavery and Politics in Antebellum Virginia* (2003); and *Righteous Warrior: Jesse Helms and the Rise of Modern Conservatism* (2008).